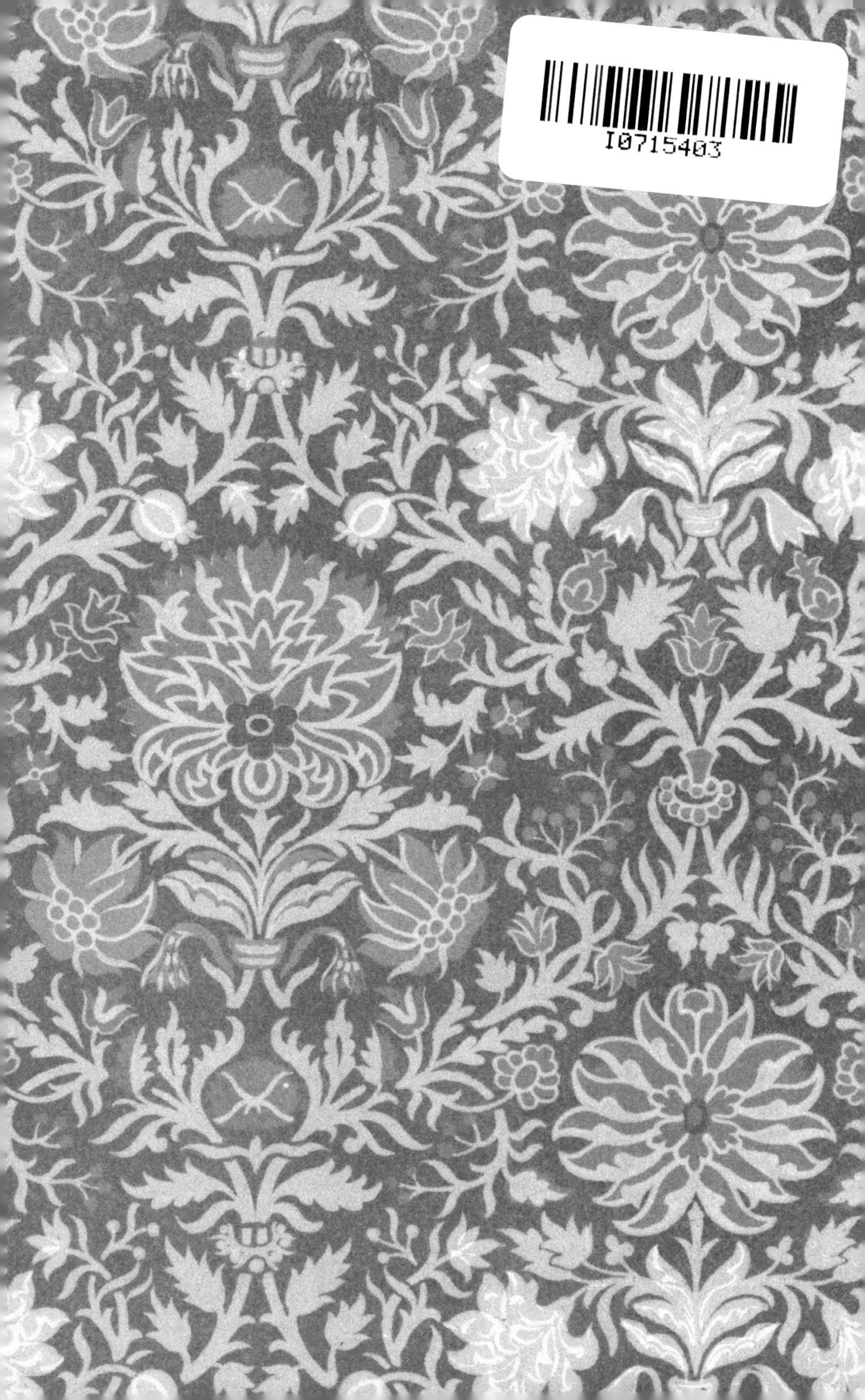
I0715403

ALBRECHT DÜRER

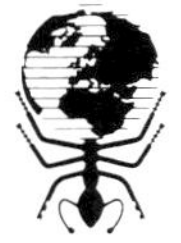

Books in the RENAISSANCE LIVES series explore and illustrate the life histories and achievements of significant artists, rulers, intellectuals and scientists in the early modern world. They delve into literature, philosophy, the history of art, science and natural history and cover narratives of exploration, statecraft and technology.

Series Editor: François Quiviger

ALBRECHT DÜRER

Art and Autobiography

DAVID EKSERDJIAN

REAKTION BOOKS

To Alessandro Nova, who also loves the North and the South

Published by Reaktion Books Ltd
Unit 32, Waterside
44–48 Wharf Road
London N1 7UX, UK
www.reaktionbooks.co.uk

First published 2023
Copyright © David Ekserdjian 2023

Printed and bound in India by Replika Press Pvt. Ltd

A catalogue record for this book is available from the British Library

ISBN 978 1 78914 764 3

COVER: Albrecht Dürer, *Self-Portrait*, 1498, oil on panel. Museo Nacional del Prado, Madrid, photo akg-images.

CONTENTS

Dz hab ich aws eim spigell nach
mir selbs kunterfet im 1484 jar
do ich noch ein kint was
Albrecht Dürer

Introduction: Life and Times

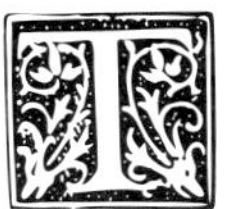he Italian Renaissance is conventionally thought of as the historical period that witnessed the rise of the individual. Yet no other artist of the day begins to compare with the northerner Albrecht Dürer in terms of the almost obsessive interest he displays in himself, his own biography, even including his dreams, and his surroundings. This introduction, both to Dürer the man and to his world, is intended to underline the extent to which this singles him out from his contemporaries, most obviously in Germany and northern Europe, but no less tellingly in Italy.

Our first sight of Dürer is in the form of a self-portrait executed in silverpoint and inscribed by the artist himself at a much later date with a text explaining that he made it at the age of thirteen with the aid of a mirror (illus. 1).[1] Subsequently, Dürer painted at least four independent self-portraits, whereas most artists of the period did not execute even one: one is lost, but the remaining three are all famously extraordinary and original, and will be explored here in some depth. At the same time, he included clearly identifiable portraits of himself with accompanying signatures and texts in no fewer than four of his religious paintings, but also once or twice used his own features less explicitly for characters within such pictures. Last but not least, he also drew himself on various further occasions in entirely unprecedented ways, most strikingly so in the case of his *Nude Self-Portrait* (illus. 2).[2]

1 Albrecht Dürer, *Self-Portrait Aged Thirteen*, 1484, silverpoint on prepared paper.

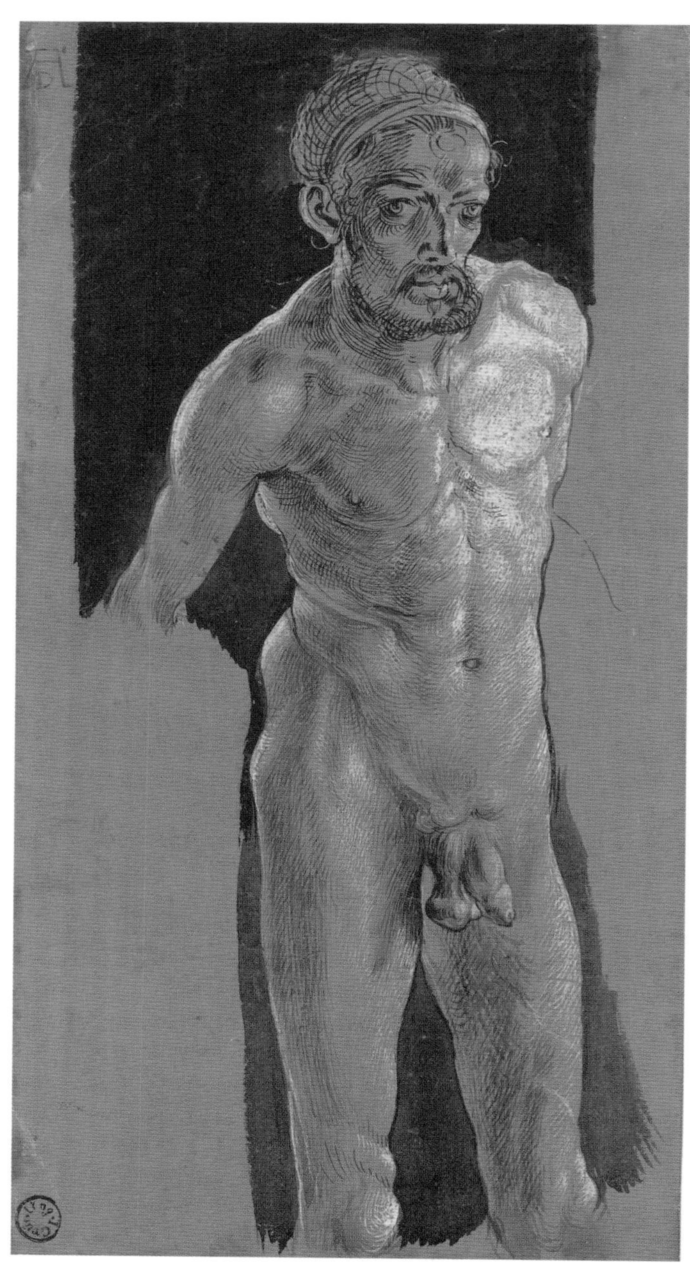

2 Albrecht Dürer, *Nude Self-Portrait*, *c.* 1499, pen and brush and black ink, heightened with white, on green prepared paper.

No less revealing is the extent to which he believed in self-commemoration, was a fanatical dater of his own productions, and equally sought to immortalize his immediate family and close circle of friends. As a rule, in the late fifteenth and early sixteenth century artists created their works for strictly professional reasons, above all to make money, but also on occasion to build their reputations. Yet many of these 'extended-family' images must have been motivated by a highly personal combination of affection and curiosity. The means Dürer employed to record his own story and that of those closest to him were multiple, because as well as his paintings, drawings and prints there is his unique concern to imprint such visual records with illuminating textual information and commentary. Last but by no means least, he was a genuine if informal autobiographer, whose letters and journals shed remarkable light upon what he was doing and what he was thinking.

Before proceeding to a detailed consideration of Dürer's self-fashioning, it seems essential to offer a very brief account of what we actually know for sure and what we may reasonably surmise concerning his biography, and at the same time to track his various comings and goings.

The principal sources of information concerning Dürer's life are his own writings, above all in the form of the *Gedenkbuch* (or *Family Chronicle*) he compiled in 1524, the diary – which is actually an account-book in diary form – he kept during his journey to the Netherlands in 1520–21, and the arbitrary selection of his letters that have come down to posterity. The *Chronicle*, which was started by his father, is only partially preserved, and both it and the diary only survive in the form of later transcriptions.[3] A whole second strand of evidence is provided by representations of places he visited and people he met, and above all his virtual obsession from the later 1490s onwards with systematically dating an enormous number of his own works. For all that, the dates are not unfailingly reliable. As a result, the picture is extremely uneven in the extent of its detail or lack of it, but it is important to add that we have more of a sense of Dürer as a person than is usually the case when it comes to Renaissance artists.

He was born in Nuremberg on 21 May 1471. It was a major cultural centre, and apart from occasional absences, including two visits to Italy, the city would remain his home for his entire life. During the Renaissance it was not really possible for important artists to work in the middle of nowhere; in consequence, Leonardo had to make his way from Vinci to Florence, but Dürer had no such need, and made the most of this good fortune in a whole variety of ways.[4]

Nuremberg had been a free imperial city since 1219, which meant that the sole jurisdiction to which it was subject was that of the Holy Roman Emperor. As a result of the Golden Bull of 1356, it enjoyed the additional distinction of being the place where each new emperor was supposed to hold his first diet, and was also the city where the crown jewels were kept. By the last quarter of the fifteenth century, it was an increasingly significant commercial and cultural centre.

Until it was destroyed by Allied bombing in 1944, Dürer's parental home on the Burgstrasse was a monument to the comparative ease of his upbringing.[5] Dürer was the son of Albrecht Senior and Barbara Holper, who was the daughter of his father's master, Hieronymus Holper (*c.* 1415–1483), and although tax records make it clear the household was not one of the most prosperous in the city, they were absolutely not starving either. Dürer's father was a goldsmith and well connected, and it was a happy chance that Anton Koberger (*c.* 1445–1523) should have been Albrecht Junior's godfather, since he was to become the most prominent publisher in all of Germany, which circumstance must have been of inestimable value to the artist when he started out as a printmaker.[6] According to his own account, his father approved of the fact that he was industrious and, albeit reluctantly, let him follow his natural inclination and become a painter. The consequence was that from 1486 to 1489 he was apprenticed to Michael Wolgemut (1434–1519), whom he was to portray at a much later date, 1516, when Wolgemut was an octogenarian. He then set out on his *Wanderjahre* in 1490 and only returned in 1494, in July of which year he married Agnes (1475–1539), the daughter of Hans Frey (1450–1523), a coppersmith, and received a dowry of two hundred florins.[7]

These contacts and relationships were only part of a whole network of connections that linked Dürer through his family background with all sorts of potentially valuable commercial associates living in their immediate vicinity. It is telling in this context that Wolgemut also lived on the Burgstrasse, just a few doors down from the parental home, which moreover was next to the house of Hans Fugger, a prominent member of the great banking dynasty. More generally, Nuremberg was a celebrated centre for metalworking, with the result that – alongside gold-smiths – armourers and braziers were among the most important tradesmen in the city, which was also noted as one of the homes of the new printing industry.

Such occupations could also lead to business relationships beyond the confines of the city, and it is telling that one of Koberger's trading partners was Anton Kolb, who worked as a draper but was also the publisher of Jacopo de' Barbari's unprec-edentedly comprehensive *Map of Venice*.[8] That work is dated 1500, and therefore both after Dürer's first trip to Venice (to be dis-cussed below) and just before Barbari's own arrival in Nuremberg. There is not a shred of evidence that Dürer saw either Kolb or Barbari in Venice, but it is not hard to see how what might be described as the Nuremberg mafia could have furnished both him and Barbari with introductions on their travels abroad.

What happened after Dürer's marriage is less straightforward, but it is generally accepted that he set out for Italy, leaving his wife behind. The evidence of a number of townscapes and landscapes powerfully suggests that both coming and going he went by way of the Brenner Pass and visited such places as Innsbruck, Trent, Arco and the Val di Cembra, although it has to be admitted that none of these sheets is securely dated and they can only be placed at this point in his career on the basis of style.[9] It is often taken for granted by believers in the idea that Dürer went to Italy in 1495 that he did not venture any further south than Venice, but in Chapter Two detailed arguments will be put forward in support of the notion that he visited both Florence and Rome.

On his return to Nuremberg in 1495 he evidently opened a workshop and was soon so fully involved in printmaking that in 1497 and then again in 1500 he engaged no fewer than three different individuals to act as salesmen of his prints.[10] By this date he was recognized as being in a league of his own among painters in the city, with his only conceivable artistic rival being the sculptor Veit Stoss (c. 1445/50–1533), who returned to Nuremberg from Cracow in 1496 and remained there for the rest of his career.[11] Stoss was one of the supreme masters of wood sculpture of all time, and although there is no evidence concerning what he and Dürer made of each other's work, it would be odd for them to have felt anything less than the greatest mutual respect. They certainly must have moved in the same circles, and Stoss's magisterial *Engelsgruss* (Annunciation) of 1517–18 in Sankt Lorenz was commissioned by Anton II Tucher (1458–1524), two of whose brothers were the subjects of portraits by Dürer.[12]

He no doubt occasionally travelled to meet prospective clients and to deliver or install works; however, apart from a trip to Würzburg with his great friend Willibald Pirckheimer (1470–1530) on official business concerning the Swabian League for the City Council, almost nothing concrete is known concerning his movements until his second journey to Italy in 1505–6.[13] As will be returned to more fully in Chapter Two, on this second visit he was definitely in the main based in Venice, as is confirmed by the evidence of his correspondence with Pirckheimer, and received one major commission there, for his *Feast of the Rose-Garlands* for the church of San Bartolomeo al Rialto.[14]

Back in Nuremberg by early 1507, in which year he signed and dated his paintings of *Adam* and *Eve*, he continued to run his workshop as before.[15] For the next decade and more, remarkably little hard evidence exists concerning any travels away from home, which does not mean he never moved an inch, but the first documented excursion was his attendance at the Diet of Augsburg in 1518, which lasted for three weeks.[16]

The last great adventure was his journey to the Netherlands, this time in the company of his wife, which is fully documented in the diary he kept of it, and it too will be explored in Chapter Two.[17] On that journey he contracted a serious illness, sometimes wrongly diagnosed as malaria, which no doubt shortened his life, although he was active to the end. He died – as is now known, of pneumonia – on 6 April 1528.[18]

In terms of Dürer's art, the first point worth making is that there was an Albrecht Dürer before the one we know best. As explained above, this was his father, who was a goldsmith and consequently had a major part in, so to speak, pointing Albrecht in the right direction. It is true that – according to his son's contribution to the *Family Chronicle* – initially Albrecht's father was not in favour of Dürer becoming a painter ('er war nit wohl zufrieden'), because he wanted him to follow in his own footsteps and become a goldsmith.[19] Nevertheless, if Joseph Koerner and others are right, as I believe, to see the *Portrait Drawing of Albrecht Dürer the Elder* in silverpoint as a self-portrait, then it must surely have been the inspiration for his child prodigy son's *Self-Portrait Aged Thirteen*.[20]

Rejecting the attribution to Dürer of the *Portrait Drawing of Albrecht Dürer the Elder* does not mean there are no family portraits by him. To begin at the beginning, a pair of portraits of his mother (*c.* 1451–1514) and father (1427–1502) have an excellent claim to be his earliest surviving paintings.[21] The latter bears the 'AD' monogram and the year 1490, and – regardless of whether both are a later addition – the date is confirmed by its appearance on the reverse of the panel (a not easily deciphered fleeing devil is represented on the reverse of its pendant). Shown in half-length against a uniform green background, both Barbara and Albrecht Senior look inwards, but appear to gaze into the middle distance rather than directly at one another, and lack the dramatic sense of engagement that would subsequently become a virtual touch-stone of Dürer's portraiture. Instead, the inclusion of their hands adds a second focus, and both of them are shown fingering rosaries, which are carefully differentiated.

The authorship of a second painted *Portrait of Albrecht Dürer the Elder* in London has excited controversy. It is routinely the case that, if there are differences of opinion, institutions tend to take a more optimistic view than the rest of the world about works in their collections, but in this instance the proposed demotion is the result of an in-house decision.[22] However, all authorities agree that there was once such a portrait, and indeed the invention is known in the form of a number of copies. This panel has an unconvincing inscription in capitals, which is surely later, along the top of its damaged background, but a version in Munich replicates what must have been the original inscription in the form of a rhyming couplet in German ('1497/ Das malt Ich nach meines Vatters gestalt/ Da er war sibenzich jar alt/ Albrecht Dürer der Elter/ AD' – 'I painted this from my father's likeness when he was seventy years old'), and this text is a virtual twin of the one on the Prado *Self-Portrait*, painted the year after, whose connection with it will be discussed below.[23] Seven years had passed since the earlier portrait, and Albrecht Senior is visibly older, but well pre-served for a man of seventy, with not a grey hair in sight. In any event, this is clearly the same man, and he is shown looking out

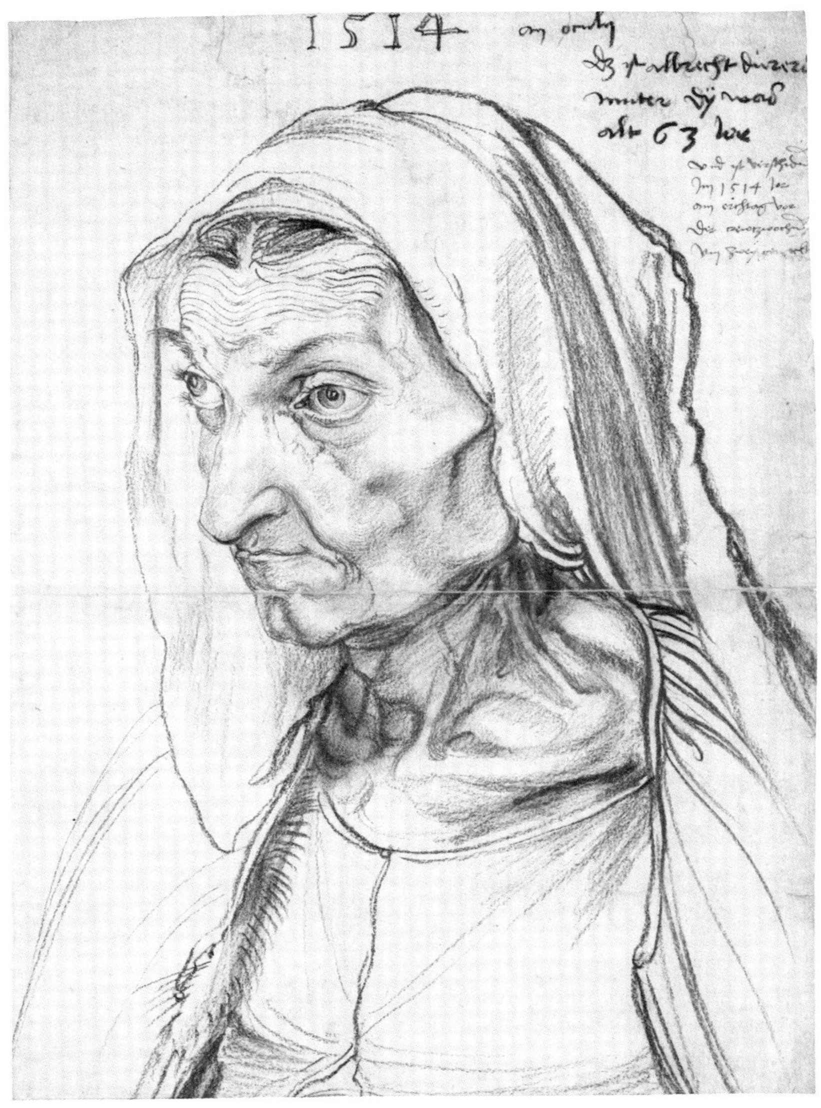

3 Albrecht Dürer, *Dürer's Mother*, 1514, charcoal on paper.

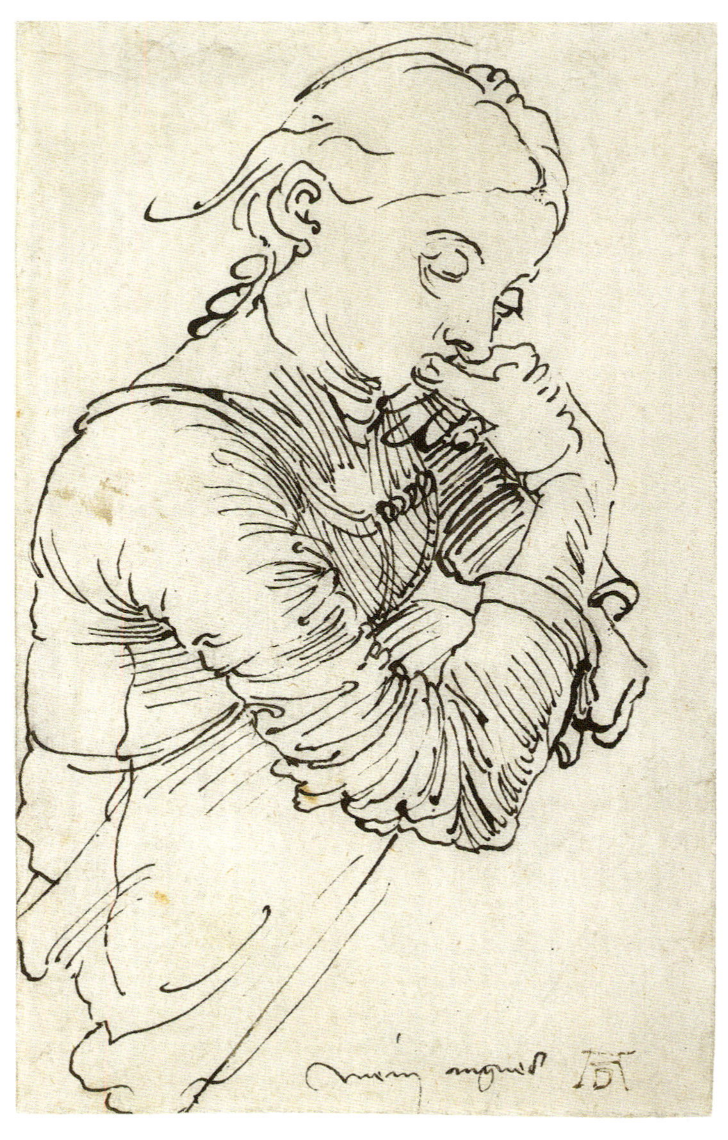

4 Albrecht Dürer, *'Mein Agnes' (Agnes Dürer)*, 1494, pen and black ink.

at the world with an almost menacingly appraising frown, as if still unpersuaded his son has made the right decision in not joining the family business.

There may well once have been drawings of Albrecht Senior, but if so they have not survived. One that has made its way to us is the depiction of Dürer's mother, a drawing now in Berlin (illus. 3), which is doubly annotated and dated 1514, and which has a good claim to be the most haunting of all his works.[24] The first inscription, which has evidently been written with the same stick of thick charcoal that was employed to make the drawing, dates it to 19 March 1514 and explains, almost as if looking in from the outside and addressing a third party, that this is Albrecht Dürer's mother – after all, he could have put 'my mother' – and that she was 63 years old. The second text, which has been added below on a smaller scale and more neatly in pen, records that she died on Thursday, 16 May 1514, at 2 o'clock in the morning. The ravages of her illness, which lasted for a year before her death and is referred to in the *Family Chronicle*, are all too painfully apparent in her sunken cheeks and raddled neck, to such an extent that she is scarcely recognizable as the woman who sat for the painted portrait 24 years earlier.[25]

For all that there is no reason to believe such a presumption, it is often claimed that Dürer's marriage was not a happy one. In truth, the evidence suggests the opposite. Drawings can be evidence, and in particular the one in pen that is thought to date from 1494, the year of their marriage, and is inscribed 'mein agnes', is an entrancingly intimate evocation of his bride (illus. 4). She looks as if she may almost have nodded off, and is clearly unaware of the fact that she is being sketched.[26] Decades later, he portrayed her on a variety of occasions, and always seemingly with affection. The earliest of the three most memorable ones, a meticulous sheet in black and grey brush extensively heightened with white, which is monogrammed and dated 1519, is an all but final study for

the artist's *Virgin and Child with St Anne*.[27] It is plain that Dürer
has arranged the pose of his wife with the picture in mind, and
areas of overlap where Jesus and Mary will go are not drawn in.
Touchingly, Agnes looks straight out in the drawing and not
– as she will in the painting, whose dynastic subject-matter may
have been bittersweet for a childless couple – slightly down to
her left towards her fictional daughter. The other two were motivated by a simple desire to record her features and costume on
their travels. The first, a sheet in brown metalpoint on grey-violet
prepared paper, is extensively inscribed with the information
that it was executed in Antwerp in 1521, and that it represents
his 'hawsfrawen' wearing Netherlandish costume he gave her
'do sy aneinander zu der e gehabt hetten XXVII Jor' ('when they
had been married for 27 years').[28] Given all the opprobrium he
tends to receive for not having taken her with him to Italy, not
just once but twice, it seems only right to point out that here
he, apparently contentedly, records their anniversary. Last but
not least, at Boppard on the Rhine on his return journey from
the Netherlands, as the inscription on it reveals, he added another
tenderly observed portrait of her to a page of his silverpoint
sketchbook.[29]

The last member of Dürer's family whom he immortalized
was his considerably younger brother, Endres (1484–1555). The
two very different likenesses of him both date from 1514, which
was the year he matriculated as a goldsmith, an event that the first
in particular may have been produced to celebrate. It is a sadly
very rubbed silverpoint head-and-shoulder-length study on
bluish-white prepared paper that represents him in essence fron-
tally, but looking away to his right. The artist has added a couplet
identifying the sitter and giving his age at top right.[30] The second
sheet shows Endres in lost profile at half-length, with his left arm
resting on what appears to be a table, and so little of his face is
visible that it is only by analogy with the first drawing that his

identity is confirmed.[31] It is not clear what purpose the study was intended to serve when it was made, but Endres is in effect a model as opposed to a sitter, and soon after Dürer exploited the pose, only minimally modifying it, in his etching the *Saturnalia* (also known as the *Desperate Man*), where the figure in question is given the artist's own profile.[32]

Turning to Dürer's drawings of himself before moving on to his painted self-portraits, the starting point is inevitably his *Self-Portrait Aged Thirteen* (illus. 1).[33] Strictly speaking, we are obliged to take the information concerning when it was executed and the related matter of the artist's age at the time on trust, but there seems no reason to doubt it. In consequence, its sheer precocity runs the risk of distracting attention from what would be an impressive technical accomplishment at any age. Seen in the light of what is to come, what is striking is its objectivity, the sense that its creator is inspecting the intently wide-eyed human specimen before him very much from the outside. As has been pointed out, a right-handed artist contemplating his reflection in a mirror and drawing it would be using what he would therefore see as his left hand to produce the work, and it is indeed omitted. Conversely, the sheet emphatically includes the right hand, and its index finger is shown suggestively pointing away to the figure's left, as if drawing our attention to something – to use the cinematic term – out of shot.

By the time Dürer came to execute his next two self-portrait drawings, unflinching directness is very much the order of the day. The former, which combines the disembodied head study with an artfully gesticulating left (and therefore actually right) hand and a cushion, is almost menacingly clear-sighted.[34] The latter, in which the subject's seeming right (and in consequence actually left) hand is propped up against his cheek, and therefore partially conceals it, is almost its converse, in the sense that the artist appears to be struggling to decipher his own features.[35] Neither drawing is dated, even retrospectively, and for Koerner the former dates from circa 1491, whereas the latter dates from circa 1493. In my opinion they belong together, and if they were both executed around 1493, which seems perfectly possible, then that obviously begs the question as to how they relate to the first of the painted self-portraits, a work in Paris that is dated 1493.[36] Seen in those terms, the second sheet cannot conceivably have been intended to lead straightforwardly to a formal portrait, but the first one is not only generically plausible as a preparatory study for such an image, but strikingly close to the Louvre *Self-Portrait*, and Koerner is surely right to see it as such.[37] The treatment of light and shadow, especially around the eyes and mouth, is very similar, as is the stern outward gaze and even the distribution of the flowing locks of hair and the hint of a wispy blond beard. It is true that the drawing is more frontal than the painting, but even here – as is commonly the case in Renaissance portraits – the nose is angled to one side in a slightly exaggerated manner in order to divide the face in two vertically.

The most extraordinary and arresting of all these drawings is the aforementioned *Nude Self-Portrait* (illus. 2).[38] Executed in pen and brush on green prepared paper, and extensively heightened with white, it does not represent the subject completely, since the right arm is only drawn in down to the elbow (the left was evidently always intended to be hidden behind the figure's back) and it also tails off around the knees, which makes one wonder whether the sheet was originally taller and was subsequently cut down by the artist to achieve an effect of near-completeness. The reason for saying so is that the overall finish of the rest could hardly be more perfectly resolved. The dating of the sheet has been much debated: Dürer unquestionably looks somewhat older than he does in his Alte Pinakothek *Self-Portrait* (illus. 10), which is dated 1500, even allowing for its possible idealization of his appearance, and yet significantly younger than he does in the *Feast of the Rose-Garlands* of 1506 (illus. 28). This would place it around

1503, as would the technique, but some scholars favour an earlier date of circa 1499.

Regardless of when it was drawn, it is both the very idea of an artist representing himself naked and the uncompromising realism of the treatment that give it a timeless immediacy, as if it had been created the day before yesterday. Some commentators have implied that the artist was eager to endow himself with a finer physique than he may actually have possessed, but that appears far-fetched, since it seems certain the work in question was not intended to have a public existence. More remarkable by far is the explicit realism of the genitalia with their peculiarly dangling scrotum, which makes this not only the first true genital self-portrait, but the first true genital portrait of any kind.[39] The appraising gaze is no less unflinching, but that was already true of the first of the two sheets discussed above, and indeed the almost uncanny similarity of their scrutiny may simply reflect the way Dürer always looked at himself in the mirror.

Another strikingly personal drawing of around 1512–13 (illus. 5) gives every indication of being the Renaissance equivalent of the current post-COVID need to send doctors photographs of our bodies for diagnosis instead of attending surgeries, since it is inscribed 'Do der gelb fleck ist und mit dem finger drawff dewt do ist mir we' ('The place where it hurts is where the yellow spot is and where my finger is').[40] Almost comically, even in this most utilitarian of drawings, Dürer seems unable to resist engaging with the viewer – in the first instance, at least, his doctor – and has also ensured that he captures his own likeness. Arguably the most gripping thing about the whole episode is the fact that the drawing was preserved, presumably because its recipient valued it as – to employ the modern terminology which had not yet been invented, but that he would doubtless have understood – 'a Dürer'.

The final drawing that belongs here is not a portrait of the artist, but instead the record of one of his dreams, which is unarguably more intensely personal than the listings of meetings and meals that fill the diary of his journey to the Netherlands (illus. 6). The sheet in question includes by far the lengthiest autograph inscription on any Dürer drawing.[41] It explains that the apocalyptic vision he has represented in the form of a watercolour, whose near-abstraction is all but unparalleled in his extensive oeuvre, is what he saw in his sleep on the night between the Wednesday and the Thursday after Whitsun 1525. He states plainly that he was frightened by it and woke up shaking with

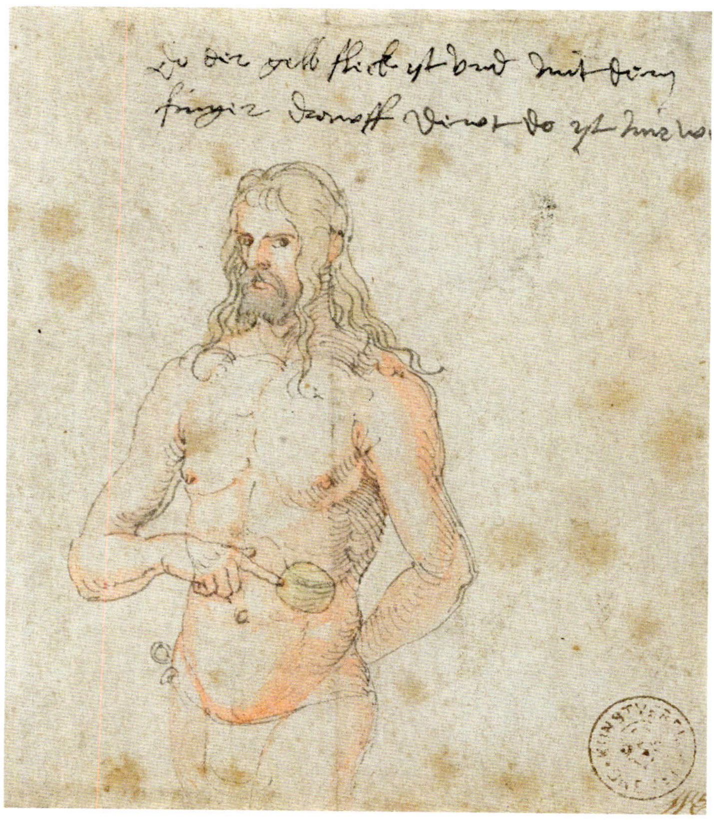

5 Albrecht Dürer, *Self-Portrait When Sick*, *c.* 1512–13, brown ink with watercolour.

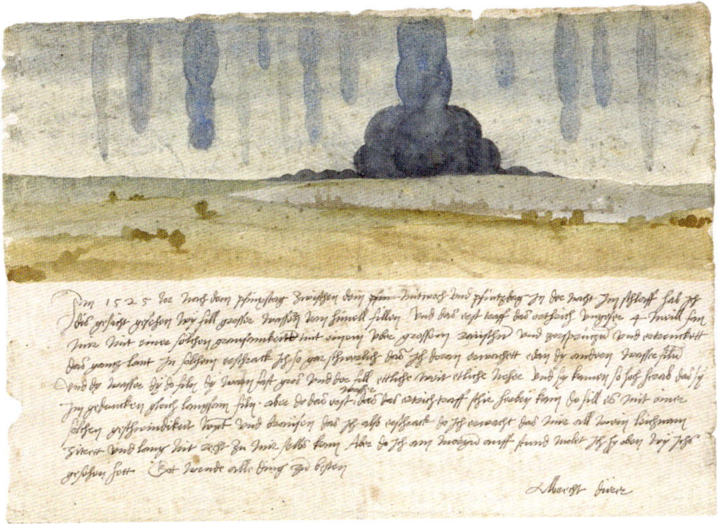

fear, before concluding by praying to God that all may be for the best ('Gott wende alle ding zum besten').

Turning, at last, to the painted self-portraits, the earliest of the three surviving ones is the Louvre *Self-Portrait* (illus. 7). As noted above, the work in question is dated 1493: this date is inscribed in gothic numerals between the splendidly elaborate red hat he is wearing and the upper margin of the image, whose large scale is inevitably emphasized by the comparatively diminutive lettering of the text to its immediate right. It is a rhyming couplet that reads as follows: 'My sach die gat/ als es oben schat', which literally means 'My thing it goes, as it stands above'. *Sach* – as it happens, a favourite word of Dürer's – is assumed to refer to his affairs, and the words seem to imply that a higher power (whether God or Fortune) will determine what becomes of him.[42] Its significance in this context will be returned to, but it seems important to add that the work is not signed, and that the reason we know it is a self-portrait is that the sitter's features are those of Dürer. The

6 Albrecht Dürer, *Dream*, 1525, watercolour.

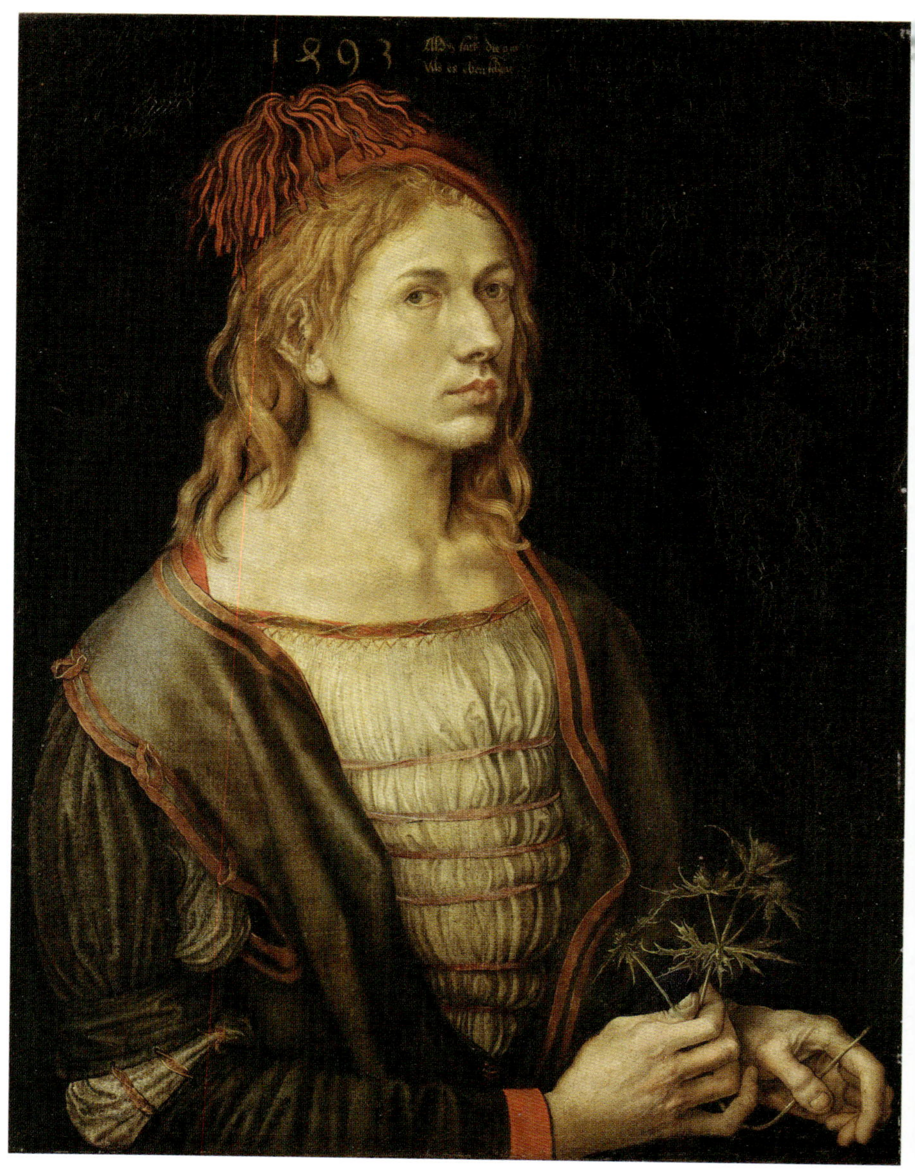

7 Albrecht Dürer, *Self-Portrait*, 1493, oil on parchment transferred to canvas.

mere fact of the subject meeting our gaze is no guarantee that it is a likeness of its creator: having sitters look directly out is a standard trope in Renaissance portraits.

The second focus of attention in the portrait is the hands at its base, and above all the plant being held in them. This is universally agreed to be eryngium (or sea holly), and its inclusion is obviously intended to have some symbolic meaning, but that of itself does not resolve the question of what its significance may be in this context. The traditional interpretation, which goes back to Goethe, is associated with *Mannstreue*, one of the German names of the plant in question, which translates as 'man's fidelity', and would therefore make it tempting to link it with his forthcoming union. In that connection, the date of the portrait has often been associated with Dürer's betrothal and marriage to Agnes Frey in 1494, but, as has recently been underlined by Jeroen Stumpel and Jolein van Kregten, in 1493 he was still away from home and may not even have been aware of any such plans, not least since the account in his *Family Chronicle* explicitly states that the agreement followed rather than preceded his return home.[43] It should be added that a slightly different gloss to the plant's amorous and aphrodisiac associations was proposed by Koerner, who speculated that it may have been intended 'to magically assist Dürer's impending sexual union', not least because of his own possible homosexuality.[44] A wholly different interpretation is offered by Stumpel and Van Kregten, who point out that many of the eryngium's other names, such as *Unruhe* (restlessness), are related to its having strong roots but a tendency to blow with the wind once deprived of them. They therefore connect its inclusion here with its appearance in the artist's slightly later engraving known as the *Small Fortune*.[45] Others have associated its presence in the engraving with good luck in love, and it must certainly have an aphrodisiac connotation in another engraving of much the same date, the *Young Woman Attacked by Death* (illus. 8), also known as the *Ravisher*.[46] Ultimately, there can be no proof that on all three occasions Dürer intended its meaning to be the same.

The Louvre *Self-Portrait* was originally painted on parchment and only transferred to a fine canvas during a restoration it underwent in 1840. This kind of support might seem particularly well suited for a painting that, regardless of precisely where it was executed, was going to need to return home to Nuremberg with the artist. As a matter of fact, however, there exist considerably more fully finished oil paintings on parchment or paper dating from the Renaissance both north and south of the Alps than is generally supposed, so not too much should be made of this detail.[47] Dürer's expression is arguably less self-assured than in later images, but what is certain is the extraordinary artistic accomplishment he reveals here, which is only surpassed by his next exploration of himself.

The work in question is of course the Prado *Self-Portrait* (illus. 9). It is inscribed in a lighter colour than its backdrop just below the window ledge: the text comprises five lines in all, with the date 1498 being followed by a rhyming couplet in gothic script that reads 'Das malt Ich nach meiner gestalt/ Ich war sex und zwanzig jor alt' ('I painted this after my person [when] I was twenty-six years old'), and is rounded off by both the artist's name and the 'AD' monogram below it.[48] Much has been made, and not unreasonably, of the splendour of Dürer's attire, but at the same time he is evidently unabashed about his profession, because the text he has elected to add to the portrait reveals that he is its author as well as its subject.

Dürer's costume is certainly very fine – the grey doeskin gloves that were a Nuremberg speciality being a particularly elegant touch – but also extremely carefully considered. In particular, the way in which the black and white of his striped headgear is echoed by the edging at the top of his jerkin, by the material covering his forearms, and even by the double cord that is attached to his coat is the mark of a dandyish attention to sartorial detail. The same goes for the decision he must have taken to have his hair coiffed in ringlets (a style that he subsequently never appears to have tired of), since all the earlier self-portraits, whether drawn or painted, show him with straight hair. Moreover, on one level recording that he is 26 is a simple statement of fact, but on another it may be a self-congratulatory trumpeting of how much he has already achieved at such a young age. In the same spirit, the inclusion of a view out of a window in a portrait is entirely unremarkable at this date, but the fact that this one discloses an identifiable

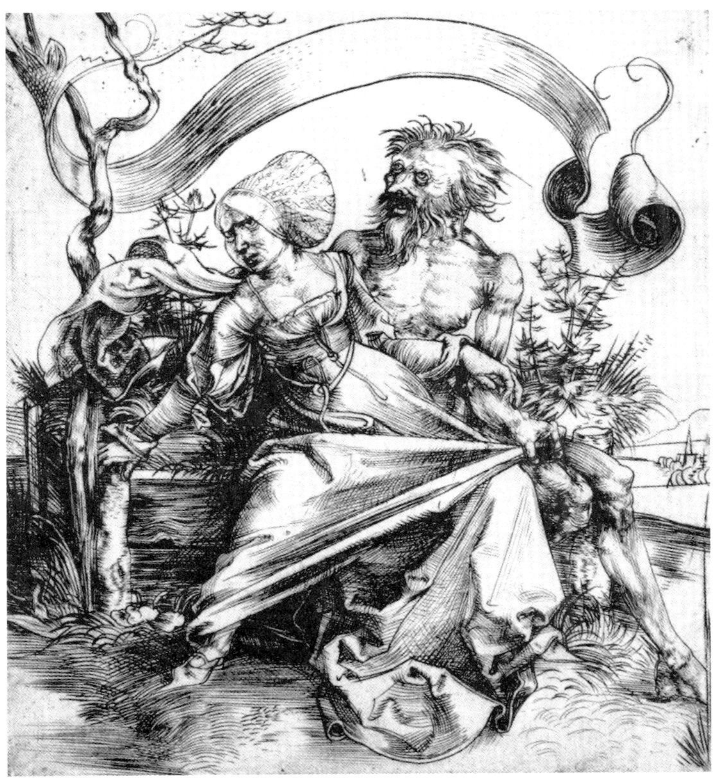

8 Albrecht Dürer, *Young Woman Attacked by Death*, c. 1495, engraving.

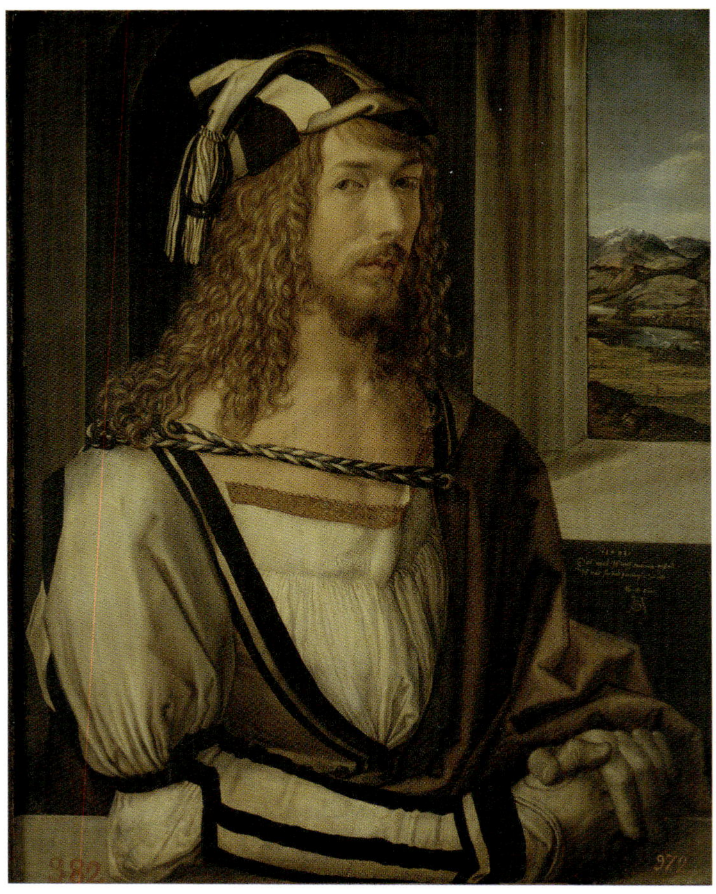

prospect of snow-capped mountains in the distance is evidently
a more private recollection of personal experiences on his journeys
to and from Italy three years earlier.

The notion that it and the *Portrait of Albrecht Dürer the Elder*
must form some species of diptych seems hard to doubt. Even
if the version of the latter in the National Gallery is not the
original, there are enough copies to confirm the fact that the

9 Albrecht Dürer, *Self-Portrait*, 1498, oil on panel.

work's dimensions were – or are – identical, as are those of the sitters within the picture field. Assuming Dürer went on the left and his father on the right, both figures look inwards in appropriate fashion. If they were indeed a pair, then the uniform background of the *Portrait of Albrecht Dürer the Elder* represents a problem: it means they make for an odd couple, and it would be tempting to suppose that the artist never finished the portrait of his father, although both the fact that it is the earlier of the two and the inscription it once bore speak against this. A different kind of explanation might be that the idea of creating a pendant self-portrait for the paternal likeness was not originally part of the plan, and that once Dürer had located himself in an interior with a landscape beyond, he intended to return to the earlier panel to modify it accordingly, but never got round to it.

As a work of art, the Prado *Self-Portrait* represents a major advance on its predecessor in the Louvre, but at the same time in terms of the psychology of its subject it presents us with an altogether more poised and confident individual. He also seems to want to play his self-assurance and panache off against the distinctly unrelaxed and almost suspicious look in his father's eyes.

The Alte Pinakothek *Self-Portrait* (illus. 10) is such an icon and has had so much scholarly wisdom devoted to it that, para-doxically, it may be deemed to require less commentary than many of his other works.[49] Perhaps the first thing to note about it is its strikingly novel golden inscription: reading from left to right, it consists of the date 1500 and a punning 'AD' – for both Albrecht Dürer and Anno Domini – on one side, and on the other a four-line text, which reads 'Albertus Durerus Noricus/ ipsum me proprijs sic effin./ gebam coloribus aetatis./ anno XXVIII.' ('I, Albrecht Dürer of Nuremberg painted myself thus, with undying [or 'authentic'] colours, at the age of 28 years.') The discovery by Dieter Wuttke of a manuscript of the writings of the humanist Konrad Celtis (1459–1508) containing no fewer than five epigrams in praise of Dürer that are not only written in the same *all'antica* script, which at this date was highly unusual on paintings north of the Alps, but employ the verb *effingere* – as opposed to such standards as *pingere* or *facere* – offers overwhelming confirmation of the source of both the text and the calligraphy found here.[50]

If all this indicates Dürer's absolute determination to break with the past at the turn of the half-millennium, then the same urge to make it new is even more blatantly apparent in the image itself. As has been pointed out, both its absolute frontality and intimidatingly penetrating gaze associate it with the traditional mode of representing the Holy Face of Christ, universally believed to be the true likeness of the Saviour transmitted to posterity on the Sudarium with which St Veronica wiped away his sweat on the way to Calvary.[51] The precise details of Christ's appearance as described in the apocryphal, but at the time undoubted, Lentulus letter are followed in the portrait, and yet Dürer squares the circle by almost miraculously producing a likeness of himself in accordance with what we know of his appearance from all the other self-portraits. Moreover, the subdued lighting, subfusc clothes and midnight black background all force us to stare into his eyes. Even the pointing right hand avoids being a distraction by closing off the composition at its base and at the same time directing us towards his face.[52] Moreover, the right hand holds a piece of his miniver lining, both a status symbol and the fur from which artists' brushes were made.[53]

What would have been by far the latest of Dürer's self-portraits – it must date from somewhat earlier than the Raphael drawing he received in exchange and inscribed with the date 1515 – is the one that no longer exists, and of which moreover there is no certain visual record, even in the form of a copy, although it has been proposed that Raphael may have employed the gift in order to insert a likeness of Dürer among the papal porters in the left foreground of his fresco of the *Expulsion of Heliodorus* in the Vatican

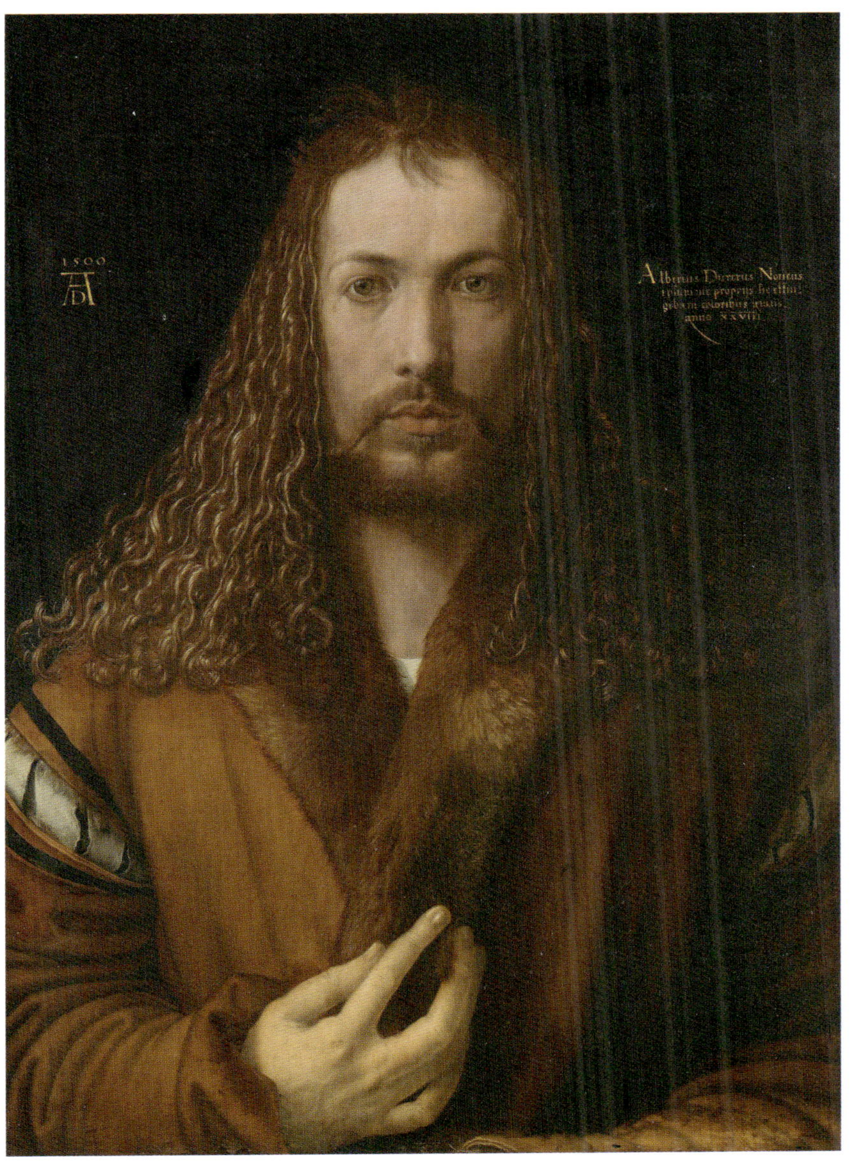

10 Albrecht Dürer, *Self-Portrait*, 1500, oil on limewood panel.

Stanze.[54] The idea is an appealing one, and both the style of the man's hair and the cut of his beard and moustache are eminently comparable with what we know of Dürer's self-image, but the features are less convincing. What is for sure is that Vasari, who is our source for the painting Dürer sent to Raphael, failed to recognize the correspondence, and instead identified the figure in question as Marcantonio Raimondi.[55]

Vasari was captivated by the Dürer *Self-Portrait* that was sent to Raphael, and discusses it at some length and in almost identical terms in his biographies of both Raphael and Giulio Romano, explaining in the latter that Giulio himself showed it to him during a visit he made to Mantua.[56] Both accounts explain that it was painted in body colour and watercolour without white heightening on a *tela di bisso* (fine linen canvas), in such a way that against the light the image was visible from either side, at which Raphael marvelled. In the Giulio biography he adds that the canvas itself was reserved for the highlights, but also that Dürer displayed amazing virtuosity in the way he used its very fine threads to render the individual hairs of his beard.

As was explained at the outset of this chapter, Dürer inserted self-portraits into no fewer than four of his religious compositions. This practice was by no means his invention, but was uncommon, and moreover more prevalent in Italy than in Germany or the Netherlands. Intriguingly, especially given the forthright way in which he presents himself, he must have sought and received patronal assent in every instance. The term *in assistenza* tends to be employed to designate such insertions, but it is important to recognize that Dürer's way of going about it is more explicit than the approach adopted by his predecessors. A select number of Italian artists seem to have included themselves in their paintings, but usually only on very rare occasions. As a rule, they also tend to leave it to the viewer to deduce that such likenesses are self-portraits by representing themselves in contemporary costume and above all by looking directly out.[57] Only even more rarely is there an inscription, as in the case of Benozzo Gozzoli in his frescoes in the chapel of the Palazzo Medici in Florence, in which he depicts himself wearing an inscribed hat, which reads 'OPVS BENOTII' and explicitly confirms his identity.[58] The only earlier artist who included his self-portrait more than once is Perugino, and even then two of the three are not thus designated and instead smuggled into larger assemblies of figures. In fact, the confirmation of his identity as the figure engaging our gaze in both the early *Adoration of the Magi* in the Galleria Nazionale dell'Umbria in Perugia and the *Donation of the Keys* in the Sistine Chapel depends upon comparing his physiognomy in them with that of the last of the trio.[59] This is the fictive independent self-portrait within Perugino's fresco cycle in the Collegio del Cambio in Perugia, which is accompanied by a self-identifying and indeed self-glorifying inscription on a separate tablet that boasts of his role as the inventor or reinventor of the art of painting. Suggestively, like Dürer's Alte Pinakothek *Self-Portrait*, it too is dated 1500.[60]

Dürer employed his own facial features and indeed flowing locks for the drummer in one of the panels of his so-called *Jabach Altarpiece*, which is undated but is usually placed around 1503–4.[61] Moreover, in the only slightly later Uffizi *Adoration of the Magi* of around 1504, it has rightly been observed that the likeness of the second king again corresponds with that of its painter.[62] Everything indicates that its original patron was the Elector of Saxony, Frederick the Wise. Dürer had painted his portrait some years before, so he would certainly have recognized the artist's insertion in his own work, but it is altogether less clear whether it would have been apparent to other viewers. It should be added that it is widely and plausibly, but not universally, believed that he employed himself as a model for a sheet dated 1522 representing *Christ as the Man of Sorrows*.[63] What seems plain, to judge by the best of the copies of the lost painting that derived from the drawing, is the fact that there was absolutely no resemblance in the final work.[64]

Dürer takes his first true bow a couple of years later in 1506, in the *Feast of the Rose-Garlands*, the altarpiece he executed for San Bartolomeo al Rialto in Venice.[65] For all that he is further back than the principal figures of donors and associates in attendance on the Virgin and Child, and therefore on a smaller scale than them, he is unmissably present. In what by this date is the approved manner for self-portraits, he looks directly out and engages the attention of the viewer, but in any event the text on the floppy sheet of paper he is holding leaves no doubt about either his identity or his being the painter of the work. Written in italic script, it states that the altarpiece took the space of five months to complete and is the work of 'Albertus Durer Germanus', and is followed by the year in the form 'M.D.VI.' and the customary, by this juncture, 'AD' monogram. Like a number of the foreground figures, Dürer is bareheaded; he is elegantly dressed in a fur-trimmed garment and accompanied by a companion. Remarkably, given how much scholarly attention the work has received, the latter's identity is far from certain, and also particularly hard to judge given the amount of damage the paint surface has suffered. The idea that it might be a portrait of Pirckheimer seems inconceivable, not only because it looks nothing like him but because he was in faraway Nuremberg and did not belong to the brotherhood of the rosary either. Alas, that only helps establish who the man is not, as opposed to who he is, and there is no way of verifying any of the other proposals.[66]

In his representation of the extremely rare subject of the *Martyrdom of the 10,000 Christians* in Vienna, which is signed and dated 1508, and which, like the *Adoration of the Magi*, was commissioned by Frederick the Wise, he once again represents himself in the middle ground and in the company of another man.[67] In this instance, instead of being pushed to the edge of the picture field they are in the centre of things, and indeed Dürer has created a kind of void to accommodate them. As with the *Feast*, there have been different suggestions concerning the companion's identity, but it now seems to be generally accepted that it represents Konrad Celtis, who was a friend of the artist, and moreover had died that very year.[68] Here Dürer, in black, is again shown brandishing a piece of paper, this time held aloft on a stick, which is inscribed in a cursive gothic script with the text 'Iste faciebat an[n]o domini 1508/albertus dürer alemanu[s]', again with the 'AD' monogram added.

The fact that the central panel of the *Heller Altarpiece* of 1509 is only known in the form of copies (its wings, which were executed by his workshop, do still exist) means that it is impossible to judge the detailed appearance and artistic quality of the self-portrait of Dürer it included. The *Martyrdom* dates from only a year before, but the new work seems to show a distinctly older man.[69] The tablet, which is inscribed with finely wrought classical capitals, reads as follows:

ALBERTIS/DVRER/ALEMANVS/FACIEBAT/POST/VIRGINIS/
PARTV[M]/1509/AD.[70]

The artist, who is standing in the middle distance far beyond the Apostles assembled around the Virgin's tomb, is shown gripping the tablet's handle with his left hand and has the loop of string that is attached to it wrapped round his wrist. Unusually, and although he is fairly centrally positioned within the composition, he is looking in from the left, not the right.

In the case of the *Adoration of the Holy Trinity* (illus. 31) of a couple of years later, Dürer is standing in the foreground at the bottom right corner of the image, but is again much smaller than the sacred personages in the heavens, or indeed than the donor, Matthäus Landauer, who kneels among them and is on the same scale as them.[71] Here too the epigraphy of the text is classical, and it is inscribed on a *tabula ansata*, which Dürer is propping up with his right hand. It reads:

ALBERTVS.DVRER/NORICVS.FACIE./BAT.ANNO.A.VIR/
GINIS. PARTV[M]/.1511. AD.[72]

The actual image of the artist could almost have been derived, admittedly in reverse, from that of his counterpart in the *Heller Altarpiece*, but his costume is not the same, and is if anything colourful and more elaborate, since he sports a fur-trimmed coat and a bright red cap and hose. In the highly resolved preparatory drawing for the altarpiece within its frame, which to a striking degree already corresponds with the final work, the self-portrait is not yet included, but that should almost certainly not be taken as an indication that it was an afterthought, not least since the donor is likewise missing.[73]

It is not clear, beyond a presumably conscious desire for variety, what motivated the changes to the adjective used to designate Dürer's nationality, which moves from 'Germanus' to 'Alemanus' (twice), before finally becoming 'Noricus' (as in the Alte Pinakothek *Self-Portrait*), a terminology sometimes associated with his joining the Nuremberg Town Council in 1509. However, given the locations of the four works and who had access to them, it seems extremely unlikely that more than at most a handful of the artist's contemporaries actually managed to see all four of them.

Other than in relation to the Alte Pinakothek *Self-Portrait*, the question of who composed all these inscriptions is seldom addressed, but the truth is that Dürer's Latinity must have been distinctly limited, if not altogether non-existent. As has been pointed out by Jane Campbell Hutchison in her biography of Dürer, at best he would have been taught the rudiments of Latin grammar and may have begun to study some Latin literature at school.[74] Admittedly, most of the Latin of the signature-inscriptions in these four works is pretty basic, but even here it would have made sense to check with a friend. Moreover, a link with Horace has been adduced in connection with the *Feast of the Rose-Garlands* text, while the employment of the form *faciebat* as opposed to *fecit* in the other three may learnedly allude to the way Pliny the Elder claims that Apelles and Polyclitus signed their works.[75]

Elsewhere, Dürer includes immeasurably more linguistically demanding Latin inscriptions of various kinds. Some of these are quotations from earlier writers, and must presumably have been supplied by learned friends, of whom Willibald Pirckheimer was only the most celebrated. A particularly striking instance of such a dependency arises in the case of the artist's drawing in pen and watercolour of *Arion*. It must have been conceived of as a finished work of art as opposed to a study for something else, and indeed is one of four such *all'antica* images that seem to form a loose set (they divide into two pairs of approximately the same dimensions and are all in the Kunsthistorisches Museum in Vienna).[76] Its hitherto unidentified inscription reads 'PISCE SVPER CVRVO VECTVS CANTABAT ARION', which turns out to be a line from a lyric by Basinio da Parma (1425–1457), his 'Basinius obsessus ab hostibus in Guardasione castello', which forms part of his poem 'Cyris'.[77]

The second sheet that belongs with it represents a *Sleeping Nymph*, and includes a four-line inscription on the fountain just behind her. The text in question was studied in depth by Otto Kurz, and his article does an impeccable job of explaining in which publications it could be found by Dürer's time, but does not speculate on how it came his way, or for that matter whether he would have been able to translate it.[78] Of the two other related drawings, the *Venus with Cupid the Honey-Thief*, which is helpfully dated 1514, is wordless, but the subject it depicts is likewise classical and is found in the poetry of ancient Greek authors such as

Anacreon and Theocritus, which once more means the artist must have been told about it by someone who was classically trained.[79] Even more blatantly, when it comes to the *Allegory of Eloquence*, it is inconceivable that Dürer – who knew no Greek – would have known the source in Lucian or thought of the subject for himself. In the event, the list of the various epithets and attributes of Hermes of which it is comprised is linguistically imperfect, since the one at top left makes Maia masculine.[80]

If the fact that Dürer lacked the linguistic tools required to gain access to a whole range of erudite classical material has largely been ignored, then its implication in connection with a number of his most iconographically demanding works is at least as important. Identification of the textual sources, where possible, is naturally a vital first step, but an arguably even more crucial issue is how easy it would have been for him to have known them. Thus in the case of a suggested parallel between the *Dream of the Doctor* and a passage in Sebastian Brandt's *Narrenschiff* (Ship of Fools), which Dürer helped to illustrate, there is no problem about his having read the relevant passage, which links an idler and a stove.[81] With his *Hercules at the Crossroads*, the ultimate source for the young Hercules choosing between Virtue and Pleasure is Xenophon, but by his time the episode had gained a far wider diffusion, and moreover the way it is interpreted in the engraving is the opposite of pedantically faithful to that text.[82] Conversely, if it is accepted that the source of the *Nemesis* is Angelo Poliziano's Latin poem *Manto* of 1482, of which there was no German translation, then it is plain that he could not have read it himself.[83]

As stated above, Pirckheimer may serve as a representative example of the kind of friend who would have been able to help Dürer with this sort of scholarly material. Their relationship is also revealing of what the artists's closest friends meant to him, and may be tracked both in visual form and in the – alas – one side of their correspondence during Dürer's time in Venice in

1505–7.[84] Two related likenesses, respectively in silverpoint and black chalk, one of which is dated 1503, both represent Pirckheimer in pure profile, which can hardly fail to draw attention to his wonky nose.[85] Clearly, Dürer felt no obligation to flatter his friend, but in the event the evidence of the engraving of him executed in 1524 makes it plain that he was one of those men who age well: he may have looked as if he was about fifty when he was thirty, but he still looked about fifty when he actually was fifty.[86] It seems only reasonable to presume that the subject composed his own text, in which the survival of his works is contrasted with the transience of his body, and there is proof positive that he was delighted by the print, because he used it extensively as a bookplate. It would be hard to imagine a grander one.

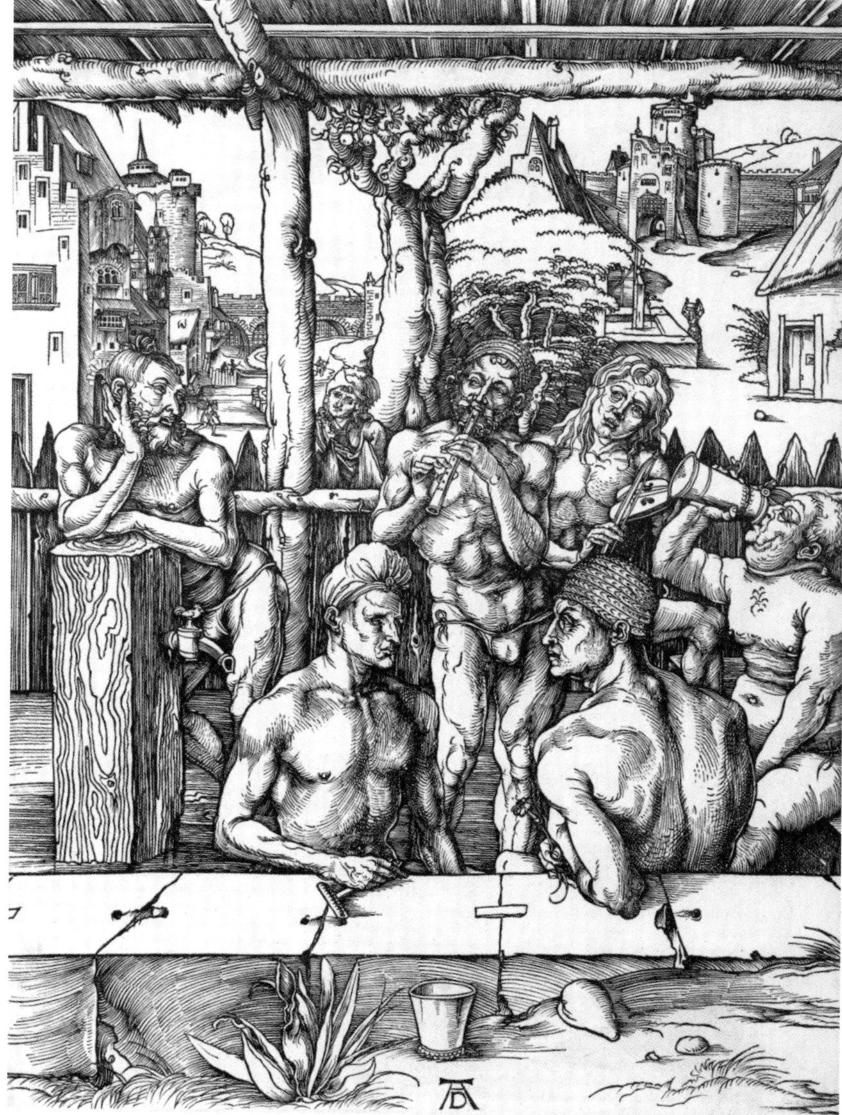

ONE

Man and the Natural World

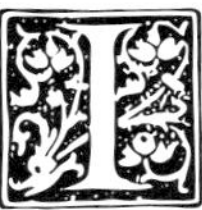n the Introduction I argued that both the nature and the extent of Dürer's scrutiny of himself, his family and his friends were without precedent, and it should therefore come as no surprise if he also looked far beyond his immediate surroundings to explore the wider world in a similar spirit. Here I will begin by examining his study of his fellow man – and crucially woman – before proceeding to investigate his relationship with the natural world, which embraced both the animal and plant kingdoms and the wider landscape.

In the Renaissance, one of the ways in which artists were judged was by their ability to represent the ideal nude figure. By the second half of the fifteenth century, especially in Italy, it had become common practice for artists to draw from the live model, for which purpose they often exploited the nearest thing to hand, namely their workshop assistants or apprentices. To begin with, these studies show the models in their everyday working clothes, but over time drawings of figures in the nude were added to the repertoire. All these life drawings were from posed male models, even if the figures they were intended to prepare within paintings were ultimately going to be female. It is far from easy to be certain when artists first employed nude female models, but it seems hard to doubt that Raphael was doing so in his final years. The quivering imperfection of the female nude in a red chalk drawing by him, which is connected with the frescoes he and his workshop

11 Albrecht Dürer, *Men's Bath House*, c. 1496–7, woodcut.

executed in the Villa Farnesina in Rome in the late 1510s, leaves little doubt that it is just such a life study.[1]

Unsurprisingly, Dürer's engagement with the nude was profoundly different in character, but, as we shall see, this does not mean that the ideal nude was of no interest to him. There is hardly any evidence in his early works that Dürer practised life drawing before he first went to Italy, but a nude study of a woman, which is dated 1493, is at least a candidate, with both her dangling head covering and her slippers seeming to support the idea that – even if somewhat modified to conform to the standard gothic figure canon – it is based on observation, very possibly in a bath house, as opposed to pure imagination.[2] In any event, it is also clear that his encounters in Italy with examples both ancient and modern profoundly affected his approach to the representation of the nude.

Ironically, for all that he would have loved to be admired in this department by his fellow artists in Italy, this was not to be. In a letter dated 7 February 1506 that he wrote from Venice to his great friend Willibald Pirckheimer back home in Nuremberg, he lamented the more general antipathy of the local painters towards his work, but also specified that 'Noch schelten sie es und sagen, es sei niet antigisch Art, dorum sei es nit gut' ('They also condemn it and say that it is not in the antique manner, and is therefore not good').[3] Intriguingly Vasari, who was otherwise a huge admirer of Dürer, in the 1568 edition of his *Lives* similarly denounces Dürer's nudes, but his negative verdict upon them at least purports to be for a different reason. He comments that – in his *Choice of Hercules* (whose subject Vasari misidentifies) – 'Albrecht sought to prove that he was able to make nudes.' He then adds:

> But although those masters were extolled at that time in those countries, in ours their works are commended only for the diligent execution of the engraving. I am willing, indeed, to believe that Albrecht was perhaps not

able to do better because, not having any better models, he drew, when he had to make nudes, from one or other of his assistants, who must have had bad figures, as many Germans generally have when naked, although one sees many from those parts who are fine men when in their clothes.[4]

In fact, however, the seemingly complementary notions that Dürer's art is not antique and that his nudes cannot hope to be good because of the ugliness of his models are arguably simply different ways of expressing a shared unease at their otherness. For Italian artists of the sixteenth century, and in spite of the stylistic gulf that separates Venetian painting around 1500–1510 from the art of Vasari at mid-century, there is a right way of doing things, and anything that does not conform must necessarily be a wrong way.

Dürer, on the other hand, was at least as fascinated by bodily imperfection as by the perfect physique, and this curiosity applied not only to men but to women. In the first category, the most evolved combination of high and low is to be found in his wood-cut titled the *Men's Bath House* (illus. 11), which must date from around 1496.[5] It includes half a dozen nude figures, some of them in posing pouches and others only represented half-length, who are organized into three loose pairs. The two in the foreground are respectively shown from the front and the back, with two musicians beyond them, the more prominent of whom adopts a classical *contrapposto* pose. The two outermost figures are also the most contrasted, with an elegantly relaxed – and again classically inspired – younger man standing up and leaning on a wooden support over to the left balanced by a distinctly overweight older man sitting glugging from a beer stein at the right margin of the composition (his chest hair is an unusual but not unique detail in this period).[6] Assuming this is not a simple genre scene, precisely what it all means is a different question, and there have been various suggestions, but the punning cock that tops the blatantly phallic tap at the young man's groin leaves no doubt that Dürer had a smutty and laddish sense of humour.

In the nature of things, as a rule prints were bound to be seen by all sorts of people, and therefore needed to maintain a certain decorum, and the chubby toper in the *Men's Bath House* is large-scale, but by no means grotesque. In contrast, there does also exist a remarkably unflinching life study on the recto of a double-sided sheet whose subject is a repulsively obese man. Moreover, just as he did when he drew his own naked body, here Dürer does not shy away from what might be described as genital portraiture.[7] The fact that the female nude on the verso of the sheet appears to be linked with the artist's studies of human proportion might lead one to wonder if this hideous vision was intended to form part of some sort of treatise, but in all probability it is neither more nor less than a singularly unappealing slice of life.

Dürer may originally have planned to produce a pair of wood-cuts, and to complement his *Men's Bath House* with a *Women's Bath House*. No such print exists, but there is a drawing of precisely that subject, which is monogrammed and dated 1496, possibly by a later hand (illus. 12).[8] There are virtually no earlier drawings of female nudes extant in the northern tradition, but this does not mean they never existed. When Jan van Eyck painted his figure of *Eve* on the *Ghent Altarpiece*, it is hard to imagine that he did not make some kind of preliminary drawing for her – what is far less easy to determine is whether it was based upon studying a life model, not least since at this date there would almost certainly have been moral concerns about women posing naked in front of men.[9] His conception of the first woman certainly conforms to what might be termed the gothic ideal of small, high breasts and a long, slim body, as it was defined in the mid-twentieth century by Kenneth Clark in *The Nude*.[10]

Having said that, bath houses would have been a natural
hunting ground for nude models, and Dürer was neither the first,
nor the last, artist to evoke such settings when seeking to give
female nudes a semi-narrative context. A notable earlier instance,
also in the form of a print, is the *Bath of Women* by the otherwise
anonymous Master PM, who was active in the Lower Rhineland
around the 1480s and '90s.[11] The four women and three children
who inhabit it are set against a plain white background, but their
remaining clothes and a bowl and a small wooden basin confirm
the accuracy of the title. This engraving only survives in a unique,
flawed impression, which has lost its bottom right corner. This
circumstance underlines the fact that, although prints were

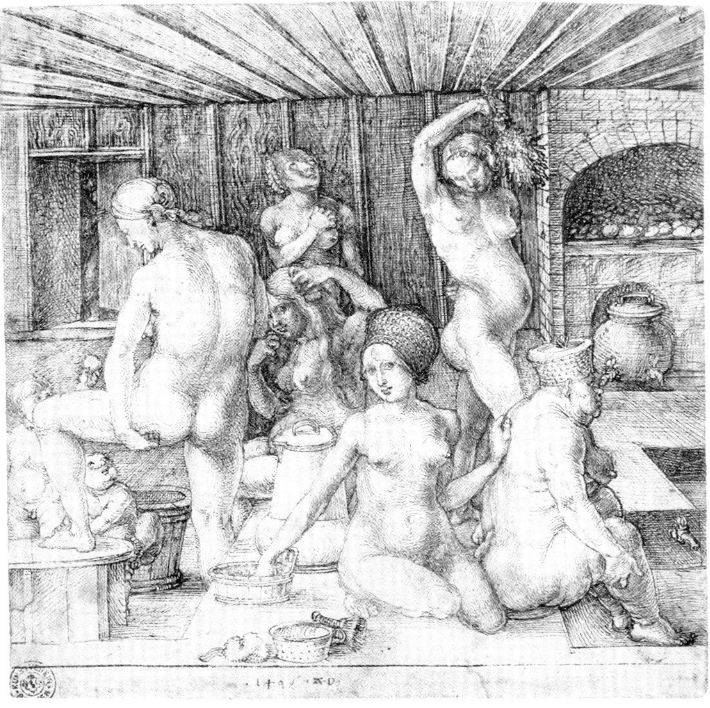

12 Albrecht Dürer, *Women's Bath House*, 1496, pen and black ink.

multiples, it would be unwise to presume that none of them are lost to us forever, a point which will be returned to in the next chapter in connection with Dürer's *Death of Orpheus*.

Like the *Men's Bathhouse*, its female counterpart features six principal figures, and is on a comparable scale, if somewhat smaller, but there are important differences. The most straightforward one concerns the indoor setting, but the women are also accompanied by two children, and in the left background (for all that he takes a bit of finding) by a bearded man furtively ogling them through a doorway. In this instance, only two of the women – the one seen from behind at the left and the one standing and turning further back and over to the right – are even vaguely classical in spirit. Once again, a single older woman with heaving thighs and bulging breasts joins the otherwise youthful company, which includes two women who look out seductively and engage the (presumptively male) viewer's gaze.[12]

In the scholarly literature on Dürer, this sheet is all but unfailingly linked with the artist's engraving of *Four Naked Women* of 1497, the first print he monogrammed and dated. The work in question is often referred to as the *Four Witches*, the title it was first given by Joachim Sandrart in 1675, but, as is surprisingly often the case with Dürer's prints, the subject-matter remains mysterious.[13] Be that as it may, the presence of a skull at their feet and a diabolical monster holding a flail emerging from flames in a room beyond at the left margin of the image confirm that this is no mere genre scene.[14] Moreover, and in spite of the closeness of date, it is not just the iconography, but equally the poses of the figures in both works, that are completely different. What they truly have in common is a similar refusal – or, as Vasari would presumably have imagined, incapacity – to idealize the female nude. However, if one thinks back to the perfection – within a non-Italian canon of beauty – of Van Eyck's *Eve*, it seems plain that no effort has been made to improve on nature here. It is true that they represent a species of northern variation on the theme of the Three Graces (since the fourth figure is only partially visible), and even echo the way the frontal, rear and profile aspects found in such groups achieve an almost sculptural 360-degree view, but that is as far as the similarities go, since these bodies are exultantly anti-classical in their proportions.[15]

Elsewhere, however, the ideal classical nude plays a significant role in Dürer's oeuvre. By virtue of their common subject-matter, the two most resolved treatments necessarily have the considerable advantage of allowing him to bring together a male nude and a female one. The earlier of the two is the engraving *Adam and Eve* (illus. 13), where he is proud to sign himself on a tablet as 'NORICVS', a self-designation that ultimately derives from the Latin name for a region corresponding to modern Austria and Slovenia, which became a province of the Roman Empire in the first century AD, but seems to refer to Nuremberg. The fact that a parrot is perched on the branch from which the tablet hangs down wittily implies that the famously 'speaking' bird is to be construed as reciting the text. The work in question is dated 1504, and therefore precedes Dürer's second journey to Italy, but reflects his debt to models south of the Alps, and above all the *Apollo Belvedere*, as will be returned to in the next chapter.[16]

A select number of drawings connected with the work have survived, as indeed, remarkably, have two trial impressions of the engraving in the course of its creation, but no doubt there were quite a few more drawings, and moreover Adam's proportions and attitude were both foreshadowed in earlier studies of a figure of *Apollo*.[17] In only one of them, a dated sheet of 1504, are both figures combined, but shown against a uniform black background. Nevertheless, this was clearly just a device to allow the artist to focus upon the protagonists in isolation, since the ground beneath their feet is already uneven, and Adam is holding onto a forked branch that emerges from the trunk of a tree.[18] The figures are

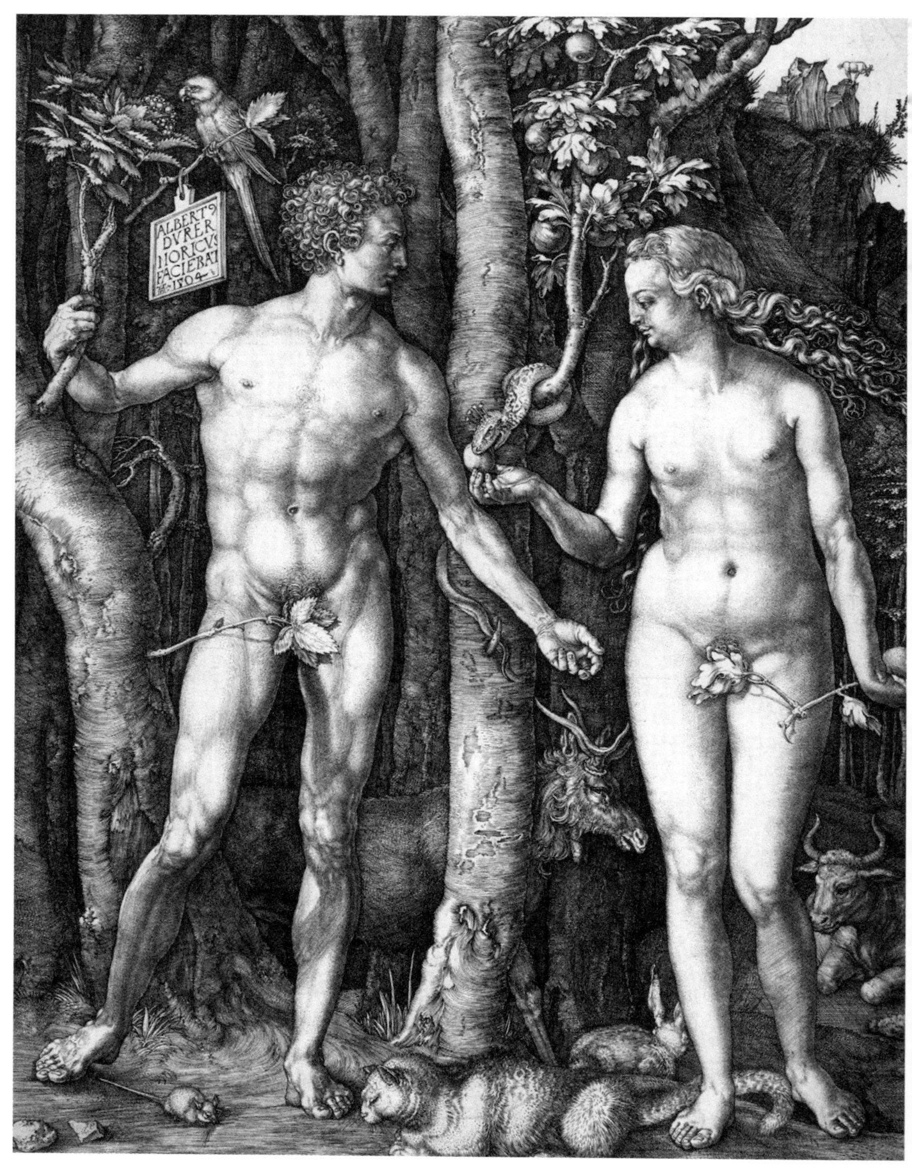

13 Albrecht Dürer, *Adam and Eve*, 1504, engraving.

represented in reverse to their arrangement in the engraving, and consequently in conformity with their alignment on the copper plate that preceded it, but the differences are otherwise minimal. When the two are compared, it emerges that the poses are essentially the same, but that certain details have been altered in the final version, where the fruits being held by both figures are modified, and Eve's flying tresses are both considerably more extensive and more finely detailed. A different and more telling change of plan involves the covering up in the print of the genitalia, which are concealed by conveniently positioned leaves (Eve's are fig leaves, but Adam's are those of some kind of mountain ash). It must be presumed that Dürer himself decided to implement this particular self-censorship, in spite of the fact that the serpent is clearly meant to be in the process of tempting Adam and Eve, who should therefore not yet be aware of their nakedness and ashamed of it (Genesis 3:7).

At the same time, he added a glimpse of pubic hair emerging from behind the leaves, a detail that appears to be virtually unprecedented in relation to female nudes.

There are also two further drawings for the figure of Eve in reverse to the print.[19] One once again sets her against a uniform black backdrop, only interrupted by an area at bottom right reserved for a couple of lopped-off tree trunks (which are absent from the sheet dated 1504). The other is in part unfinished, with Eve's left hand being the obvious missing element, but also lacks shading on her left leg, which was traced through onto the verso – a simple way for the artist to be able to see it the right way round. Importantly, it bears witness to Dürer's systematic endeavour to create ideal nude figures, because it is organized around a vertical pen line bisecting Eve but also has incised lines round her head and a number of pricked points arrived at mathematically. For the rest, both studies are so remarkably close to the first drawing that one is tempted to wonder why all three were required, which only serves to underline Dürer's well-nigh infinite capacity for taking pains.

Two final drawings connected with *Adam and Eve* remain to be discussed.[20] One of them is a sheet executed in pen and ink with two complete studies of hares and one partial one – presumably all sketched from a single specimen.[21] As will be returned to more fully in due course, such studies were not made by Dürer with particular projects in mind, and in that sense they are not truly preparatory, but he would always have been aware at the back of his mind that they might come in handy one day. Conversely, the other sheet is a genuine working drawing, and one of the rare instances of Dürer emulating an approach to the representation of details that had only relatively recently been pioneered in Italy by Leonardo da Vinci.[22] It comprises several distinct studies, all blatantly drawn from life, for the upper body, and especially the right arm and hand of Adam. Interestingly, the two halves of the upper body are examined separately, and whereas the central study of the right arm adds a fig in the palm and the associated leaf and branch, which must be invented, the left arm at upper left is shown holding a vertical staff, as opposed to the irregular branch in the finished version. The reason is entirely straightforward: the staff would have helped Dürer's model to hold the pose. For the rest, there is one further study of the right arm, a larger close-up in which Adam is holding a fruit that looks more like an apple than a fig and finally three independent studies of his right hand. Of these, it is the middle one that ended up being used. Somewhat unexpectedly, a small detail of a rocky outcrop is added to these figure studies, and although it does not exactly correspond with its counterpart in the engraving, it must surely be a first idea for the sliver of distant landscape in the print.

If all the surviving preparatory drawings for Dürer's engraving were evidently executed at a stage when the final appearance of the work had been established, the same does not go for the

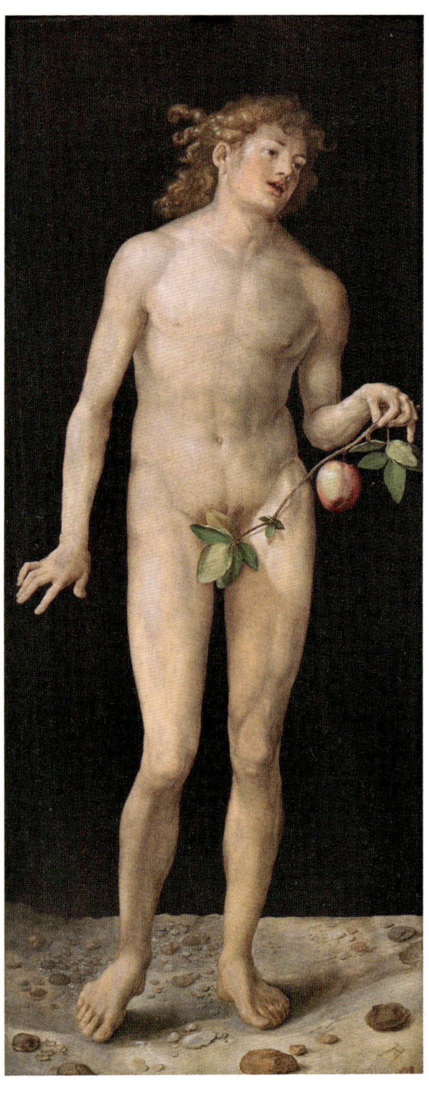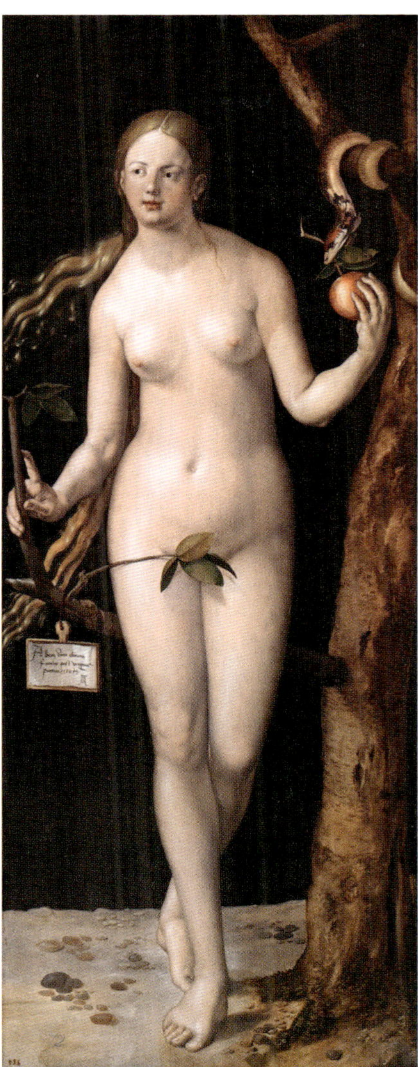

14 Albrecht Dürer, *Adam and Eve*, 1507, oil on pine panel.

studies connected with his paired paintings of the same subject, which are signed and dated 1507 (illus. 14).[23] In this case, he dubbed himself 'ALEMANVS' instead of 'NORICVS', but was arguably even more resolutely content about his northernness.

The earliest record of what would appear to be these monumental panels dates from around the next decade, when they were owned by Johann Thurzo (1464–1520), the Bishop of Breslau, who was related, via his brother, to the Fugger family of Augsburg. In view of the fact that he also acquired a Virgin and Child from the artist in 1508, and was a cultivated patron of the arts, it seems entirely possible that he was their original patron, for all that this has often been doubted.[24]

Regardless of their patronage and planned setting, it is clear that they must have been ordered the previous year, when Dürer was still in Italy, since two of the five related drawings, all but one of which are double-sided, bear autograph inscriptions with the date 1506 (another is monogrammed and dated 1507).[25] Two of them – respectively for *Adam* and *Eve* – reveal Dürer starting out by in effect replicating the attitudes of both figures in his own engraving of a couple of years before.[26] They are the same way round as their counterparts in the print, of which he must have had an example with him to consult, but whereas the Adam is virtually identical, and even has a branch drawn in to cover his nudity, Eve's right arm is less fully stretched out and her left one below the elbow is bent and concealed behind her back rather than hanging down fully visible by her side. A number of other drawings reveal the fact that at a later stage Dürer contemplated showing Eve with one arm outstretched above her head and brandishing an apple.[27] In the event, however, he opted to represent her with her legs crossed and both arms lower down.

Dürer's engagement with ideal nudes ultimately led to his posthumously published treatise, the *Vier Bücher von menschlicher Proportion* (Four Books on Human Proportion) of 1528, although it is only its illustrations of the body type that is eight heads tall that conform to the ideal.[28] His desire to represent physical perfection was evidently balanced by an equal determination to record what in his day would have been thought of as freaks of nature, regardless of whether they were animal or human oddities. The most obvious examples of this are his engraving the *Monstrous Sow of Landser*, which must date from around 1496, and his dated drawing of 1512 the *Conjoined Twins of Ertingen*.[29] In both instances, it is known that the artist was working at second hand from images in broadsheets rather than directly from nature.

At the same time, he was consistently fascinated by what he would have regarded as exotic people and their attire, seemingly wherever he encountered them. In the mid-1490s he studied the characteristic dress of Venetian women on his first visit to the city, and while there also copied representations by Gentile Bellini of people sporting turbans.[30] A quarter of a century later, he would adopt much the same approach on confronting Livonians wearing their outlandish national dress in the Netherlands.[31] Tellingly, his response to the Africans who crossed his path is strikingly empathetic. This was by no means a given at this date, but equally it would be wrong to suppose that he was the first Renaissance artist to accord such people real dignity: a haunting exception dating from 1459 is Benozzo Gozzoli's frescoed portrait of a black attendant on the east wall of the chapel of the Palazzo Medici in Florence.[32] In his woodcut of the *Adoration of the Magi* in the *Marienleben* and his painting of the same subject, both of around 1504, the physiognomy of the black king is already carefully observed and is not simply a type, and the same goes, at a later date, for the African heads in two woodcuts of coats of arms, respectively those of his friend Christoph Scheurl (1481–1542), around 1512–14, and of the artist himself, which is dated 1523.[33]

However, it is in two drawings of Africans that Dürer's affectionate curiosity about his fellow man – or indeed woman – is most compellingly displayed. The first of these is a study in black chalk, which is monogrammed and dated 1508 and depicts a bearded black man who is shown turning to his right and pensively looking in that direction. Given the nature of the medium, but also the fact that the skin is not especially dark, it is both his facial features and curly hair that identify him as an African. Nothing is known about where he and Dürer met, but, given the date, the presumption has to be that it was in Nuremberg, where Ethiopians (who were Christians) were by no means unknown. Nothing suggests that the drawing was made with a painting or print in mind, but the artist would of course have known that such a head might come in handy in the future for another *Adoration of the Magi*.[34]

Conversely, the making of his exquisite silverpoint drawing of Katherina (illus. 15), an elegantly dressed black woman who accompanied João Brandão and is often erroneously presumed to have been his servant, is recorded in the diary of his journey to the Netherlands, where he tersely notes, 'Ich hab mit dem Steft konterfet sein Mohrin' ('I portrayed his [Brandão's] moor [the word is feminine in the original German] with the stylus').[35] At the top of the sheet in question Dürer has added the year – 1521 – her first name and her age (twenty).[36] These details all seem to confirm the warmth of the bond between artist and sitter, while the sheet itself is the very opposite of a cartographic record of human topography. Remarkably, it has been – surely rightly – pointed out by David Bindman and Henry Louis Gates Jr that this is the earliest known likeness of a named black individual by a European artist.[37] At a later date, and in the context of his *Four Books on Human Proportion*, he trots out what, for the period, must have been the standard line, stating that 'black people's faces are rarely beautiful to look at,' but his own art belies the bigotry.[38]

A delight in extremes of expression and unflinching contemplation of facial imperfections runs through Dürer's oeuvre.

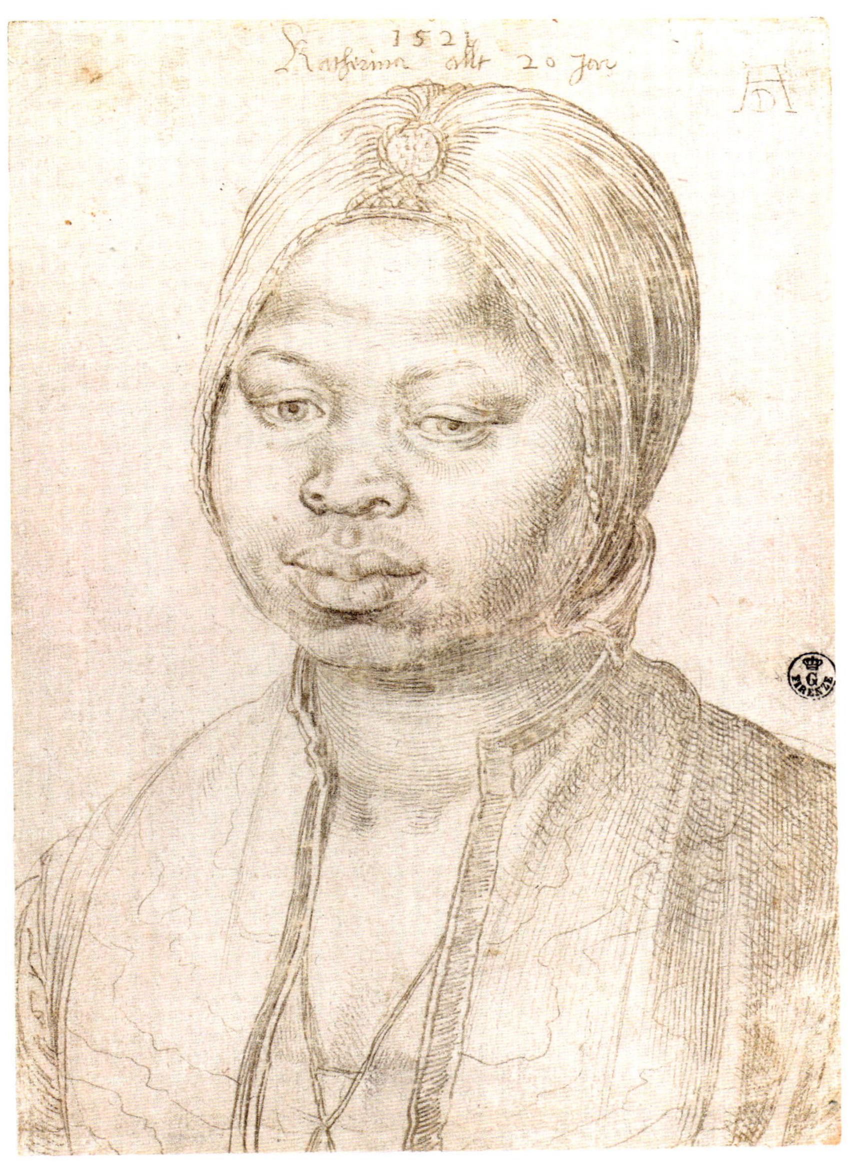

15 Albrecht Dürer, *Katherina*, 1521, silverpoint.

It is certainly no coincidence that most of these explorations are
confined to the private realm of drawings, and went no further.
This is as true of the infectious teeth-baring grin of the pen and
wash 'villana Windisch' of 1505 – to quote the artist's own inscription – as of the open-mouthed *Suffering Man* and the agonized
Dead Christ, both in charcoal and dated 1503.[39]

Moving on from the capturing of emotions to physiognomy,
the unforgettable crooked nose and *di sotto in sù* perspective of the
charcoal portrait drawing of Dürer's friend Conrad Merkel have
often been regarded as a one-off.[40] Yet this may simply be a question of survival, since, as Dürer notes in the diary of his journey
to the Netherlands, 'Auch hab ich den Walen mit dem krummen
Nasen konterfet, mit Namen Opitius' ('I also portrayed the Italian
with the crooked nose called Opitius'), an individual whose identity remains a mystery.[41] What is more, for all that he is no Conrad
Merkel, the bearded man located at the top right-hand corner
of his *Christ among the Doctors* of 1506 (illus. 30) boasts a nose that
bends resplendently to the right.[42] In the same spirit, Dürer
does not conceal Felix Hungersperg's wandering left eye in the
more detailed of his two portrait drawings of him executed in
1520.[43] Moreover, as discussed in the Introduction, all the extant
likenesses of his friend Willibald Pirckheimer – two related
drawings dated 1503 and an engraving of 1524 – positively revel
in his irregular profile.[44]

Dürer was by no means the first artist to record the wonders
of the animal kingdom with an accuracy worthy of a natural his-
torian, and importantly to employ colour in his drawings in order
to do so. His great precursors in this department were Pisanello
and Leonardo: there are a number of captivating watercolours
either by the former or from his circle that testify to this, while the
latter produced memorable studies of cats and of a bear.[45] However,
it is extremely unlikely that Dürer was aware of these earlier works,
and would therefore have presumed he was ploughing a lone

furrow. In any event, being the first is far less important than being the best, and what is indisputable is that nobody else looked as carefully as he did or left such a rich legacy of animal images of different kinds, all of which testify to his almost limitless curiosity in this realm. For these, as for his studies of landscape, he tended to employ both watercolour and body colour, but crucially they are drawings, not paintings, and even the most immaculately resolved of them would not have been regarded by either Dürer or his contemporaries as finished works of art in the way that paintings were.

More generally, there is something approximating to a consensus about the extent of Dürer's oeuvre, but the one area where almost the opposite is now the case is in relation to his nature studies. In 1985 Fritz Koreny was responsible for a transformational exhibition, 'Albrecht Dürer und die Tier- und Pflanzstudien der Renaissance' (Albrecht Dürer and Animal and Plant Studies in the Renaissance), at the Albertina in Vienna, whose catalogue radically reduced the corpus of Dürer's nature studies of all kinds and proved immensely influential on subsequent scholarship.[46] Extremely recently, however, and most dramatically in Christof Metzger's catalogue of a more comprehensive show at the very same institution in 2019–20, a significant number of the botanical illustrations have been rescued from the outer darkness into which they had been cast for decades.[47] Even Solomon might have hesitated before passing judgement on these conflicting visions, but happily there is more than enough common ground between the two conceptions for the present overview.

The reason for describing Dürer's approach as founded on curiosity is that only a relatively minor part of this activity made its way into his finished works of art, whether paintings or prints. It is true, as we shall see, that he sometimes added them to the mix, but only occasionally are they essential components of his narratives. Most straightforwardly, if any artists in Dürer's day had the chance to study an actual lion, they would have been only too well aware of how useful this opportunity was for the correct representation of St Jerome's all but obligatory companion, and it would not have been hard to tweak their drawings from the life if the context required them to undergo minor modifications. After all, if it is effortlessly easy for us to tell the difference between lions in paintings that are based on direct observation and those that are not, it cannot have been much harder to do so at the time.

In order to survey this material coherently, it seems best to examine it in terms of categories – 'phyla' is the technical term – and to proceed from the smaller to the larger animals. This will mean beginning with insects, reptiles and sea creatures, before moving on to birds, and concluding with mammals. At the same time, and regardless of what kinds of animals are involved, there is always bound to have been a profoundly different approach to the everyday and the exotic: cats, dogs and horses were lurking round every corner – and may well have been part of an artist's home – whereas hamadryas baboons were not.

Entomology proves only to have been a minor concern for Dürer.[48] Controversy still surrounds the authorship of a celebrated watercolour of a male stag beetle, which bears a later Dürer monogram and the not necessarily reliable date of 1505.[49] However, regardless of whether this is the original or not, it must at least be an accurate record of a Dürer drawing, which was copied incessantly in the sixteenth century, but more crucially was also quoted by the artist himself in his *Virgin and Child with a Multitude of Animals* of around 1503, and also in his panel of the *Adoration of the Magi* of 1504 (illus. 36).[50] In both instances, the stag beetle is joined by other insects and small creatures: in the former there is a whole procession of them across the foreground consisting of a snail, a dragonfly, another butterfly (possibly a cabbage white), a ground beetle, a frog and a spider crab, while in the latter two butterflies (a small white and a large heath) and what seems to be the same ground beetle are included in the left foreground.

The accuracy of these representations indicates that at least some of the creatures here were the objects of previous studies, whether along the same lines as that of the *Stag Beetle* or of a less detailed character. A pen and ink drawing of around 1494, unknown to Friedrich Winkler when he compiled his great catalogue of Dürer's drawings in the 1930s, combines a sand lizard (another appears in his engraving *Knight, Death and the Devil* (illus. 53)), another

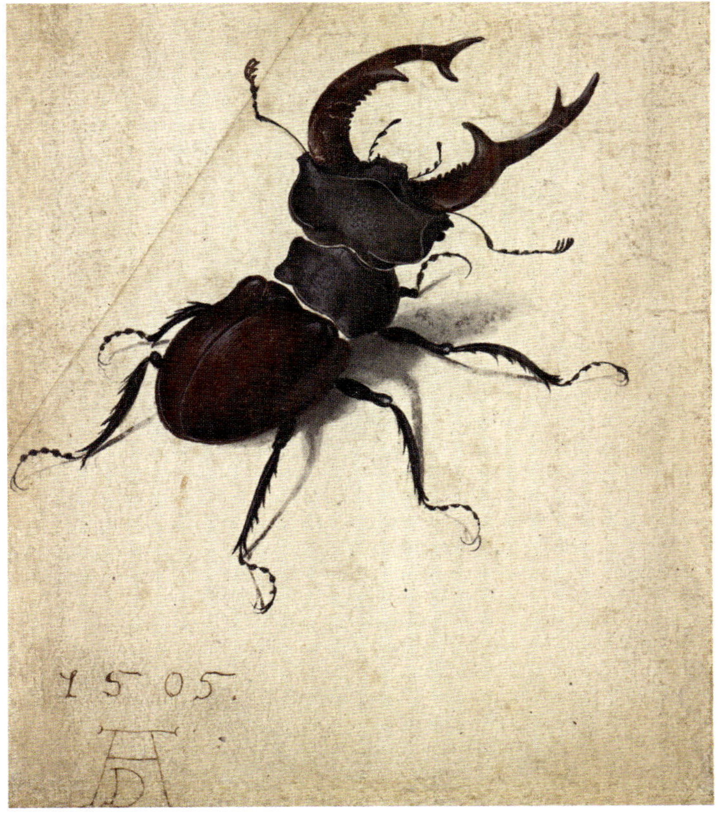

16 Albrecht Dürer, *Stag Beetle*, c. 1501, watercolour and body colour, heightened with white.

small white butterfly, and two frogs, one of which matches its counterpart in the *Virgin and Child with a Multitude of Animals*.[51] The apparent repetition of the ground beetle in the *Virgin* and the *Magi* also points in this direction. Yet Dürer's sole Homeric nod in terms of his utter reliability as a recording angel of members of the animal kingdom he had actually seen (imaginings being a wholly different matter) was in relation to an insect. Around 1495 he produced an engraving that is traditionally called the *Virgin and Child with a Dragonfly*, but in fact the insect in question is a species of hybrid that combines the long body of a dragonfly with the wings of a butterfly.[52] The explanation may be a simple one: Dürer's deep passion for natural history manifested itself above all after 1500 or so.

Moving on to sea creatures, but saving Dürer's walrus for later, the only autograph extant study is of a lobster.[53] It was presumably drawn during the artist's sojourn in Venice in the mid-1490s, and would no doubt have had a particular appeal for someone from landlocked Nuremberg. Elsewhere, in other prints and drawings by the artist, such as his engraving the *Sea-Monster* and his drawing *Arion*, his aquatic fantasies give one the impression that they are based upon observation, whether of a turtle's shell in the former or of actual fish in both.[54]

The distinction between the everyday and the exotic outlined above is particularly acute in the case of birds. Dürer departs from convention in his *Virgin and Child with a Siskin*, because the goldfinch was the bird customarily preferred by virtue of its symbolic association with the Passion of Christ.[55] Be that as it may, siskins – like other small birds – were doubtless routinely kept in cages, which would have meant they were easily studied in detail, and this one is shown flying about but attached to a string.

Conversely, Dürer's four full-dress watercolours of larger species, which are all on parchment, perhaps to confer a special dignity upon them, are of dead specimens. The first is the undated

Dead Duck, which has been identified as featuring a female common pochard (*Athya ferina* L.).[56] No doubt availability was the simple motivation for drawing it, not least since the male of the same species is an altogether more distinctive and glamorous bird. The depiction of dead game birds hanging from hooks goes back to classical antiquity, but was also something of a speciality of Jacopo de' Barbari, who even executed a pioneering independent still-life painting that includes a hanging partridge.[57]

There is a second watercolour on parchment of a dead bird, which is monogrammed and dated 1512, but is probably actually of around 1500, and represents a European roller. Moreover, although it lacks the nail and string – not to mention the cast shadow – that serve to anchor the common pochard to its sur-roundings, this specimen must in fact have been hung in exactly the same way.[58] Clearly the appeal here relates to the radiant luminosity of the bird's plumage, but, as is dramatically under-lined by the inferiority of the trio of derivations from it by Hans Hoffmann, it is also distinguished by the delicacy and brilliance of its execution.[59]

As has been pointed out by Koreny, study of birds' wings had a very specific ulterior motive because they were ideally suited to be employed to represent the wings of angels and other celestial creatures.[60] In Exodus (25:20) and Ezekiel (10:5–22) cherubim are said to have wings, and in Isaiah (6:2) the same goes for ser-aphim. By extension, the visual tradition tended to endow angels with wings, and predictably Dürer sought to make his as convinc-ing as possible by basing them upon birds' wings. The care he took is demonstrated by a pen and ink drawing for his engraving of *Nemesis*: the sheet shows the figure in reverse with a single smaller and more schematic vertical wing, and then adds a detailed study of the wing in isolation, again aligned vertically, but the same way round as it will be in the finished print.[61] Interestingly, when they are carefully compared, even this rendition differs considerably from the altogether more detailed wing in the engraving. It should therefore come as no surprise if another drawing of a European roller, likewise dated 1512 but probably of around 1500, and presumably executed at the same time from the same specimen, comprises a single extended wing (illus. 17).[62] Finally, in the case of the *Wing Study of a Lapwing*, although the doubts about Dürer's authorship have been even more vigorous than usual, on balance it seems hard to conceive who else could have drawn it.[63]

There are a select few other studies of birds by Dürer, some of which appear in surviving drawings and prints. However, the

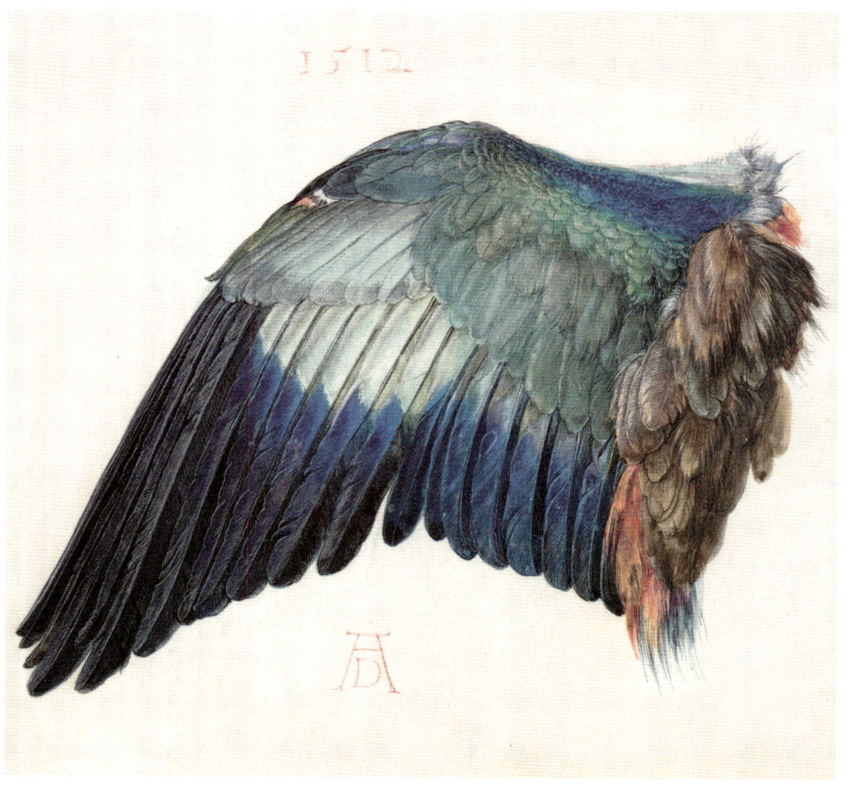

17 Albrecht Dürer, *Wing of a European Roller*, c. 1500, watercolour and body colour, heightened with white and gold, on parchment.

idea that there were once more is supported by their occasional appearance alongside birds for which no drawings are preserved. Thus a drawing of a parrot appears in the *Virgin and Child with a Multitude of Animals* and, as has been discussed, in the engraving *Adam and Eve*, and Dürer's drawing of a stork is likewise quoted in the former. In all probability, therefore, there must once have existed a study of the green woodpecker next to the parrot in the left foreground of the drawing.[64]

Dürer's attitude to animals was entirely consistent, regardless of whether they were commonplace or he knew he was unlikely to see another of the same species ever again. Strictly speaking, we do not know if he kept pets, but would sentimentally like to imagine he did, and Dürer's friend and fellow Nuremberger, the jurist and diplomat Christoph Scheurl, tells an admittedly tall tale about the artist's dog kissing his master's face on a still wet self-portrait drying in the sunshine.[65] Be that as it may, he had certainly observed the sleepy contentment of which cats are capable, and introduced just such a one into the forest floor in his afore-mentioned engraving of Adam and Eve (illus. 13). What is more, even the proximity of a mouse, whose tail Adam has inadvertently trapped under his right foot, cannot rouse it. The Book of Genesis has nothing to say on the subject, but it seems plain that Dürer, perhaps recalling a passage that foresees harmony among all creatures led by a little child (Isaiah 11:6–9), imagined a similar peacefulness in Eden.

When it came to dogs, the sheer number of different breeds meant there were far more possibilities, and Dürer made the most of them. This is above all apparent in his prints, whose doggy population was to prove particularly irresistible to his Italian ad-mirers, as will be explored briefly in the next chapter. Even more blatantly than was the case with birds, there must have been numbers of life drawings of which we can only dream. In the en-graving of his vision of Christ, Dürer's St Eustace is accompanied

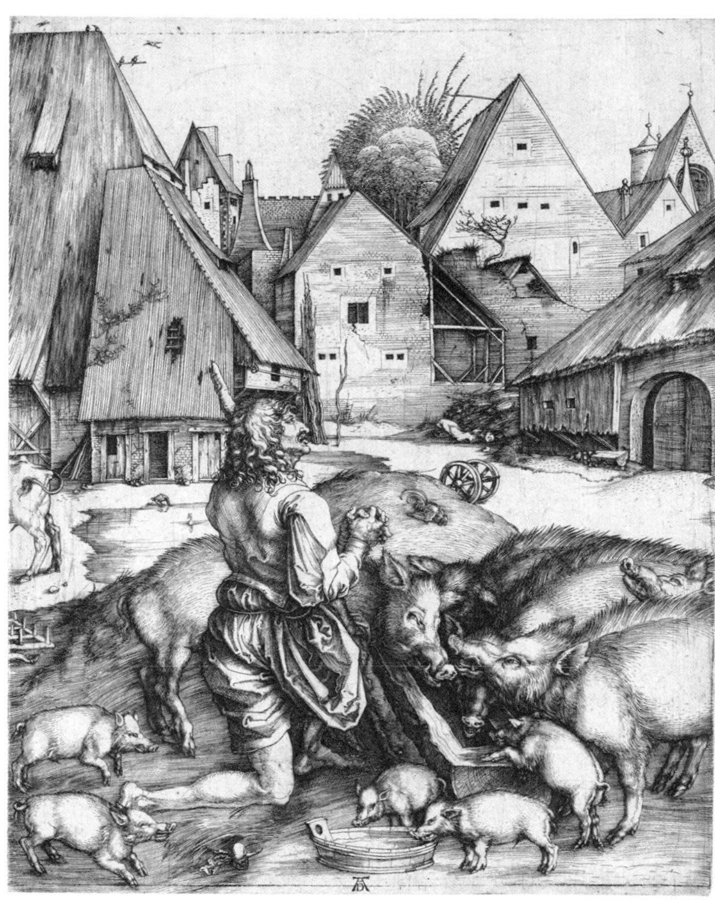

by five greyhounds: each of their attitudes must have required an individual study, quite possibly all drawn from the same canine model, but only one such sheet has come down to us.[66]

Direct observation of farmyard animals must have been equally straightforward, and the seething mass of swine and piglets in the artist's engraving of the *Prodigal Son* – especially seen in conjunction with the piglet-free preliminary drawing for it, where not a single

18 Albrecht Dürer, *The Prodigal Son*, c. 1496, engraving.

animal is identically posed – bears eloquent witness to his unfailing self-scrutiny.[67] Studies of cattle, an elk, a bison and, above all, a dead stag with an arrow through its head all reveal a similar attention to detail, which could then feed into later productions, such as the *Adam and Eve* and the *St Eustace* (illus. 51).[68]

The most celebrated of all Dürer's animal portraits is the monogrammed and dated *Hare* of 1502 (illus. 19), which was extensively copied in the sixteenth century, not least by Hans Hoffmann.[69] Its sole rival used to be the *Squirrels*, a drawing which is now also given to Hoffmann. In his consideration of it, Koreny observed that it is impossible to be certain whether either squirrel – or both

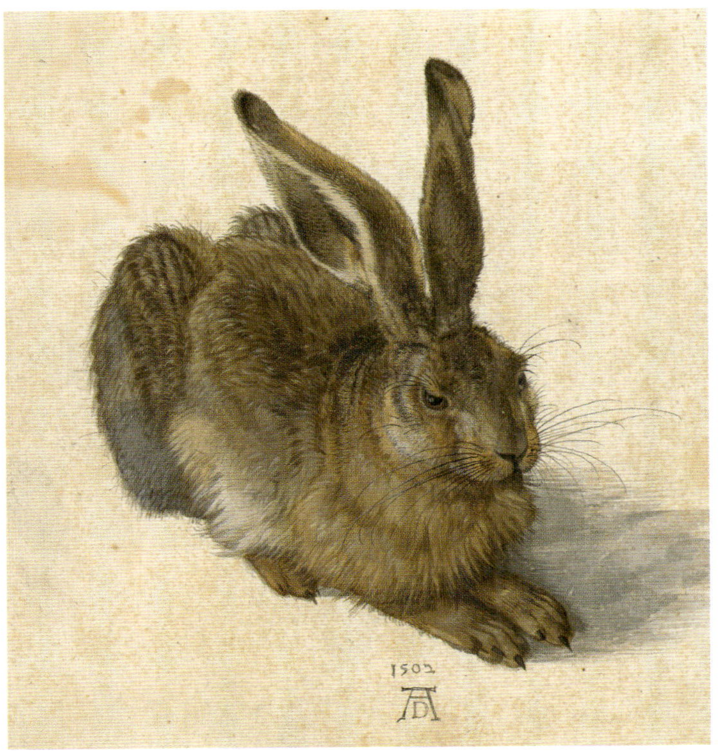

19 Albrecht Dürer, *Hare*, 1502, watercolour and body colour.

– may hark back to a lost Dürer prototype, and strictly speaking this is undeniable, but it is nevertheless striking how much more animated they, and in particular the foremost one, are than any of Hoffmann's own independent inventions.[70]

During his time in the Netherlands, Dürer made the most of his encounters with a variety of more exotic animals. Around 1498 he had of course already included a chained Hanuman langur, which was evidently based on a now lost life study, in his *Virgin and Child with a Monkey* engraving (illus. 26), and was now able to add a hamadryas baboon in watercolour on a sheet of pen studies.[71] It is accompanied by a lynx, a chamois and three studies of lions, which he may have drawn when he visited the zoo (Tiergarten) in Brussels.[72] They are not the only lions he drew in that period, and in his diary the artist refers to having seen lions (*löben*) and drawn one in silverpoint from a living specimen in Ghent on 10 April 1521.[73]

As has been demonstrated, Dürer was meticulously accurate when it came to reproducing animals he was able to see in the flesh, but that prerequisite was not always feasible. The principal *raison d'être* of his Netherlandish journey was to see a beached whale, but he did not manage it.[74] In the case of both his drawing *Walrus* and his drawing and woodcut *Rhinoceros* (illus. 20) he himself reveals the fact that he is working at one remove through the inscriptions he added to them – admittedly only obliquely in relation to the first.[75] The hitherto unnoticed clue is in the length of the walrus, which he gives as twelve Brabant ells, which is around 8.4 metres (27 ft 6 in.), whereas the largest adult male walruses only reach a length of about 3.7 metres (12 ft), or significantly less than half the size (his account also exaggerates the size of the whale). The text of the *Rhinoceros* drawing, which is the basis for a nearly identical legend on the print, explicitly states that the creature was delivered to Lisbon as a gift for the king of Portugal. It is impossible to reconstruct exactly what Dürer had to go on, but inevitably neither is an accurate portrait. Typically, he nevertheless cannot resist introducing a few tiny tweaks between his drawing of the rhino and its final resolution in the woodcut, such as the enlargement of the horn on its back and extension of what might be described as the craquelure of the armour plating around its neck.

Having examined Dürer's engagement with his fellow man and the wonders of the animal kingdom, it now remains to explore plants, trees and landscape.[76] In so doing, it also makes sense to include his representations of man-made objects, buildings and cities. He directed an identical attention towards all of them, for two connected reasons: the first is that he was attracted to them by his immense curiosity, and the second is that he knew such accurate transcriptions had the potential to make his finished paintings and prints feel more compellingly real to the beholder. The majority of his surviving drawings of this kind that portray larger-scale motifs seem to belong to very particular periods of his life, above all when he was travelling and visiting new places.

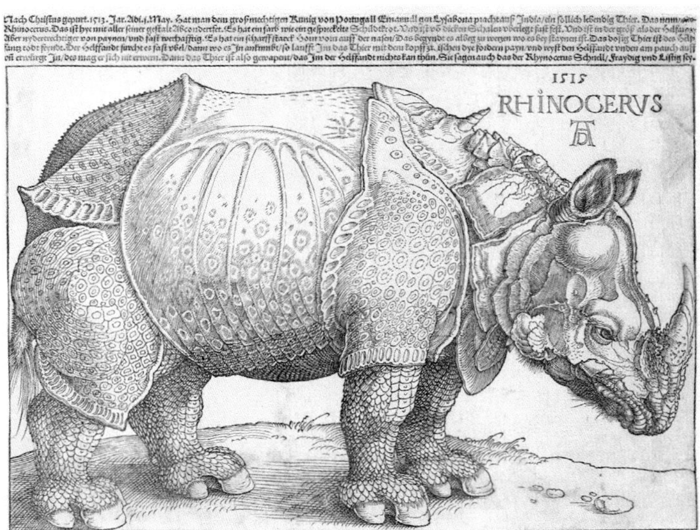

20 Albrecht Dürer, *Rhinoceros*, 1515, woodcut.

Nevertheless, there is firm evidence that he also subjected his more immediate surroundings to similar scrutiny. Moreover, this has to be one of those areas of his artistic practice where all manner of wonders are irretrievably lost. In theory, he may never have bothered to pin down his impressions of the canals and buildings of the most photogenic of all cities, Venice, but it hardly seems likely.

In the case of Dürer's explorations of still-life details and elements of interiors in his drawings, it almost invariably seems that they are not directly preparatory for specific works. The sole exception is the substantial sheet with two pen and ink studies for a pair of scales, which must have been made for the engraving *Melencolia* (illus. 54), and not just used in it, although even in this instance they are somewhat modified in the print.[77] Elsewhere, one has a sense of the artist taking note of his surroundings with no particular project in mind, if naturally always aware that they might turn out to serve a purpose one day.[78]

Dürer's use of watercolour and body colour for so many of the studies of nature we do still have may well have guaranteed their survival, but it has to be assumed that the highly detailed landscapes of his fifteenth-century Netherlandish predecessors, and most notably Jan van Eyck, were based upon the observation of the world beyond the workshop. What is less straightforward are the way or ways in which they achieved their illusions of authenticity.

The simple answer would be to presume that they made record drawings, conceivably in watercolour and/or body colour, and employed them as the basis for their topographical fictions. After all, the use of colour on paper or parchment would not have been alien to all of them. From this point of view, it is immaterial who painted the astoundingly convincing *bas-de-page* landscape prospect with the *Baptism of Christ* on one of the pages of the *Turin Book of Hours*, but it already triumphantly demonstrates an equivalent

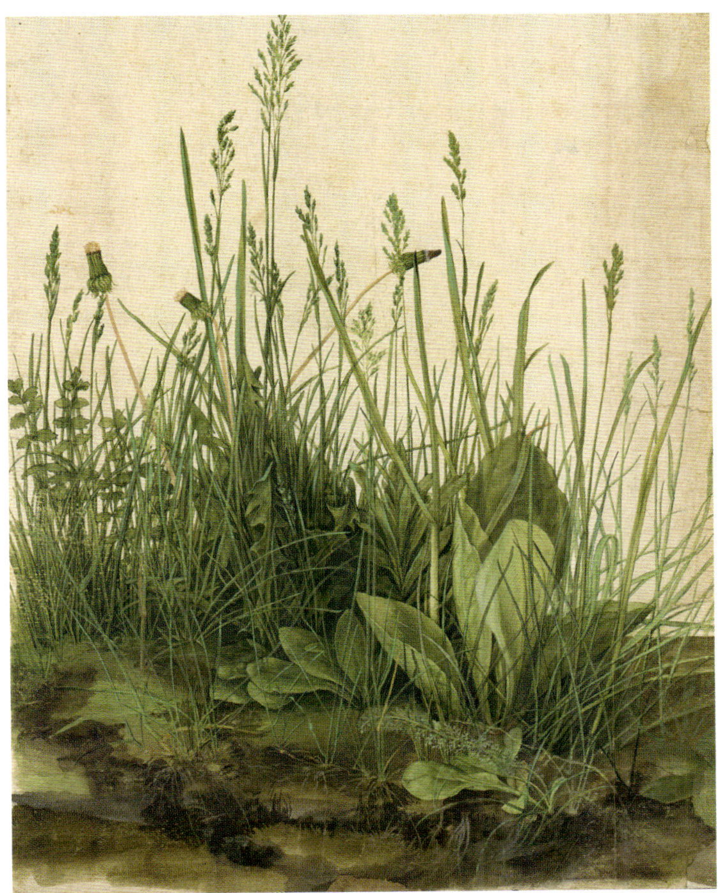

passion for landscape.[79] Almost no comparable Italian studies are known, but that too may be a reflection of what has survived. A stunning sheet, which is customarily attributed to Marco Basaiti for no very good reason, is actually so strikingly close in its overall configuration to the middle distance of Giovanni Bellini's *Sacred Allegory* as to tempt one to wonder if the artist Dürer hailed as 'still the best in painting' was not its creator.[80]

21 Albrecht Dürer, *Great Piece of Turf*, 1503, watercolour and body colour.

The other possibility is that they simply looked more intensely than we are accustomed to, and registered what they saw. In two of the early biographical accounts of Adam Elsheimer, he is said to have done precisely this, although the fact that it was deemed worthy of note may well indicate quite how rare a gift his ability to do so was. In the paragraph Carel van Mander devoted to the then still living artist in his *Schilder-boeck* of 1604, he writes, 'He does not busy himself with drawing, but rather sits in churches or elsewhere to look at the works of the great masters, impressing everything securely in his memory.'[81] It may be objected that Van Mander is referring exclusively to works of art, but the complementary account provided by Sandrart in the substantial biography in his *Teutsche Akademie* of 1675 is more comprehensive. According to Sandrart, who lists and describes a number of his paintings:

> So profound were Elsheimer's works, for his memory and imagination were thus constituted, that if he only saw a few beautiful trees (before which he had often sat or lain half or even whole days) they were so firmly engraved on his mind that he was able to render a complete and natural likeness of them at home, without preliminary drawing. This can be judged by the fact that he impressed the Vigna Madama in Rome so firmly in his mind that he was able to incorporate it without any drawings and with greatest skill into his landscapes. Every tree is recognizable from its special type, from its stem, foliage and leaves in all parts as well as from colour, shade and reflection, quite similar, natural and vivid, a manner which not everybody can achieve and which is difficult without the aid of the actual object or a drawing.[82]

Turning to specific sheets, the supreme botanical microcosm is indisputably the *Great Piece of Turf* (illus. 21), which leaves all the other studies of wild flowers, regardless of whether they are autograph or not, in the shade.[83] As with the comparable animal studies, the primary reason for making them is to try to see and record the world as it is, and any subsequent exploitation of them is an additional but by no means guaranteed benefit. What seems clear, and may well not simply be an accident of survival, is the fact that there are almost no detailed coloured drawings of nature by Dürer that are securely datable after 1510 or so, when he was nearly forty. In this context, it is worth underlining the fact that, in a letter of 1520 to Georg Spalatin, he himself makes reference to the prospect of fading powers in terms of both eyesight and manual dexterity ('Dann so mir abgeht am Gesicht und Freiheit der Hand, würd mein Sach nit wohlstehn').[84]

At home in Nuremberg and in the surrounding countryside, he was not particularly attracted to grand structures or scenes, but it would be misleading to imply that he was simply a Christopher Isherwood-style camera.[85] In his representations of individual trees or the rocky corners of quarries, he tends to be punctiliously accurate in his observations, but quite free in his touch.[86] However, the supreme accomplishment of his more expansive landscapes is their celebration of topographical precision or their romantic atmosphere. Thus the *Wire-Drawing Mill* (illus. 22) and the *Church and Cemetery of Sankt Johannes, Nuremberg* both artfully communicate a sense of their timeless fidelity to what the artist saw, whereas the *Willow Mill* and the *Fisherman's House on a Lake* appear to freeze a moment in time, above all by virtue of their atmospheric skies.[87]

Unsurprisingly, on his travels Dürer likewise reacted to the landscapes and architecture he encountered in more or less the same ways. A group of studies is generally agreed to chronicle his journeys to and from Venice in 1495. When he reached Innsbruck, for instance, he executed two depictions of the central courtyard in the Hofburg (the Habsburg residence) from the north and the south, but also a view of the city under a cloudy sky across the reflective surface of the water that separated him from it (illus. 23).[88] In the nature of things, it is by no means always possible to judge the accuracy of his *vedute* (views), to employ the term favoured at a later date, because so much has changed in the last five hundred years. Tellingly, however, a recent photograph showing the view from Cembra to the northeast confirms the basic accuracy of his watercolour of the same prospect.[89] There are a number of other watercolour and body colour drawings of identifiable locations, which were referred to very briefly in the previous chapter, that make it possible to track the routes he took on his way to Italy and his return home. Conversely, it would appear that no comparable sheets date from his second Italian journey.

After a hiatus of around a quarter of a century, Dürer's journey to the Netherlands in 1520–21 yielded a substantial group of drawings, which, with two memorable exceptions, display a completely different technique and approach.[90] The odd ones out are both horizontal pen studies – one of the port at Antwerp, the other of the view of the zoo in Brussels from the Imperial Palace – both of which Dürer has inscribed with the location and the

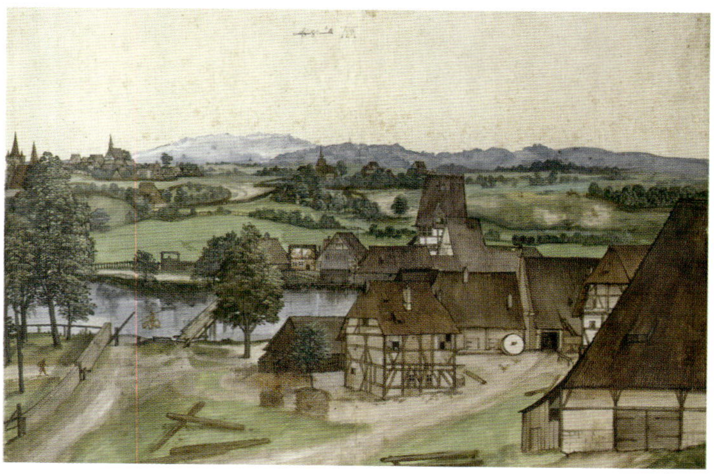

22 Albrecht Dürer, *Wire-Drawing Mill*, c. 1494, watercolour and body colour.

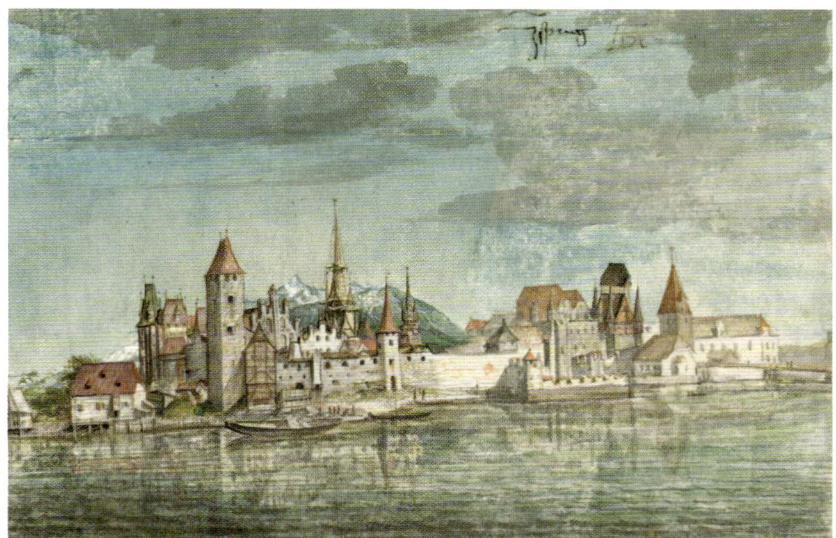

date 1520.[91] For the rest, they all belong to the so-called Silverpoint Sketchbook, and are divided between standard representations of buildings or landscapes and highly original half-length portraits, which show the subjects against memorable town- or landscape backdrops.[92]

In conclusion, and not least because Dürer is far too great an artist to require protection from what might be seen as a mild criticism, it seems worth observing that in his paintings – as opposed to his nature studies in watercolour – he was perhaps surprisingly indifferent to the challenges posed by the dramatic potential of light. It is true that in his early painting of *St Jerome* in the National Gallery all the colours of the evening sky beyond the kneeling figure of the saint in the wilderness are gloriously brought to life, but this is an exception and absolutely not the rule.[93]

Tellingly, Dürer never painted a night scene, and yet impressively realistic depictions of the darkness of night, often pierced by artificial light, had been painted, above all in illuminated

23 Albrecht Dürer, *View of Innsbruck*, *c.* 1495, watercolour and body colour, heightened with white.

manuscripts, nearly a century before his day. There are fine examples in the *Très Riches Heures du Duc de Berry*, in the *Turin Book of Hours* and supremely in Barthélemy d'Eyck's *Le Livre du cuer d'amours espris*, where, uniquely, there is a solitary interior night scene alongside the more customary exteriors.[94]

Moreover, for all that the earliest night scenes give every indication of having been the work of manuscript illuminators, by the second half of the fifteenth century the first nocturnes on panel had come into existence. There is good evidence that two entirely separate treatments of the *Nativity by Night* were executed by Hugo van der Goes in the 1470s: both are now lost, but they are known in the form of a number of copies and adaptations. Of these, a panel by Geertgen tot Sint Jans in the National Gallery, which reflects the composition of what appears to be the later of the two, is currently and convincingly dated around 1490.[95] At least on his journey to the Netherlands in 1520–21, if not before, Dürer can hardly have failed to come across the odd night scene, not least in the hellish visions of Hieronymus Bosch, but he never succumbed to the appeal of the genre.[96]

TWO

Study, Travel and Influence

From a modern perspective, it may seem paradoxical that Dürer's dazzling originality was founded upon his virtually ceaseless study of the works of artists both ancient and modern, but in that respect, as in so many others, he was neither more nor less than a child of his time. What is more, for all that a number of his direct copies, such as the ones after Mantegna, which must have been an early education in the reach and power of the print, bear dates that prove they were made when he was in his early twenties, he arguably never stopped learning from others.

In this connection, his various travels are bound to be of particular relevance, since seeing original works of art and meeting new people have the potential to be life-changing experiences. A considerable body of evidence indicates that Dürer visited both the Lower and the Upper Rhine and Italy in the years between 1490 and 1495, but it is altogether harder to be certain exactly where he went and precisely what he may have seen, and moreover the whole idea of an Italian journey before 1500 has been explicitly denied.[1] Here it will be contended that he did not simply visit Venice in the mid-1490s, but also reached both Florence and Rome at that time. Especially in the case of the latter, the evidence in the form of borrowings from ancient works of art is controversial to say the least. Indeed, there is considerable reluctance to believe that he even went to Rome on his second Italian journey of 1506.[2] Be that as it may, there is incomparably more hard evidence, not least in the form of his correspondence and journal (as referred to in the Introduction), not only concerning Dürer's return to Italy, but especially about his journey to the Netherlands in 1520–21. Both will be exhaustively investigated in this chapter, not least in order to distinguish between certainties and hypotheses. In conclusion, Dürer's influence on the works of other artists – above all but not exclusively in Italy – will also be addressed. In order to present all this very diverse material coherently, it seems to make sense, as indicated by the title of this chapter, to divide it into three sections, respectively devoted to study, travel and influence.

As Dürer recounts in his *Family Chronicle*, at the end of 1486 his father arranged for him to be apprenticed to Michael Wolgemut in Nuremberg for three years ('in die lehr jahr zu Michael Wolgemuth, drei jahr lang jhm zu dienen').[3] Given the extraordinary accomplishment of the drawn *Self-Portrait Aged Thirteen* and the only moderate standard of his new master's paintings, of which the *Portrait of Levinus Memminger* is a characteristic example, it is tempting to wonder how much he can have learnt from the experience.[4] Having said that, the technical demands of painting in oils on wood panels, canvas or fine linen are entirely separate from the arts of employing metalpoint or pen in the context of drawing, which we may presume Dürer picked up almost literally at his father's knee, and would have been fundamental for his future development. He simply states that he learnt, but adds that he was bullied by many of his fellow apprentices.[5]

In the *Family Chronicle*, what happened next is hilariously tersely recounted:

Und da ich aussgedient hat, schickt mich mein Vater hinweg, und bliebe vier Jahren aussen, bis dass mein vatter mich wieder fodert. Und alss ich im 1490 jar hinweg zog, nach Ostern, darnach kam ich wider, alss man zehlt 1494, nach Pfingsten. [And since I had completed my service, my father sent me from there, and I stayed away for four years, until my father called for me again. I went away after Easter 1490 and returned after Whitsun 1494.][6]

The impressive level of his work in painting prior to his departure is demonstrated by the paired portraits of his father and mother, since the reverse of the former is dated 1490: the same date accompanied by the 'AD' monogram also appears on the front of the panel, but this may well be a later addition.[7]

Where he went and what he did is almost entirely unknown, the only concrete clue being provided by his slightly younger contemporary and close friend, Christoph Scheurl, who in 1515 implies that Dürer's father planned to send him to study with Martin Schongauer (c. 1450/53–1491) in Colmar. This intention evidently followed on his apprenticeship with Wolgemut, since Scheurl records the fact that he was a welcome guest of the artist's brother in 1492, but that 'he had never been a pupil of Martin's, indeed he had never even seen him.'[8] The simple reason was that by the time he reached Colmar, Schongauer was no longer in a position to take pupils, having died in February 1491.

Be that as it may, the importance of Schongauer's work for Dürer cannot be emphasized strongly enough. The most obvious way in which he proved influential was as both the most technically brilliant and the most inventive printmaker of his time. Compositions such as his *Temptation of St Anthony* and *Christ Carrying the Cross* set a standard in the still relatively novel medium to which the young Dürer could aspire.[9] At the same time, no doubt as a result of his personal contact with the family in 1492, Dürer owned three pen drawings by Schongauer, which he inscribed with their dates and the artist's initials, and in one instance with a line of text: 'Das hat hubsch martin gemacht. Im 1469 Jor' ('This was done by beautiful Martin [the standard punning nickname for Schongauer] in the year 1469').[10] Even more remarkably, as was demonstrated by Fritz Koreny in an article of exceptional importance, the watercolour and body colour *Study of Peonies* by Schongauer must also have been known to Dürer, who indeed presumably owned it, since he copied it so punctiliously in his *Virgin and Child with a Multitude of Animals*.[11]

In the case of another pen drawing, which was inscribed by Dürer and no doubt likewise owned by him, he states, 'D[a]z hat wofgang pewrer gemacht Im 1484 Jor' ('This was made by Wolfgang Peurer in the year 1484').[12] Nothing is known about this individual, but it has been plausibly suggested that he may be identical with the otherwise anonymous Master W. B., not least because 'P' and 'B' (like 'D' and 'T' in the case of Dürer himself) were interchangeable in the German vernacular at this period. W. B. – alias Beurer/Peurer – was clearly an artist to whose portraits, such as the *Portrait of a Man* of 1487, Dürer looked for inspiration, although it remains unclear if he was based in Nuremberg or elsewhere.[13] Regardless of whether he came across the sheet in question at home or on his travels, there is no doubt that he subsequently turned it into one of his first engravings, the so-called *Grosser Postreiter* or *Great Courier*, simply adding a landscape and making the most minimal of modifications to such details as the horse's tail.[14]

Like Schongauer, in addition to being a painter the Master W. B. was an important early printmaker, and the appeal of prints to the youthful Dürer is plain. Another figure best known by his initials, the Master LCz, had a slightly different but no less direct influence on his art, in this case above all by virtue of a single engraving. For when around 1503–4 Dürer came to devise his woodcut of the *Flight into Egypt* for the *Marienleben*, he incontrovertibly took the Master LCz's engraved treatment of the same subject as his model. He not only borrowed the general disposition of the figures, with Joseph over to the right leading the way, looking back over his right shoulder and with a diagonally angled walking stick over his left one, but, even more clinchingly, repeated the iconographically highly unusual motif of the ox of the Nativity accompanying the ass on the Flight.[15]

Another destination must have been Basel, where he appears to have worked on the illustrations for a number of printed books. Thus the woodblock for the title page of Nicolaus Kessler's 1492 (second) edition of the *Letters of St Jerome* bears an admittedly not autograph inscription on its reverse that reads 'Albrecht Dürer von Nörmergk', while various drawings connected with a projected but ultimately unrealized edition of the *Comedies* of Terence have been plausibly attributed to him, and are undeniably superior to the end products in the form of woodblocks.[16]

Among the early sources for Dürer's biography, both Carel van Mander in 1604 and Joachim Sandrart in 1675 claim that he visited the Netherlands during his *Wanderjahre*, but there is no hard evidence to support this.[17] On the contrary, at no point in the diary of his journey in 1520–21 does he make a single reference to any previous acquaintance with the places he visits or the sights he sees of the sort one might reasonably expect if he knew them of old.

Turning to art from south of the Alps, Dürer may very possibly have been acquainted with such works at home in his native Nuremberg. If so, the pieces in question are almost bound to have been prints, which exist in the form of multiples and must in any event have been more likely to travel than drawings, which at this period tended to remain within painters' workshops.

There survive no fewer than twenty drawings from his hand that reproduce a whole array of engravings from the admittedly even larger series known as the *Tarocchi di Mantegna*.[18] In all these sheets, Dürer is not satisfied simply to replicate his models, but instead at least in part translates them into his own visual idiom.

What is more, in the case of the singularly undistinguished *Tarocchi*, he decisively improves upon his prototypes, and also on occasion adds coloured washes to his translations. Each pair of images would yield a similar result, but a comparison between the original of *Prudence* and Dürer's version of it may serve to underline the gulf that divides them. Moving from the bottom up, Dürer adds foliage and the odd stone to the neutral ground of his model and considerably enlarges the dragon, while at the same time cropping it at the edge of the composition and rendering it more ferocious. When it comes to the figure, the drapery folds are artfully gothicized, but the main difference concerns the facial features, which are unmistakably 'Dürerized' – even when it comes to the reflection in the mirror.[19] Unlike all the other Italian sources he copies and adapts at the outset of his career, the *Tarocchi* were demonstrably known in Nuremberg at that time, where a number of them were reproduced – likewise with what might be described as localizing modifications – in Michael Wolgemut's workshop in connection

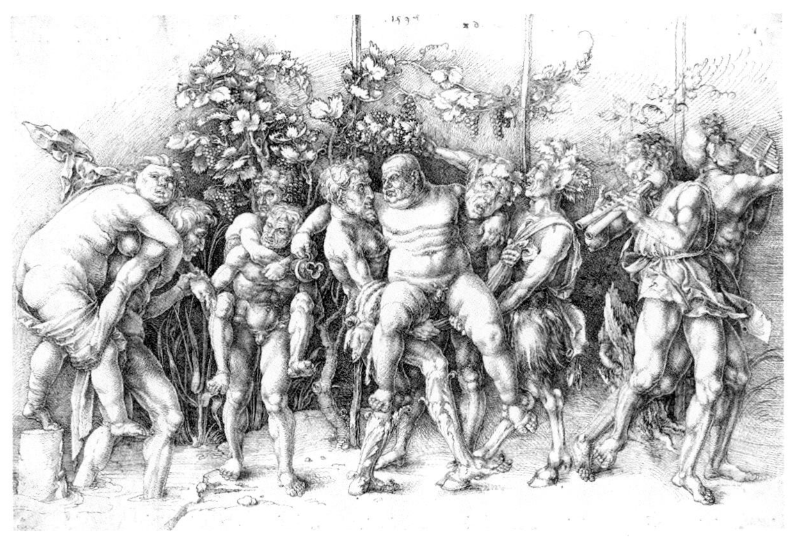

24 Albrecht Dürer, after Mantegna, *Bacchanal with Silenus*, 1494, pen and brown ink.

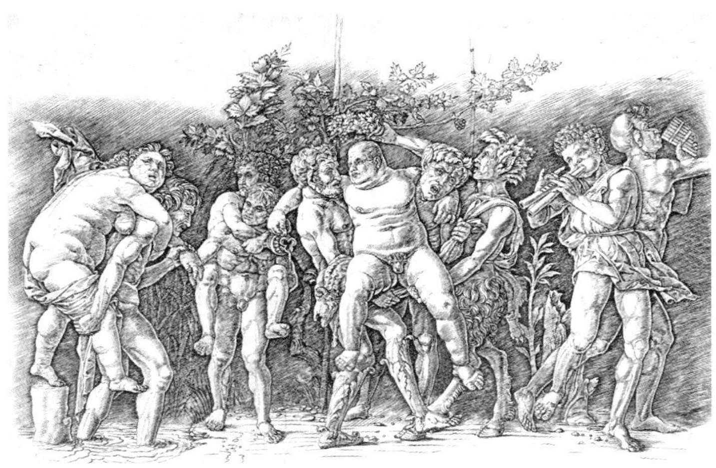

with Peter Danhauser's projected but never published *Archetypus triumphant is Romae*, which was being planned there around 1493–7.[20] It is also tempting to wonder whether Dürer would have found these mediocrities so absorbing after reaching Italy, where he would be surrounded by works of real distinction.

The *Tarocchi* copies are not his only early drawings after Italian prints: two celebrated sheets by Dürer, which are both monogrammed and dated 1494, are copies of Andrea Mantegna's *Bacchanal with Silenus* and the right half of his *Battle of the Sea-Gods*.[21] Traditionally, it has been assumed that Dürer's prime motivation in making these drawings was to learn a new visual language through their example, but recently Andrew John Martin and Christof Metzger have rightly insisted upon the fact that, in their words, 'Dürer made significant changes in both copies after Mantegna.'[22] If Dürer had access to both these prints, then it is hard to imagine he was not also familiar with the left half of the *Battle of the Sea-Gods* and the *Bacchanal with a Wine Vat*, and a case can be made that he may have adapted a heroically Apollonian figure in the latter for a woodcut of *St Christopher*, which bears a later 'AD' monogram and

25 Andrea Mantegna, *Bacchanal with Silenus*, c. 1470–75, engraving with drypoint.

a hopelessly misguided date of 1525. Its status within his oeuvre is extremely controversial, but there is no denying the connection with the Mantegna print, and it would be an odd coincidence if a spurious association with his name had been added precisely to a print that quoted from another by the Italian artist he most revered.[23]

In the case of the most tantalizing of all these early derivations, Dürer's drawing of the *Death of Orpheus*, the ostensible source is a late fifteenth-century Italian engraving, generally thought to be Ferrarese. However, it is now widely accepted that their common prototype must in fact have been a now lost work by Mantegna. I have previously argued that there are concrete reasons to attribute the invention to Mantegna, perhaps above all because the distinctive attitude and costume of the figure of the maenad seen from behind are also quoted in Perugino's *Battle of Love and Chastity*, which was painted for the Studiolo of Isabella d'Este in Mantua.[24] It may be unwise to speculate unduly concerning which differences between Dürer's solution and that found in the Ferrarese print go back to Mantegna, but it is tempting to assume that both the presence of the central clump of trees and the substitution of a modern lute by a classical harp reveal Dürer's greater fidelity to their common model.

If Mantegna's authorship of the lost original is accepted, and it seems hard to doubt it, there remains the question of whether both the Ferrarese engraver and Dürer had access to a highly finished drawing by him or to a print. In this connection, it is important to stress that the earliest Italian engravings often seem to have been produced in extremely small editions: the Hamburg *Death of Orpheus* engraving is a unique impression, and there are only two of the *Prevedari Engraving* by Bramante, which means that in both cases their loss would have resulted in posterity remaining entirely unaware of their ever having existed.[25] The fact that the *Death of Orpheus* drawing is dated 1494 may be decisive in this connection, since if it is accepted that Dürer did indeed make a journey to Italy, but not until the year after, the dated copy drawings must have been executed in Nuremberg before his departure for Italy in 1495. According to the biography that Joachim Camerarius included as a preface to his 1532 Latin translation of Dürer's *De Symmetria*, in 1506 the aged Mantegna summoned the younger artist to Mantua, but death intervened and they never met. It is impossible to know if there is any truth in this account, but it does inevitably recall the similar near miss with Schongauer.[26]

On the other hand, in certain instances it is clear that his sources must have been drawings as opposed to prints. The idea that Dürer visited Venice on his first Italian journey is fairly well established, not least because one of his letters of 1506 to Willibald Pirckheimer seems to allude to a previous sojourn eleven years earlier, and it is supported by at least one copy drawing.

Conversely, there has been a tendency to resist the notion that he might have travelled further south on this first journey, but not for any very good reason. An opposite scenario will be put forward here, above all because in the case of four works that give every indication of being after Florentine models, it is hard to resist the temptation to suppose that cumulatively they provide decisive evidence of a visit to the city. In theory, drawings can travel and so can copies of them, but it is undeniable that access to them would have been far easier on the spot. Even working on the assumption that Dürer's versions were made elsewhere, they did of course end up in Nuremberg, but it does also seem reasonable to contend that his interest in Italian art far exceeded that of his fellow artists in Nuremberg or in Germany more widely.

Three of the four sources referred to above have been exten-sively discussed in the literature on Dürer, but the third has hitherto not been recognized. The first is a sheet that represents two naked men carrying off two equally naked women.[27] No existing

prototype for it is known, but it has not unreasonably been presumed that it must be a basically faithful copy of a now lost
drawing by Antonio Pollaiuolo in the spirit of his celebrated
Battle of the Nude Men. Moreover, as will be returned to in the next
chapter, Dürer also seems to have been acquainted with the
Pollaiuolo painting of *Hercules, Nessus and Deianira*.[28]

The three other connections all associate Dürer with the
Florentine painter Lorenzo di Credi. The first is a monogrammed
and dated drawing of 1495. It is executed in pen and black ink
on prepared paper, heightened with white, and shows the Christ
Child seated on the ground. In attitude, he is related to representations of his counterpart in a number of paintings by Lorenzo
di Credi, but is only perfectly matched by the same figure in a
tondo by him in New York.[29] In that painting the Child is sitting
on a drapery and supported by a bundle, but neither features in
the drawing, which suggests that they were not present in Dürer's
model, and that it was rather a highly finished preparatory study,
whose technique he has endeavoured to imitate. In the case of the
second drawing, which is a sheet of miscellaneous studies in pen,
one of them represents another seated Christ Child, which does
not exactly correspond to any known invention of Credi's, but
has long been suspected of deriving from a prototype by him.[30]
What is more, it is hard to doubt that these studies were drawn
in Italy, since the sheet bears a watermark found on paper that is
known to have been used in Venice.[31]

The final connection is between another Christ Child, this
time in Dürer's engraving of the *Virgin and Child with a Monkey*, which
is customarily dated around 1498 (illus. 26), and the same figure
in the *Madonna di Piazza* in Pistoia Cathedral (illus. 27).[32] The altarpiece was commissioned from Andrea del Verrocchio in the late
1470s, and documentary evidence proves that it was nearing completion in 1485. It is now widely accepted that Lorenzo di Credi
as opposed to Verrocchio was responsible for both the preliminary

drawings for it – one for each of the attendant saints by him survive – and the finished work.[33]

In consequence, if Dürer did actually reach Florence in 1495, then he might also have made a pilgrimage to Pistoia to see it, but it is altogether more likely that he copied a now lost study for the central group of the Madonna and Child. Verrocchio had died in 1488, and the contents of his *bottega* may well have passed to Lorenzo, who could as easily have allowed Dürer to copy three drawings as one. It is true that Dürer's Child is not absolutely identical to his counterpart in the Pistoia altarpiece, but there can be no doubt of the correspondence, and two obvious – and not mutually exclusive – explanations for the minor differences between them suggest themselves. One is that some of the divergences may reflect slight variations from the final resolution of the pose in the drawing Dürer saw, while the other is that it served his purpose to modify some of the actions of the Child. In the altarpiece, his right hand is raised because he is blessing the figure of St John the Baptist on his right, whereas in the engraving he and the Virgin are the only people present, and he is holding a struggling bird in his right hand and teasing it with what appears to be a handkerchief he holds in his left one.

The generally agreed dating of the *Virgin and Child with a Monkey* is based upon its style, but it is inconceivable that it was created as late as 1507, when Dürer returned to Nuremberg from Venice. On the other hand, it must be later than the sublime *Fisherman's House on a Lake* in a combination of watercolour and body colour from which the building in the print was derived – and reversed in the process.[34] That drawing, together with a whole group of closely related nature studies, is convincingly placed around 1496, not least because of their stylistic kinship with various dated topographical studies by the artist, which will be discussed briefly below.[35] The reason for labouring the point about the dating of both the coloured landscape drawing and the engraving is that they cannot possibly have been created only after Dürer's return from his second journey to Italy. In the context of the attempt to deny his first journey ever took place, the derivation of the Madonna and especially the Child in the *Virgin and Child with a Monkey* either from a drawing by Lorenzo di Credi or from the altarpiece it prepared is of crucial importance. The idea that any of the three Credi drawings, far less all of them, was in Nuremberg is almost impossibly far-fetched. Taken together, if that were felt to be necessary, they immensely strengthen the plausibility of the idea of Dürer in Italy in 1495.

Many art historians are intensely reluctant to accept the notion of artists travelling without – so to speak – their permission, or strictly that of the documentary record. In that connection, it is revealing that a contract drawn up on 12 December 1505 concerning the young Raphael, when he was almost exactly the same age as Dürer was in 1494–5, provides a whole list of places where he might conceivably be found: 'Perugia, Assisi, Gubbio, Rome, Siena, Florence, Urbino, Venice, and other places'.[36] For Dürer, there could have been no certainty that his first visit to Italy would not also be his last, and it is therefore not exactly far-fetched to imagine that he would have wanted to see Rome.

At that date, the great achievements of Michelangelo and Raphael in the Vatican were yet to come, and the main attraction would unquestionably have been the ancient sculpture the Eternal City had to offer. Over a quarter of a century ago, I argued in a short and seemingly entirely ignored article that a much-admired Dürer sheet is not, as has been supposed, a life study of the back view of a female model, but rather a virtual restoration and completion of a celebrated classical statue, at the time in the courtyard of Casa Sassi in Rome, a male torso in marble that was displayed in a niche in such a way that it could only be seen from the rear. The full argument does not need to be rehearsed here, but it seems important to underline the fact that the artist switches from the neater technique of pen to the looser brush precisely at the limits of the torso.[37]

Altogether more recently, I have made the case in another article that in northern Europe prior to 1500 or so knowledge of and borrowings from classical sculpture were not nearly as uncommon as tends to be presumed.[38] I only fleetingly discussed Dürer in that context, but the Louvre drawing is not the sole example of a possible borrowing from the antique. In the *Large Woodcut Passion*, both the prints of the *Capture of Christ* and the *Flagellation* feature contorted male figures lying or sitting on the ground, respectively representing Malchus, the servant of the High Priest, who is being assailed by St Peter, and one of Jesus' tormentors, who is straining to tighten his bonds.[39] In both cases, it is tempting to wonder if the source of inspiration was not one of the great treasures of the Vatican, the *Torso Belvedere*, which was recorded at an admittedly somewhat later date lying on its back as opposed to sitting up.[40] What is more, the *Flagellation* also includes the figure of a flagellant in the attitude of the so-called *Niobid Pedagogue*, albeit in reverse. That statue was not rediscovered until a considerably later date, but a number of early derivations seem to confirm the fact that artists must have had access to some other variant of the figure, whose pose is demonstrably not unique, since other versions of it are known.[41]

Another sculpture that inspired Dürer is the *Apollo Belvedere*. It is not known precisely where or when it was discovered, but by the late 1490s, and quite possibly somewhat earlier, it was in the garden of Cardinal Giuliano della Rovere at San Pietro in Vincoli, as is demonstrated by its having been copied at that point in the Codex Escurialensis.[42] As has already been mentioned in the previous chapter, Dürer adapted the statue's pose both in two closely related drawings of Apollo and for the male protagonist in his engraving *Adam and Eve*, and particularly clearly in a dated preparatory study of 1504 for the print. The overall visual

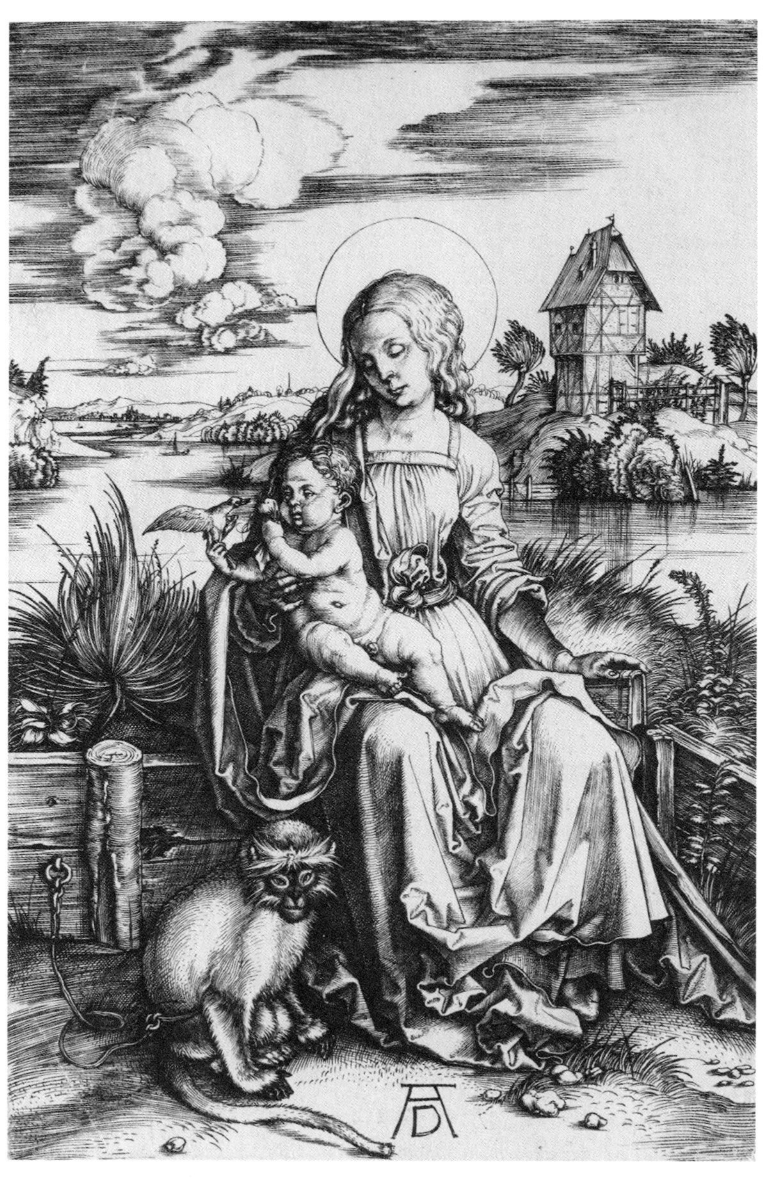

26 Albrecht Dürer, *Virgin and Child with a Monkey*, c. 1498, engraving.

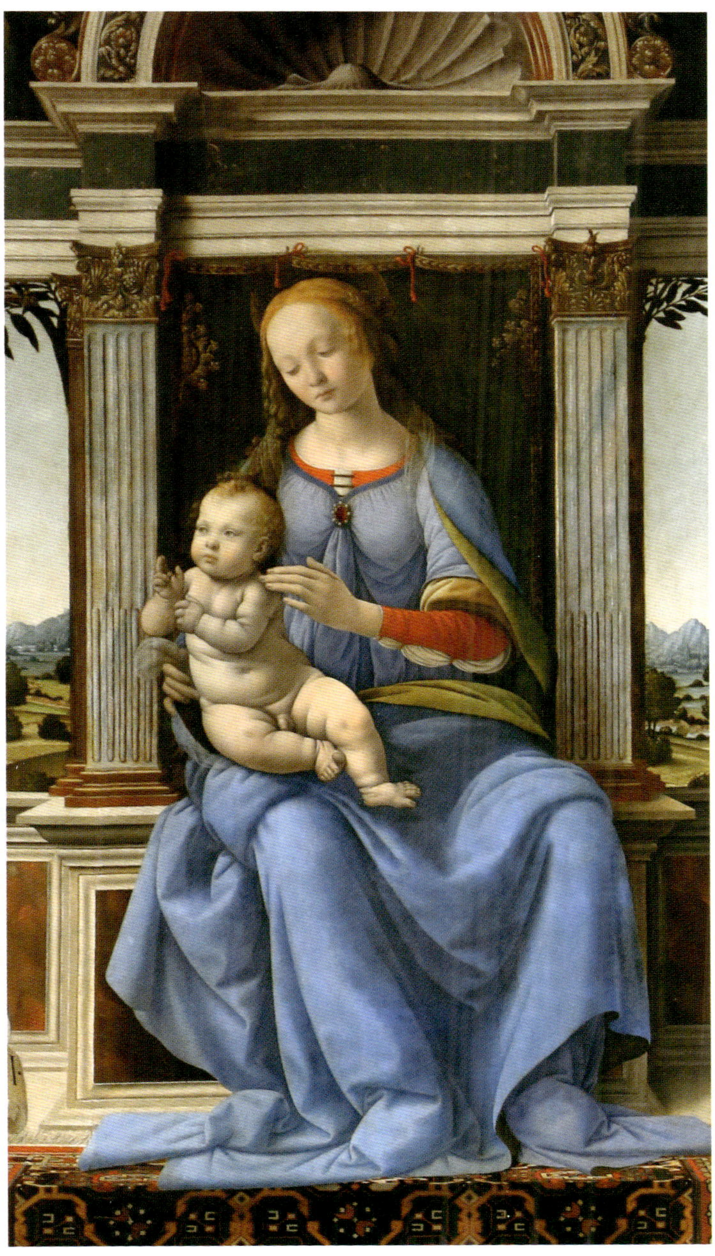

27 Andrea del Verrocchio and Lorenzo di Credi, *Madonna di Piazza* (detail of Virgin and Child), *c.* 1475–85, oil on panel.

correspondence is very convincing, with such elements as the raised left heels and the pure profiles of the heads being particularly striking. At the same time, it is important to underline the degree to which the whole conception of the male nude in these works is completely alien to the German visual tradition.[43]

A further Roman antique source employed by Dürer is the horse of the *Equestrian Statue of Marcus Aurelius* on the Capitol, which he looked to in devising the mount of the Knight in his engraving of the *Knight, Death and the Devil* of 1513 (illus. 53).[44] Unlike the other quotations and adaptations, which relate to works completed before he travelled to Italy for the second time in 1505–7, it might appear that this one could be the consequence of his study of the group then, always assuming, as will be argued below, that he went to Rome in 1506. In fact, however, the pose of the horse is already virtually identically established in a monogrammed and dated drawing of 1503, so it too could be a work of art he saw on his first Italian journey.[45] The same uncertainty arises in connection with Dürer's use of the *Mazarin Venus* in a drawing of the *Temptation of St Anthony* in the Albertina, which dates from 1521.[46] Lastly, there is a single somewhat earlier drawing of 1514 by Dürer, his *Venus with Cupid the Honey-Thief*, where the attitude of the goddess must derive from some Roman numismatic source, but where the ubiquity of such coins means the connection cannot be used to support the notion that the artist visited Rome.[47]

If Dürer was in the main settled in Nuremberg in the decade between 1495 and 1505, and busy establishing his workshop, that naturally does not mean that he never went anywhere else, but as a matter of fact there are no documented journeys elsewhere. Moreover, there is no particular indication of his having drawn strength from his northern contemporaries at this period, and it seems likely that he instead simply relied upon all his accumulated experiences of Italy. A case in point is the recollection in his *St Onophrius* in Bremen of the figure of Job from Giovanni Bellini's

San Giobbe Altarpiece, a work that must date from before 1484 and that he could therefore certainly have seen in the mid-1490s.[48] In much the same spirit, right at the end of his career he would recall the side panels of Giovanni Bellini's *Frari Triptych* of 1488, which, to quote Michael Levey, 'are the germ which, thirty years after his first visit to Venice, produced his *Four Apostles*'.[49]

It is impossible to know whether Dürer had been dreaming of returning to Italy virtually ever since he got home, but the arrival in Nuremberg of Jacopo de' Barbari in 1500 can hardly have failed to provoke all sorts of fond memories of its beauties.[50] In any event, as on the previous occasion, he does not appear to have been in the least deterred by the prospect of leaving his wife behind. On the contrary, his correspondence with his friend Pirck-heimer – from which, frustratingly, only Dürer's letters survive – indicates her professional usefulness to him as his representa-tive at such events as the Frankfurt Easter Fair, and also explains that his mother was similarly put to work.[51]

In Venice, Dürer produced only one major painting, but it was one of the most ambitious and important ones of his entire career. The extent to which it reveals him employing what might be called Venetian dialect has been much debated, and will be explored in depth below. It has also been plausibly suggested that he may in effect have received the commission in Nuremberg, and that it may have motivated his trip to Venice.[52] The work in question, which has come to be known as the *Feast of the Rose-Garlands*, was executed for the chapel of the recently founded guild of the German merchants in Venice in the church of San Bartolomeo al Rialto, which was in the immediate vicinity of their headquar-ters, the Fondaco dei Tedeschi, whose exterior would be frescoed a few years later by Giorgione and Titian.[53] The *Feast* was subse-quently acquired by the emperor Rudolph II, which explains its presence in Prague, but is alas in a very severely compromised state of preservation.[54]

The guild's chapel was dedicated to the Madonna of the Rosary, which was the Dominican equivalent of the Franciscan devotion to the Immaculate Conception, for all that there was no historical association between San Bartolomeo and the Dominicans. The devotion's point of departure was the foundation by Jacob Sprenger of a Rosenkranzbruderschaft (Brotherhood of the Rosary) in 1475 in Cologne, which led to the establishment of numerous such confraternities both north and south of the Alps, but it does appear to have enjoyed particular favour among Germans.[55] Two principal iconographic strands rapidly evolved, both ultimately based upon German print prototypes. The former concentrated upon the Virgin and Child handing out rosaries to the faithful, among whose number were typically both the pope and the emperor, respectively at the heads of representatives of the clergy and the laity.[56] The latter showed the fifteen mysteries of the rosary, customarily in roundels, accompanied by various Dominican saints.[57] It was not until as late as 1571 that the Feast of the Rosary was instituted by Pope Pius V, as commemorated in an altarpiece of 1609 by Francesco Vanni, but by that date the devotion had existed for almost a century.[58]

Dürer's composition belongs to the first of these two types. Moreover, as has been pointed out, its main lines are so directly related to the solution found in an anonymous German woodcut of 1476 representing the *Distribution of Rosaries*, which accompanied the statutes of the aforementioned Cologne brotherhood, that it seems hard to doubt that he was instructed by his patrons to employ it as his point of departure when it came to inventing his altarpiece.[59] Such contractual arrangements, known in the Italian context as *modo et forma* agreements, were standard in the Renaissance, but were almost never designed to restrict an artist's creativity.[60] In the present instance, once the source is recognized, it is arguably more rewarding to analyse the differences between the prototype and the derivation than to enumerate the

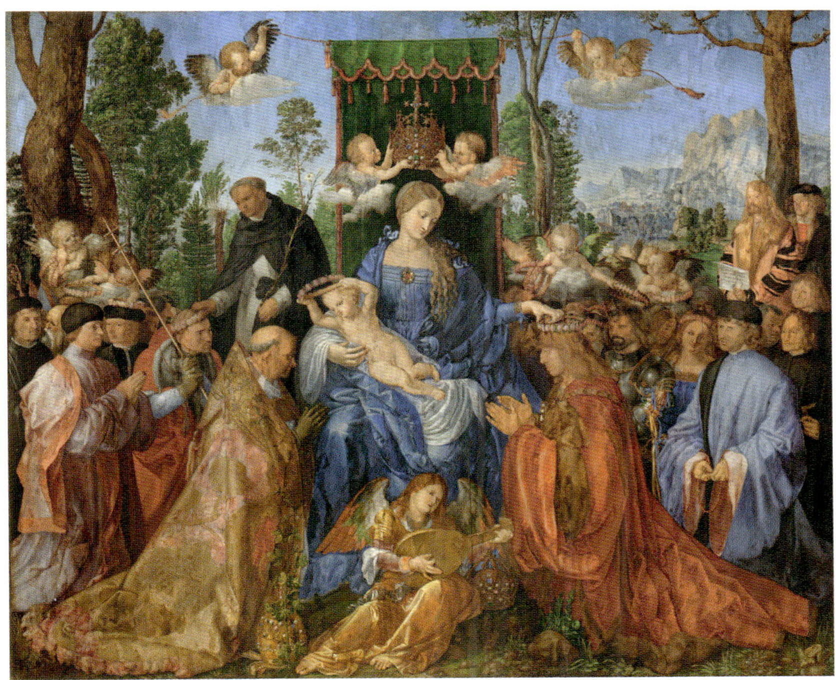

correspondences, but both aspects will be explored here. Sadly, as is nearly always the case with Dürer, there are no exploratory or inventive preparatory drawings for the work (as opposed to detailed studies), so it is only possible to examine the first and last stages of the process, rather than chronicle the progress from the one to the other.

In the woodcut, the Virgin and Child turn respectively to their left and right and are placed at the centre of the composition. They are represented in front of a cloth of honour and two angels are shown holding a crown above the former's head. Dürer follows its example, but has them crowning the principal figures to their sides with rose-garlands instead of merely handing them out. The identities of the recipients are not quite the same, either: the

28 Albrecht Dürer, *Feast of the Rose-Garlands*, 1506, oil on poplar panel.

Christ Child gives his garland to a cardinal holding a tall cross, while Mary offers hers to a crowned and bearded figure in armour holding an imperial standard, who is presumably the emperor. In the altarpiece, their roles are reprised by the pope to the proper right and Maximilian, king of the Romans (who did not become emperor until 1508), to the proper left, but in a sense they are more faithfully echoed by the next most prominent figures in its design, a cardinal with a double cross, who is being crowned by St Dominic, and a bearded soldier in armour, who is about to be crowned by a putto-angel.

Dominic himself must be the friar to the immediate right of the Virgin and Child in the print. He is not performing an action, but is paired with a nun on the other side, who is therefore presumably to be identified as St Catherine of Siena, the most revered female Dominican saint, who is likewise part of a passively kneeling threesome, joined by two members of the laity. Apart from them, the only other accompanying figures are a man with a boy and a woman with a girl in the foreground, all of whom already hold their garlands aloft. When Dürer adapted this conception, he made two main changes to the personnel. One was to increase their number, albeit only slightly, since there are only half a dozen genuinely distinct figures to either side, admittedly backed by a species of chorus of indistinctly visible extras, and the other was to portray those in the front row, who almost without exception are men, as actual individuals. At the same time, he also replaced the children at the feet of the Virgin with a single musician angel in a blatant homage to local tradition, and specifically to Giovanni Bellini's latest production, the *San Zaccaria Altarpiece* of 1505.[61]

Moving on from the dramatis personae to the whole compositional arrangement, one of the most striking decisions Dürer took, inevitably with the consent of his patrons, was to modify the vertical format of the woodcut and instead opt for a horizontal arrangement. A connection has often been proposed with a Venetian picture type exemplified by Giovanni Bellini's *Virgin and Child between St Mark with Agostino Barbarigo and St Augustine* of 1488 in San Pietro Martire on Murano, but such paintings are not customarily altarpieces, and are incomparably more sparsely populated than the *Feast of the Rose-Garlands* and lack its notably elaborated northern landscape background.[62] What Dürer elected not to do was to adapt the traditional format of the Madonna and Child with Saints altarpiece, otherwise known as the *sacra conversazione*, presumably because he did not feel he could accommodate a sufficient number of figures on an adequate scale.[63] His familiarity with it may be taken for granted, but is further confirmed by a monogrammed and dated drawing of 1511, which is a textbook emulation of the Venetian type.[64]

In terms of technique and related matters, there are obvious similarities but also significant differences. With a single exception, all the extant preparatory drawings for the work are executed in brush heightened with white on Venetian blue paper, and fall into three main categories, namely studies of single figures (which are in essence limited to those parts of them that are visible), bust or head studies and hand studies.[65] The technique is a version of local ones, but Dürer had employed all these methods before apart from the last category. However, as far as we know, no earlier work had been as meticulously prepared, and moreover a sheet of studies of hands in silverpoint on prepared paper by Alvise Vivarini indicates the kind of drawings he may have learnt from.[66] In addition to using Venetian blue paper, he did not employ azurite, as was customary in Germany, but instead ultramarine, which was favoured throughout Italy.[67] Inevitably, he used poplar panels, but conversely failed to follow local practice when it came to the arrangement of the thirteen individual planks that make up the painted surface, since they are aligned vertically, whereas in Venice (but not in the rest of Italy) it was customary for them to be aligned horizontally.[68]

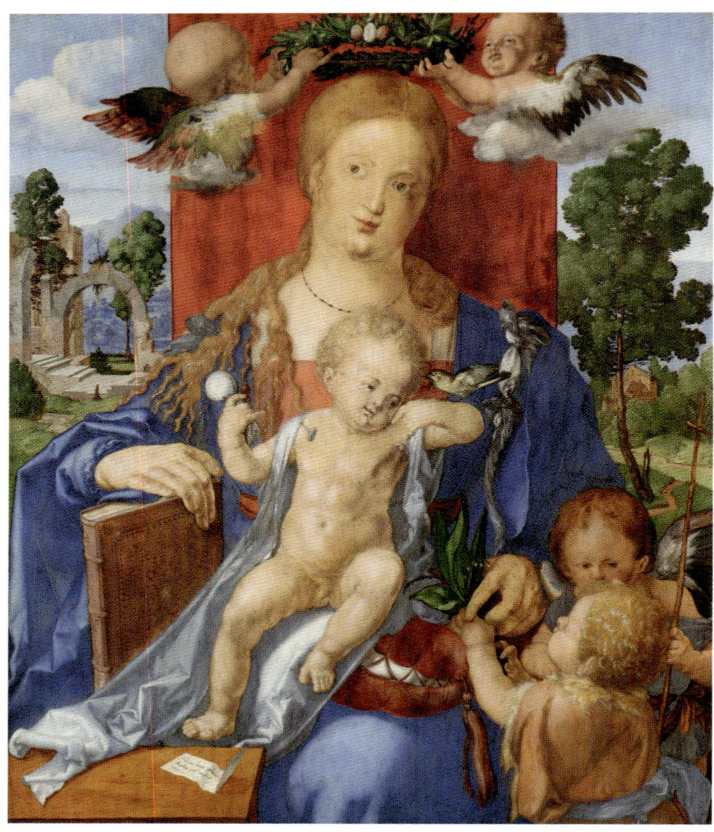

All in all, the extent to which the *Feast of the Rose-Garlands* does or does not feel Venetian is a matter of one's expectations, because in truth it looks nothing like any previous German – or indeed northern – altarpiece, but equally nothing like any previous Venetian one either. Dürer himself reports that it eventually won plaudits from the Venetian establishment – both from initially suspicious fellow painters and from grandees such as the doge and the patriarch – but at the same time it has to be admitted that it had no effect on local painting.[69] Giovanni Bellini expressed

29 Albrecht Dürer, *Virgin and Child with a Siskin*, 1506, oil on poplar panel.

the wish to have a work by Dürer, and by implication a picture, but it was from his engraving of the *Prodigal Son* that he quoted the back end of a bull.[70] Giorgione may also have been an admirer. There is no obvious reason why Dürer should not have brought examples of his work to Venice, as he was to do on his later journey to the Netherlands in the 1520s: if so, that might explain the uncanny – if hitherto unobserved – resemblance, admittedly in reverse, of the pose of the knight saint in Giorgione's *Castelfranco Altarpiece* to that of St Eustace in Dürer's earlier *Paumgartner Altarpiece* (illus. 33).[71]

In Italy, Dürer also produced his comparably half-and-half *Virgin and Child with a Siskin* (illus. 29), which it is tempting to describe as a Giovanni Bellini or Cima da Conegliano with a German accent, and his *Christ among the Doctors* (illus. 30).[72] One of these

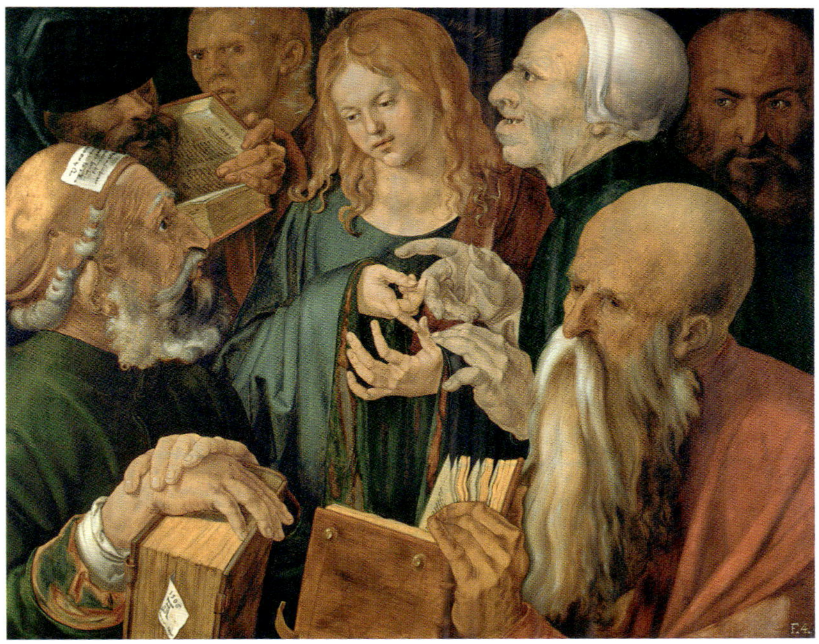

30 Albrecht Dürer, *Christ among the Doctors*, 1506, oil on panel.

must be the work he refers to in his quirkily hybrid semi-Italian as a 'Quar' (that is, 'quadro', 'painting'), which is likely to have been the *Virgin and Child*.[73] The reason is that two drawn copies of the *Christ* add the word 'ROMAE' to the celebrated 'opus quinque dierum' ('the work of five days') inscription on the slip of paper emerging from the book in the bottom left-hand corner.[74] In the late summer of 1506 Dürer expressed the hope that he might accompany Maximilian to Rome if he went there for his coronation as Holy Roman Emperor. In the event, the royal journey never took place, but while there Dürer could also have dealt with financial losses referred to in his *Family Chronicle* around this time, and a fleeting visit might equally explain the exceptional speed of the work's execution.[75] Regardless of where the picture was painted, it unquestionably conforms to a quintessentially Italian tradition of dramatic half-length narratives, not least in the form of the admittedly later treatment of the identical subject by Bernardino Luini.[76]

After Dürer's final return from Italy, it might not seem unreasonable to presume that he would no longer have had any contact with Italian art and artists, but on the contrary there is incontrovertible evidence that he did. In his specific case, moreover, the difficulty of reconstructing the particulars of a life lived over five hundred years ago are compellingly underlined by a single piece of evidence, which could so easily not have survived. A red chalk drawing by Raphael for figures in one of the frescoes in the Stanza dell'Incendio in the Vatican bears an inscription dated 1515 in Dürer's handwriting, in which he states that he was sent it by Raphael:

> Raffahel de Vrbin der so hoch peim/ pobst geacht ist
> gewest hat der hat/ dyse nackette bild gemacht Vnd hat/
> sy dem albrecht dürer gen nornberg/ geschickt Im sein
> hand zw weisen ['Raphael of Urbino, who was so highly

esteemed by the Pope, made this naked picture and sent it to Albrecht Dürer in Nuremberg to show him his hand'].[77]

This date, taken in conjunction with the use of the past tense, cannot relate to the writing of the inscription, but must instead refer to the making of the drawing.[78] As was brilliantly observed by Rolf Quednau, this particular sheet was carefully selected by Raphael, since the pose of its main figure is a mirror image of that of the executioner in the recipient's 1510 woodcut of the *Beheading of St John the Baptist*, one of the Dürer prints singled out for individual mention by Vasari.[79] Vasari adds that Dürer started the ball rolling by sending Raphael 'la testa d'un suo ritratto condotta da lui a guazzo su una tela di bisso' ('a self-portrait head in gouache on a canvas of silk fabric'), and that Raphael riposted by sending 'molte carte disegnate da man sua' ('many sheets drawn by his hand'), but in the absence of this drawing there would be no proof that they were actually in touch.[80]

It is incontrovertible that Raphael was an admirer of Dürer's art, but it has tended to be supposed that – for all that Vasari alleges Dürer held Raphael's drawings very dear ('furono carissime ad Alberto') – nothing in his work betrays a reciprocal esteem. Nevertheless, a number of his works do in fact appear to reflect knowledge of works by Raphael, and intriguingly they are by no means all productions of his Roman years.[81]

In the case of a drawing of the *Holy Family*, which is datable to around 1521, Friedrich Winkler noted a possible connection with Raphael's *Canigiani Holy Family*, and although he could not decide if the resemblance was merely coincidental, it has recently been reaffirmed by Peter van den Brink.[82] However, even disregarding the known connections between the two artists, two additional factors speak in favour of the link. One is the extremely singular compositional arrangement of the *Holy Family*, while the other is the fact that, as with the Raphael sheet inscribed by

Dürer, the drawing that reached him need not have been identical to the final work.

It has recently been proposed by Christof Metzger that a study of a *Nude with Head Tilted Back* of 1515 was inspired by the pose of Christ in Raphael's *Baglione Entombment* of 1507, which he would have known via a drawing.[83] Once again, the attitude is suggestively close, although admittedly not identical, but the plausibility of the link is strengthened by the existence of a compositional drawing of the *Entombment* dated 1521. In at least three specific respects, it matches Raphael's groundbreaking response to the challenge of how to represent the subject: the action moves from right to left towards the mouth of a cave-tomb, the bearer at Christ's head walks gingerly backwards, and a single figure fills the gap between the two porters at either end of his body.[84]

A final Dürer borrowing appears to derive from a Marcantonio Raimondi engraving after Raphael or possibly a preliminary drawing for the print in question. For, as I have pointed out elsewhere, he must have been familiar with Marcantonio's *Dido*, which was adapted and reversed in the woodcut designed by a member of his workshop of the *Coat of Arms of Christoph Scheurl*, which is customarily dated to around 1512–14.[85] It is worth adding that the idiosyncratic diagonal division of the figure's torso exposing the left breast was derived by Raphael – who also used it in his *Lucretia*, likewise engraved by Marcantonio – from the standard classical mode of representing an *Amazon*, as in a characteristic example in Oxford, and only serves to confirm that it was not Dürer's invention.[86] It seems that more works by Raphael must have come his way at a later date, because during his journey to the Netherlands he met Tommaso Vincidor, gave him six guilders' worth of his best prints, and was promised 'des Raphaels von Vrbin Ding' ('things by Raphael of Urbino'), who had died the year before, in exchange.[87]

Before concluding with a very brief survey of the effects of Dürer's prints in Italy, the related questions of which works of

art he saw on his journey to the Netherlands and what he did
with them need to be addressed. The first point worth making is
that he was demonstrably not only interested in the art of his
contemporaries. Various references in his admittedly famously
telegraphic diary confirm his admiration for what he might almost
have regarded as the work of the Old Masters, with his reaction
to the Van Eycks' *Ghent Altarpiece* being among his most expansive
pronouncements: 'Darnach sahe ich des Johannes taffel; das ist
ein über köstlich hoch verständig gemähl, und sonderlich die
Eva, Maria und Gott der vater sind fast gut' ('Then I saw the St
John picture, which is a delightful and ingenious painting, and
in particular the figures of Eve, the Virgin and God the Father are
outstanding').[88] A little earlier, in Cologne, he simply explains that
he paid the price of a visit that same day to the barber to have
the *Dombild* opened up for him (a common necessity in the case
of folding altarpieces, which were routinely kept shut, as were,
generally, the chapels that contained altarpieces), but helpfully
names its creator, which is how we know it is the work of Stephan
Lochner: 'hab 2 Weisspfenning geben von der Tafel aufzusperren,
die Meister Steffan zu Cöln gemacht hat.'[89] In Antwerp he drew
one of the bronze figures on the tomb of Isabella of Bourbon,
while in Bruges he saw Michelangelo's *Virgin and Child*, which he
wrongly believed to be made of alabaster.[90]

Inevitably, during these months he met many local artists, was
made much of by them and on occasion drew their likenesses. He
tends not to write about their art, and certainly not in any detail,
but, as in the case of the tomb and Michelangelo's *Madonna*, he was
by no means exclusively interested in paintings. In fact, the only
contemporary work he discusses in his diary is Gossart's *Middelburg
Altarpiece*.[91] In Antwerp he met and drew Lucas van Leyden, noting
that he was an engraver and describing him as 'ein kleins männ-
lein' ('a small little man'), and Conrad Meit, the good sculptor,
'desgleichen ich kein gesehen hab' ('whose like I have never seen').[92]

Moreover, he was famously awestruck by the treasures of the 'neuen gülden Land' ('new golden land'), which he described in detail, summing up his response by writing, 'Und ich hab aber all mein Lebtag nichts gesehen, das mein Herz also erfreut hat als diese Ding' ('In all my life, I have never seen anything that brought such joy to my heart as all these things').[93] Understandably – and in this context his going there did not make much of a difference – his work was immensely influential in the Netherlands both before and of course thereafter.[94]

Just as Dürer learnt from others, so countless others learnt from him, not just north of the Alps but in Italy. Sadly, because of the north–south divide that still all too often tends to bedevil the history of art, many of these Italian reflections and borrowings have yet to be recognized, but they reveal exactly what the Italians most valued about his art, and are full of surprises. This arises not only from the fact that their homages are by no means guaranteed to celebrate what is most admired today, but that they on occasion single out details that do not seem to accord with our idea of their taste. A telling instance is the quotation in a drawing by that paragon of elegance Parmigianino of Dürer's gothic horror figure of Death from his *Promenade* engraving.[95]

As a matter of fact, Dürer was not the first northern printmaker whose works were quoted by Italian artists. Botticelli derived one of the devils in his *Mystic Nativity* in the National Gallery from a print by the Master E.S., while the pose of Perugino's *St Sebastian* in Stockholm is quoted from the Master of 1446's *Flagellation*.[96] Similarly, more than one artist borrowed from Schongauer's *Peasant Family Going to Market*, while Vasari referred to the teenage Michelangelo having copied his *Temptation of St Anthony*, and a candidate for the painting in question has recently reappeared.[97]

To return to Italian artists looking at Dürer's prints, it emerges that they study them for four main reasons.[98] The first is to copy whole compositions, the second is to pick out single figures or heads, the third is to copy animals, and the fourth is to replicate landscapes. A whole book on the subject would be required for a comprehensive survey, so it is to be hoped that a few examples of the various kinds of derivations will suffice here.

An excellent example of the borrowing of an entire invention, which also underlines the long reach of Dürer's work across time, given that it must date from after 1573, is Biagio Betti's *Christ among the Doctors* in San Silvestro al Quirinale in Rome, since, apart from the reversal of the composition, it is a remarkably faithful repetition of the woodcut of the same subject in the *Marienleben*.[99] In the case of single figures or heads, a sheet by Perino del Vaga in the Ashmolean Museum in Oxford is a particularly graphic example of such homage, since it includes copies of no fewer than nine heads variously extracted from three separate woodcuts from the *Apocalypse*, the *Christ Carrying the Cross* from the *Large Passion*, and the *Four Naked Women*.[100] When it comes to animals, both exotic and homely ones appealed, and Perino is again involved: he copies the unicorn from the *Abduction of Proserpina*, but also the dog from the *Visitation* in the *Marienleben*.[101] In very much the same spirit, Garofalo is no less gripped by a sheepdog from the *Annunciation to Joachim* in the same series than by the monkey that gives its name to the *Virgin and Child with a Monkey*.[102] Turning, finally, to landscapes, Fra Bartolomeo produced meticulous pen copies of two elements of the landscape of the *Sea-Monster*, while Antonio di Donnino del Mazziere translated elements from the backgrounds of the *Madonna with the Pear* and the *Offer of Love* into red chalk.[103]

All these examples date from the sixteenth century, but, as will be explored in the Conclusion, interest in Dürer and his work has never faded, and shows no signs of being about to do so.

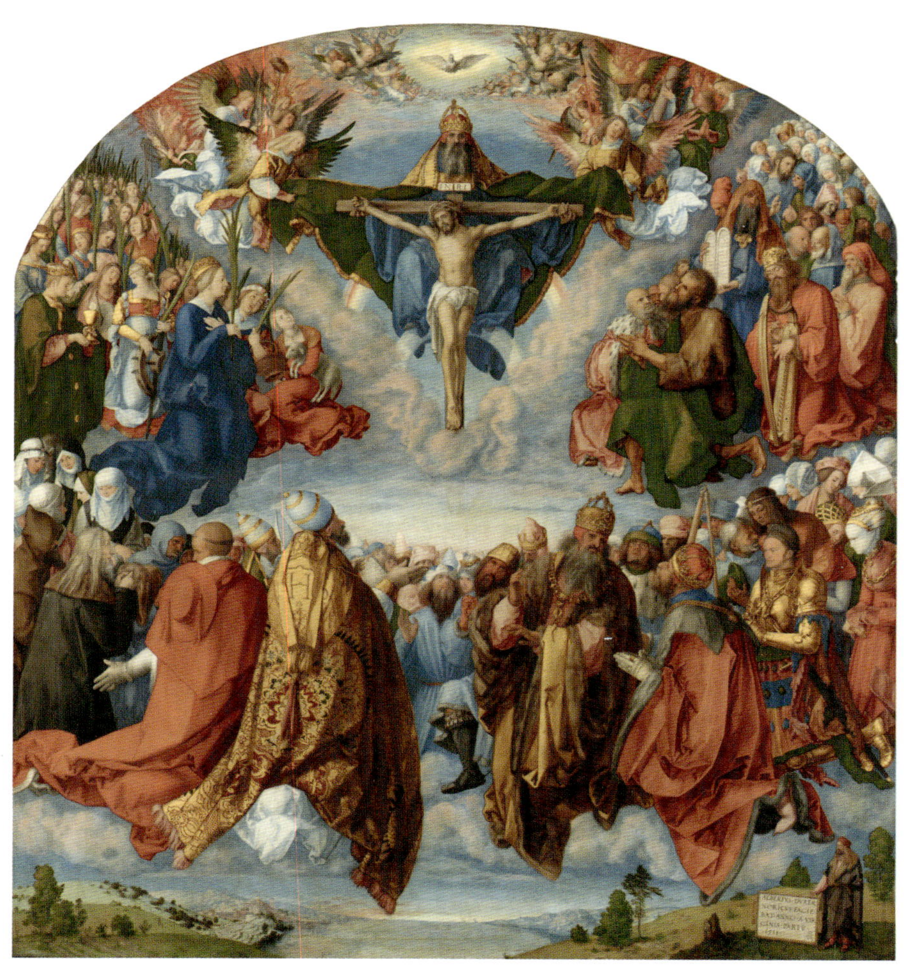

THREE

Paintings

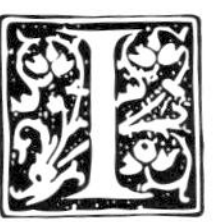In Dürer's day, paintings were what mattered. In response, he explored all the principal genres available to him, namely religious art, mythology and portraiture, on both a monumental and an intimate scale. He was plainly keenly aware of the private appeal of drawings and perhaps even more acutely of the exciting possibilities offered by the fact that prints are of their nature multiples and could earn him a lot of money, but both media were ranked far, far lower than paintings. In that sense, Dürer would have taken it for granted that he would above all be judged by the merits of his works in paint, and he was manifestly not indifferent to the judgement either of his own age or of posterity.

In examining his achievements in this field, it therefore seems crucial to grasp the nettle, and both to acknowledge the unevenness of his painted oeuvre and to examine why these works are sometimes disappointing. At the same time, it would be quite wrong, however, to fail to recognize that at his best Dürer is a wonderful painter. Given the seemingly effortless power of his drawings and prints, there could be a temptation to imagine that it was the sheer scale demanded by much public art that defeated him, but the truth is that such monumental works as the *Adam* and *Eve* and the *Four Apostles* are his absolute masterpieces in painting.

In this connection, it is crucial to underline the poignant fact that this is not a purely modern subjective prejudice. During his

31 Albrecht Dürer, *Adoration of the Holy Trinity*, 1511, oil on limewood panel.

Venetian residence in 1506, he executed his most ambitious religious painting, his altarpiece of the *Feast of the Rose-Garlands*, for the German church of San Bartolomeo al Rialto, which is discussed in the previous chapter. In terms of its physical survival, the centuries have not been kind to the work, which makes it peculiarly hard to judge its original appearance and strength, but it is striking how little influence it had on Venetian or other Italian painting of the time. It might appear tempting to suppose that this was merely part of a more widespread Italian distaste for northern European art, but the evidence of the international appeal of Dürer's prints refutes this presumption.

When completing his catalogue of Dürer's paintings, Fedja Anzelewsky approached the task chronologically, but in addition sensibly divided the works by broad categories, starting with – to employ his terms – Christian iconography followed by non-religious iconography, and then divided between mythology and allegory on the one hand and portraiture on the other.[1] Much the same structure will be followed here, with the proviso that the religious paintings will be further subdivided into works that were public and those that were private, naturally acknowledging that there may be the odd case where a measure of uncertainty remains. The one other point to make at the outset is that in the context of portraiture it seems distinctly artificial – and equally counterproductive – to exclude all consideration of his approach to the same challenges when it came to drawings and prints, not least since the sitters are not infrequently the same individuals.

It would appear that Dürer's first public religious commission was an immensely ambitious altarpiece, of which only parts have survived. In 1717 Matthaeus Faber provided an impressively full account of an elaborate triptych in a chapel of the Schlosskirche at Wittenberg, without stating who painted it. It must have been commissioned by Frederick the Wise in 1496 when he visited Nuremberg and also had his portrait painted by the young prodigy.[2]

As we shall see, for the rest of Dürer's career his large-scale religious commissions would prove to be fairly evenly divided between grand patrons and altogether more modest local ones. The triptych's outer wings depicted the Annunciation, as usual with the Archangel Gabriel on the left and the Virgin Mary on the right. When it was opened, its centrepiece was an image of the Virgin with the Christ Child on her left arm and holding a cross in her right, surrounded by angels and crowned by two of them, with Eve and devils and a serpent under her feet. She was flanked on her left by a second figure of the Virgin, here pierced by a sword and surrounded by her Seven Sorrows, and on her right by a third representation of the Virgin, this time surrounded by her Seven Joys. Faber further transcribes various Latin texts that accompanied the images.[3]

If various surviving paintings by the young Dürer were indeed parts of this vast ensemble, then only the elements of the left wing remain, but they are not all together. The sorrowing Virgin is in Munich, while her Seven Sorrows are in Dresden, and – allowing room for the inscriptions – their dimensions match up. The existence of reliably accurate drawn copies of six of the seven narratives, which are accompanied by others of five of the seven Joys of the Virgin, means that the main lines of their compositions are not lost to us.[4] The principal anomaly, apparently undiscussed in the vast scholarly literature on the artist, is the fact that Faber's listing follows standard convention in giving the subjects of the last four Sorrows as Christ Carrying the Cross, his Crucifixion, Deposition and Entombment, whereas what Dürer actually painted was Christ Carrying the Cross, his Nailing to the Cross, Crucifixion and Deposition (another surprise is the choice of the Circumcision as opposed to Simeon's prophecy at the Purification of the Virgin as the first of the Sorrows).

Two preparatory drawings for the left wing survive. The first is a sketchy idea for the Virgin, flanked by the Crucifixion,

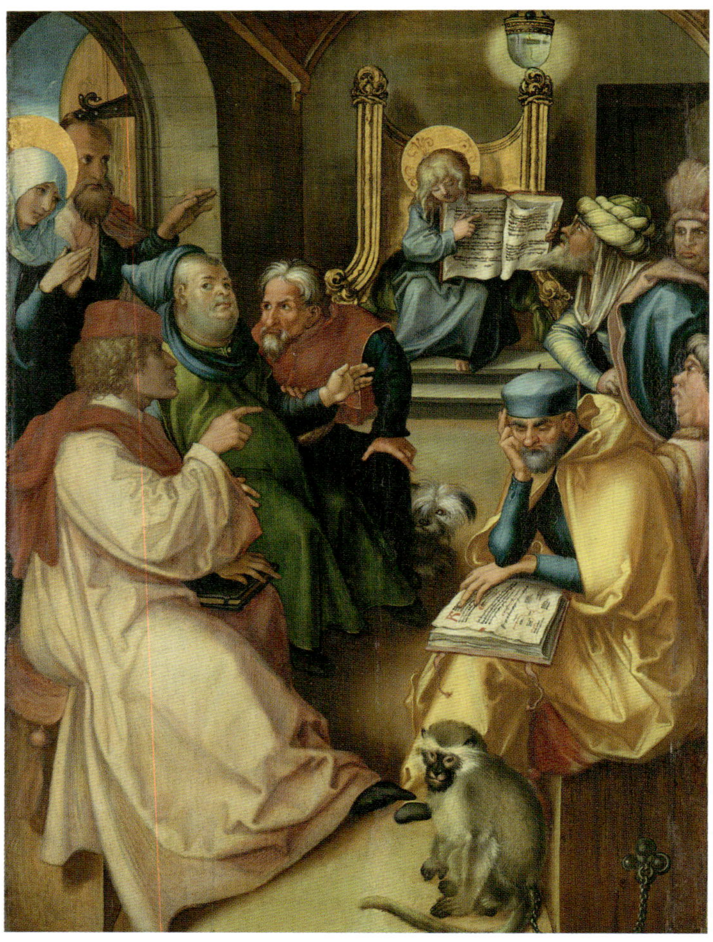

and what appears to be a subsidiary scene of Cain slaying Abel above it.[5] The second is a final study, corresponding in every detail, for the man drilling a hole in one of the arms of Christ's cross in the scene of the *Nailing*.[6] Many of these narrative scenes are intriguingly related to later representations of the same subjects either in the *Marienleben* or in one of the artist's three

32 Albrecht Dürer, *Christ among the Doctors*, 1495–6, oil on panel.

series of prints of the Passion, with the comparisons between
the different versions often making it plain how evolved Dürer's
art already was at this early date. In particular, a number of the
compositions – and especially the *Nailing to the Cross* and the
Crucifixion – are strikingly bold in their viewpoints, with the former representing Christ virtually upside down and the latter
adopting a radically angled asymmetrical presentation. A singular oddity, given the artist's more general indifference to artificial light effects, is the radiant circle projected by the hanging
glass lamp above the young Christ in the scene of his disputation
with the doctors (illus. 32). Dürer also appears to have been involved in a second work for Frederick the Wise around this date,
but seemingly slightly later, which is likewise first recorded in
the Schlosskirche. This was the so-called *Dresden Altarpiece*, whose
small scale begs the question as to whether it was not originally
intended for a more private setting. It combines a central Virgin
Adoring the Christ Child, now usually thought not to be by
Dürer, with half-length representations of Anthony Abbot and

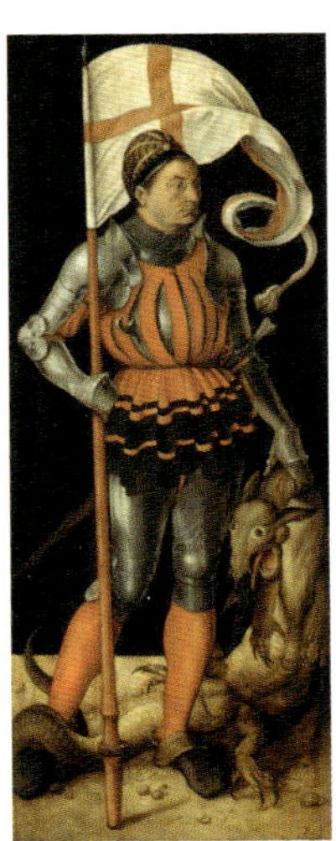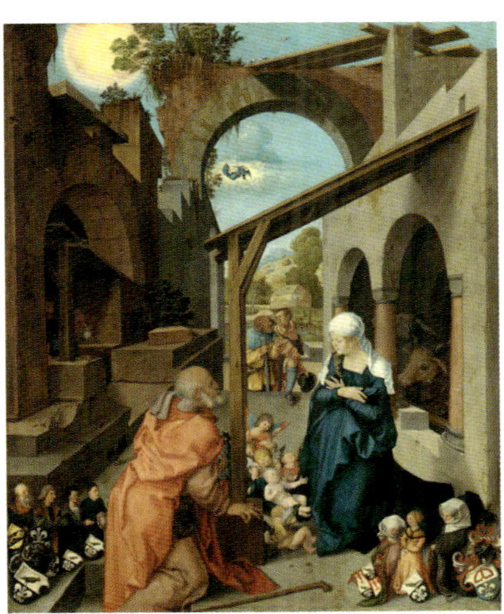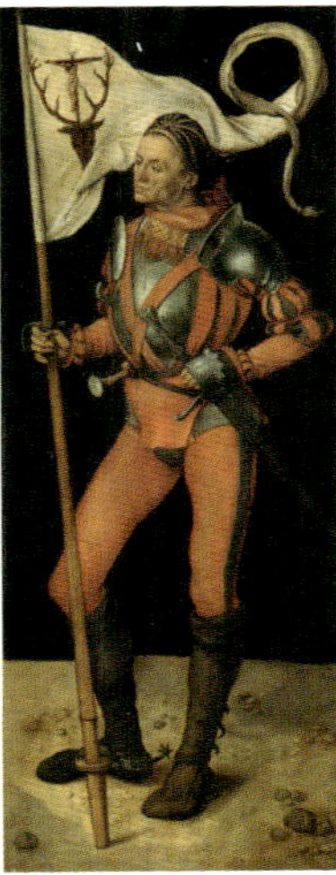

33 Albrecht Dürer, *Paumgartner Altarpiece*, c. 1498–1500, oil on limewood panel.

Sebastian, who were both saints associated with plague and healing.[7]

A similar combination of a narrative central scene flanked by two attendant saints in the wings is found in the *Paumgartner Altarpiece* (illus. 33), which was painted for the family's chapel in the Katharinenkirche in Nuremberg.[8] Generally dated around 1498–1500 or a bit later (it is clearly not as assured as the so-called *Christmas* engraving of 1504[9]), it represents a very definite advance on the artist's previous work, perhaps especially when it comes to the paired soldier saints, George and Eustace, whose poses convey their relaxed confidence and whose armour is lustrously brought to life. These latter are plainly portraits of actual individuals, their heads evidently based upon life studies, while seven further members of the family, accompanied by their coats of arms, are represented on a diminutive scale to the sides of the *Nativity*. The plunging perspective employed for the setting is carefully planned, and the Romanesque arches of the ruined stable may well be intended to evoke a past glory, whereas the farmhouse in the landscape beyond is reassuringly local and contemporary.

Two variations on the theme of the Lamentation again allow us to observe Dürer refining his art as he matures. The earlier of the two, which was executed for the Holzschuher family, was originally intended for their family chapel in the church of Sankt Johannes in Nuremberg, and is intimately related to the corresponding scene in the *Large Passion*. It includes no fewer than ten diminutive male donors and four female ones kneeling in prayer in the predella zone of the scene, which is set in front of the cave where Christ is to be buried, and completed by a grand prospect of Calvary juxtaposed with an elaborately detailed panorama of Jerusalem, imagined as set beside a wide lake with tall mountains beyond.[10] It is customarily dated around 1500, and by implication after the *Paumgartner Altarpiece*, but if so it hardly represents any sort of improvement upon it, and probably instead precedes it. Such a dating also makes sense in relation to the notably more impressive *Lamentation* for Albrecht Glim, given that the donor's first wife, who is represented here, died in 1500 (he later remarried).[11] In terms of the iconography and the arrangement of the composition, the two major differences are that the scene diverges from the precedents of the *Holzschuher Lamentation* and the one in the *Large Passion*, and instead now takes place at the foot of the cross, with Christ's head to the left, not the right. In both respects, it follows the final narrative of the *Seven Sorrows* altarpiece, but there is a world of difference between them, above all in terms of the monumentality and conviction of the figure style and the assured naturalism of the landscape topped by melodramatically looming black clouds.

In the case of the so-called *Jabach Altarpiece*, all that remain are four dismembered fragments of the triptych in various locations. The first two must present its appearance when closed – showing a scene of Job mocked by his wife with two musicians in attendance – while a further pair of panels are the cropped elements of its wings when open, with Joseph and Joachim on the left and Simeon and Lazarus on the right, uniquely for Dürer set against a gold ground decorated with arabesquing foliage, with their names in a hybrid of Latin and German within their haloes.[12] It has been argued – wholly convincingly, given the presence of both women's husbands together on one of the wings – that the missing central element must have comprised a group of the Virgin and Child with St Anne.

The representation of Job's wife pouring a wooden bucket of water over his shaven head and boil-infected body as he sits on a dung heap is entirely unparalleled, and only in part sanctioned by the Old Testament account, but the background details are precisely drawn from verses: 'The fire of God is fallen from heaven' and 'The Chaldaeans made out three bands, and fell

upon the camels' (Job 1:16–17). The figures' costumes are contemporary and, as has already been discussed in the Introduction,
the drummer is a self-portrait of Dürer. Given the association
of both Job and Lazarus with plague and healing, it seems clear
that the work, whose original patronage and context are unknown,
was commissioned either as a thanksgiving or as a protection
against the threat of sickness.

Dürer's *Feast of the Rose-Garlands* has already been examined in
Chapter Two, so the next work of substance to be considered is
the *Martyrdom of the 10,000 Christians*, which is signed and dated 1508
and depicts a story that is often attributed to the ninth-century
scholar Anastasius Bibliothecarius.[13] Its commission represents
a renewed act of patronage on the part of Frederick the Wise,
and it is generally assumed that it was placed in the Schlosskirche
at Wittenberg, which housed a large quantity of relics, including
some bones of the 10,000 Martyrs, which explains the choice of
subject.[14] Given its comparatively small scale and the meticulously detailed treatment of both the figures and the landscape,
it is nevertheless at least worth wondering whether it might not
have been intended for a more private setting. What is plain is
the fact that the artist was only too well aware of the importance
of satisfying such a prestigious patron, who was paying him a
truly princely 280 guilders, and in two letters to Jacob Heller of
28 August 1507 and 19 March 1508 he explained that the latter
would simply have to wait for his own altarpiece, which was much
more substantial, but paid the artist only two hundred guilders.
Dürer had previously produced a woodcut of the same (far from
common) martyrdom subject around 1496, and that work served
as the basis for the new composition, but they are by no means
identical.[15]

In the following year, 1509, Dürer signed and dated the *Heller
Altarpiece* itself for the family chapel dedicated to St Thomas
Aquinas in the Dominikanerkirche in Frankfurt.[16] If only it had

not been destroyed by fire, its main panel would no doubt have had a good claim to be the artist's supreme achievement in the field of the altarpiece. As it is, even on the basis of the known copies – and indeed the nearly twenty highly finished drawings for single figures, heads, hands and feet (which are briefly returned to in the next chapter) – the assured monumentality of the conception comes across clearly. The composition is divided into two zones, a common enough solution for the subject in Italy, but maybe less so in Germany, with the earthly company consisting of the Apostles crowded so closely round the Virgin's tomb that it almost disappears. Interestingly, they are shown without identifying attributes, but the aged kneeling figure in blue and orange in the foreground must be Peter, while the one peering into the tomb, which is empty but for a cloth left behind by the Virgin on her ascent, must be doubting Thomas (in the Italian tradition often shown receiving her girdle). In the upper zone, the kneeling Virgin, her hands joined in prayer, is represented being crowned simultaneously by Christ and God the Father, with the Dove of the Holy Spirit above to complete the Trinity, and with all of them ringed by a cloud-borne assembly of child angels playing musical instruments, and cherubim and seraphim. Dürer's satisfaction with the overall scheme is demonstrated by its repetition in the woodcut of 1510 on the same theme for the *Marienleben*, where the main (but only minor) iconographic difference is that Christ and God are no longer wearing, respectively, a papal tiara and a species of imperial crown.[17]

The *Adoration of the Holy Trinity* in Vienna (illus. 31) is comparable in scale to the *Martyrdom of the 10,000 Christians*, but took three years to finish.[18] There is a complete study for the painting in its frame, which is dated 1508 in the artist's hand, yet the finished work is dated 1511.[19] It is the only one of Dürer's altarpieces whose original frame survives, in Nuremberg, and therefore separately from the painting, which, happily, is housed in a faithful copy of it. Its unidentified carver evidently followed a revised design by the artist, since so many of the details of its ornamentation differ from what is projected in the drawing. The work in question was painted for Matthäus Landauer's All Saints Chapel in the Zwölfbrüderhaus in Nuremberg. The work's iconography is explained by its destination, since its main field shows the adoration of the Trinity by an assembly of saints, who in effect stand for All Saints.

On the basis of the differences between the 1508 study and the painting itself, it seems reasonable to presume that while the theme was determined by the patron, the precise details of how to distribute the attendant figures were left to Dürer's discretion. In any event, since artist and patron were both living in Nuremberg, meeting to discuss the finer points would not have been a problem.

In relation to the carved lunette and its predella, whose theme of the Last Judgement also extends to the trumpet-blowing angels found in the drawing and then carved in the round on the frame, the only differences concern the absence of the lily and sword to either side of Christ, also found in the *Last Judgement* in the *Small Woodcut Passion* of around 1509–10, which therefore falls between the two.[20] In contrast, the main panel has been substantially modified. In the drawing, the four zones – upper and lower as well as left and right – are already established, but they are far less populous, and only some of their inhabitants are in their final locations. To the proper right of the Trinity, the upper tier of figures is introduced by the Virgin, accompanied by an assembly of female saints, with Catherine – armed with her wheel and crown – in front. They are balanced by John the Baptist (both he and the Virgin echo their positions in the lunette), just conceivably with Landauer behind him. Down below, the group to the proper right consists of saints, who include a pope (with the keys of St Peter), a cardinal and a bishop, while the only two identifiable figures

on the left are Moses with the tablets of the law and David with
his harp.

In the painting they are both on the same side, but appear
behind John the Baptist on the upper level, where the Virgin is
again backed by female saints, whose palms designate them as
martyrs, with Catherine, Dorothy, Agnes, Barbara and Christina
all being identified by their attributes. Higher up, angels with the
Instruments of the Passion (reading from left to right, two sets
of flails, the sponge on a pole, the spear and the column) are joined
by a heavenly host of cherubim and seraphim seemingly fading
away to infinity. Nearer to earth, the idea appears to have been
to place the rulers of the church – two popes and a cardinal –
on the proper right, and the emperor and kings of this world
on the left, in both cases with holy women who are not martyrs
behind them. The most prominent male figures are almost all
turned away from the viewer, and at least one portrait has been
added to each side. The one next to the left margin is the wiz-
ened Matthäus Landauer (in fact, he was born in 1451, so was only
sixty), and there is a sublimely evanescent black chalk study for
his head, which is inscribed 'landawer styfter' ('Landauer the
donor') and dated 1511 by the artist. The identity of the counter-
pointing warrior on the other side is less certain, although he is
probably Wilhelm Haller, Landauer's son-in-law.[21] The final difference between the drawing and the painting is the addition of
Dürer's self-portrait set against the panoramic landscape backdrop, but in truth – and in spite of his absence from the drawing
– such an insertion may well always have been part of the plan.
Landauer was by no means the grandest of Dürer's patrons,
but the surface perfection and lavish use of gold leaf here are
unrivalled.

With the exception of an abortive project for a Virgin and
Child with Saints altarpiece he was working on in 1521–2, which
will be examined in detail in the next chapter, the last years of

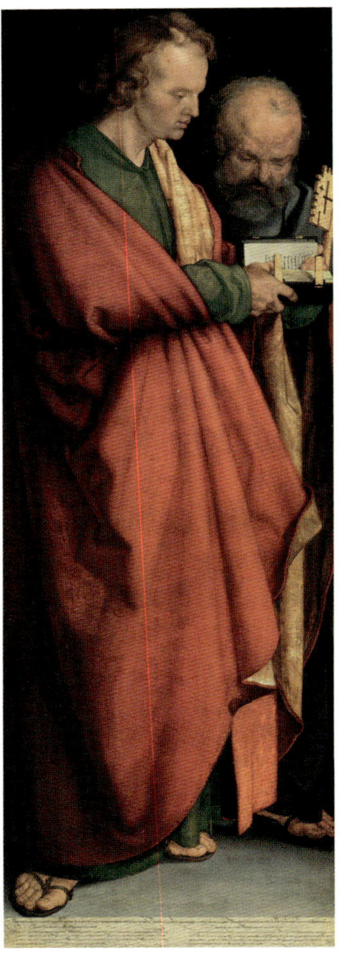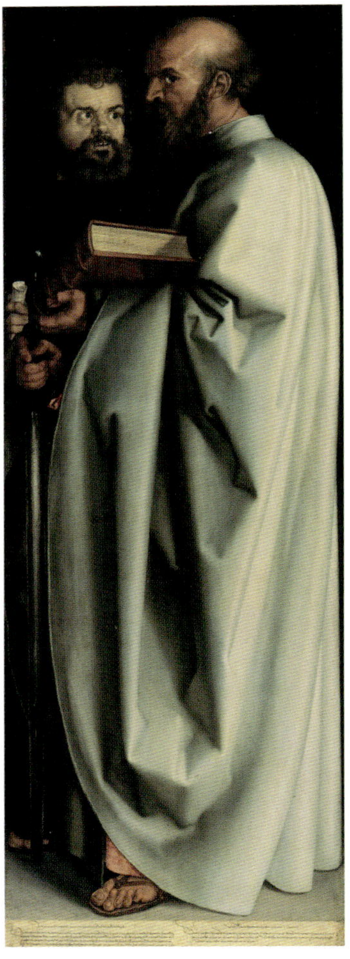

Dürer's career only saw him engaged with one monumental commission. Happily, this concluding achievement represents an uplifting finale. The *Four Apostles*, which is monogrammed and dated 1526, was executed by Dürer as a gift for the Nuremberg Rathaus (town hall), where the two sides were to remain for over

34 Albrecht Dürer, *Four Apostles*, 1526, oil on limewood panel.

a century (illus. 34).[22] Documentary evidence in the form of a payment of one hundred guilders on 19 September of the same year in the town registers is an indication of a desire on the part of the city to show its gratitude to the artist, but does not alter the fact that his original act of generosity was intended as a *Gedächnis* (memorial), and in a sense represents a variant of a Renaissance tradition – at least south of the Alps – for artists to adorn their family chapels with works of art.[23]

The major difference here is not just that the pair of paintings were destined for a civic as opposed to an ecclesiastical context, but also that they are explicitly Protestant images. Each of the four figures has an extensive text from Luther's German translation of the New Testament positioned beneath him, and in addition the text of the first verses of his Gospel, again in German, is legible on the open book in John's hand (Mark holds a scroll that is inscribed, in Latin, 'EVAN. MARCI CAP I'). Slightly unexpectedly, the words below John are Peter's, while those below Peter are John's, and the same criss-cross arrangement obtains for Mark and Paul.

In view of the fact that Luther was excommunicated at the Diet of Worms in 1521, and that his almost equally contentious publication of the New Testament in the vernacular followed the year after (the complete translation of the Bible was not issued until 1534, after Dürer's death), the decision to celebrate his rejection of Catholicism and his new evangelical Christianity was not only bold but related to events of the day. Even as recently as 1520–21, when, as stated above, Dürer was planning an entirely standard *sacra conversazione*, which would have been intended to go above an altar in a Catholic church, there was not yet any such thing as Protestantism.

The title *Four Apostles* is distinctly misleading. Both John and Peter, who are paired on the left wing, are numbered among the original twelve disciples, but neither Paul nor Mark was one of their number. A different way of thinking about all four would therefore be to see them as corresponding mixed couples, since Peter and Paul, each shown with their most familiar attributes (the keys and the sword), are routinely paired, while John and Mark are both evangelists, and hold their Gospels. Moreover, in Luther's *Septembertestament* of 1522, he writes that John's Gospel, Paul's Epistles and Peter's First Epistle General are the 'rechte kern vnd marck allen buchern' ('the true heart and core of all books'), which is certainly suggestive, although it does not explain why one of John's epistles and Peter's Second Epistle are cited in preference to those books named by Luther. Much has also been made of the passage where Christ sends the Apostles forth 'by two and two', and commands that they should take nothing for their journey, 'But be shod with sandals' (Mark 6:7–8), as Dürer's figures indeed are. However, it is worth adding that the otherwise faithfully followed full-length study for John, which is dated 1525 in the artist's hand, shows him barefoot.[24]

In the last analysis, the work's great strength is the compelling immediacy of the four heads, which are artfully contrasted, with the intensely contemplative expressions of John and Peter being set against the energized animation of Mark and Paul. The surviving studies for three of the four heads will be returned to in the next chapter, but here it seems worth underlining the extent to which Dürer's mastery means we are bound to believe in them as real presences.[25]

Turning to the artist's small-scale religious compositions, it is unsurprising that the overwhelming majority of them revolve around the theme of the Virgin and Child, and it is with them that I shall begin, before moving on to other subjects.

There is a good deal of controversy concerning precisely which Madonnas traditionally agreed to be by Dürer are actually his work. As is often the case when it comes to the first steps of even the greatest Renaissance painters, the fact that their signature style is not yet established, combined with a dearth of connected drawings and a lack of documentation, hampers a clear understanding of their artistic beginnings. Until recently, two paintings of the *Virgin and Child*, which were both added to his corpus in an article of 1961 by the great Roberto Longhi, were very widely agreed to be autograph works by Dürer.[26] Of late, doubts have been raised about both of them, and the whole issue has been carefully discussed by Peggy Grosse, who ends up denying them to him but argues that they must date from the period around 1490–1510 (others have contended that they are much later emulations and part of the so-called Dürer Renaissance).[27]

Leaving them to one side, the first universally acknowledged Virgin and Child by Dürer is the *Haller Madonna*. It was painted for a relation of his mother-in-law, but the family connection is hardly a close one.[28] It too is undated, but the fact that – for all its independence of spirit – its mood is so profoundly Venetian and specifically Bellinesque makes it hard to see how it could have been painted by a German artist who had never been to Italy. As was discussed in Chapter Two, there has recently been a vigorous onslaught on the whole idea that Dürer made a first Italian journey around 1495 before his documented one in 1506, but the existence of the *Haller Madonna* is arguably one of the most powerful pieces of evidence for such a journey. It is certainly hard to see how it can date from 1507 or later, and indeed it has never been placed that late, which would allow of only two possibilities – either that it is not by Dürer at all, or that its Italianate manner is the result of an exclusively long-distance acquaintance with that country's art.

In terms of its actual dating, it seems hard to separate it overmuch from the Prado *Self-Portrait* of 1498, since not just the landscape glimpsed beyond but the hair of the Christ Child look so similar. However, at the same time, the *Flight of Lot and His Daughters* on the reverse does not appear to be as evolved as the

Job element of the *Jabach Altarpiece*, whose vignette of the destruction by fire of a different city set beside a watery distance is blatantly by the same hand. The reason for the inclusion of an episode that at this date was all but unrepresented is unexplained, not that Lot lying with his daughters would have been any less mysterious.[29]

The next Dürer *Virgin and Child* is a dramatically cropped image of the type known in Italy as the 'Madonna del latte', monogrammed and dated 1503, which some authorities regard as a product of the so-called Dürer Renaissance.[30] The theme is also found in Dürer's drawings and prints, but the two distinctive aspects of its treatment here are the affection and intimacy of their embrace and the way in which the Infant Jesus' features are all but hidden from view. If autograph, it is evidently related in some way or other to Jacopo de' Barbari's *Ill-Matched Couple*, which is likewise dated 1503, and in all probability depends upon it.[31]

The *Virgin and Child with a Siskin* of 1506 has already been discussed in the previous chapter and will be returned to in the next one. During the final two decades of Dürer's career, Madonnas play only a small part. The first of these five small paintings, which are all monogrammed, is a dated panel of 1512. It represents Christ in a reclining pose adapted from an earlier drawing, as will also be more fully explored in the next chapter, and shows him holding an unusual attribute in the form of the end of a sliced pear in his left hand.[32] Conversely, both the apple he holds and the carnation proffered by his mother in another close-up *Virgin and Child*, this time of 1516, which is painted on parchment on panel, are entirely standard attributes by this date.[33] Perhaps unexpectedly, given their more general prevalence in the art of the period, what makes it unique is the inclusion of haloes (here calligraphically linear ones), which he tended to eschew. The next *Virgin and Child* by Dürer, a panel that is likewise dated 1516, is entirely self-contained, but plays ingeniously with the idea that the Child has been distracted by something that prompts him to look away to his right.[34] The slightly later *Virgin and Child with St Anne*, which was painted for Gabriel III Tucher and is dated 1519, is his next-to-last – but arguably best – word in paint on the devout and tender love of Mary for her baby, here fast asleep.[35] It has the added bonus of a St Anne based upon a life study of the artist's wife Agnes, as already discussed in the Introduction, which is one of a small group of four related sheets variously connected with the project.[36] It was followed by a *Madonna* of 1526, which returns to the motifs of fruit and flowers, but here shows the pear in the Virgin's hand and the Christ Child with a tiny flower.[37]

Moving on to consider Dürer's other small-scale religious paintings, constraints of space mean it is not possible to do equal justice to all of them, but at the same time they are not so numerous that any need to be omitted. Viewed as a whole, they represent a strikingly heterogeneous array of works, divided as they are between narrative and iconic images of Christ, the Virgin (without the Christ Child) and a number of saints.

Taking them in chronological order, the earliest – apart from two controversial narrative panels, which appear to be the work of a single artist – is the *Christ as the Man of Sorrows*.[38] It depicts Christ wearing the Crown of Thorns and holding a flail and a besom, both associated with the Flagellation, which have left his body covered with blood. His hands and right side reveal the marks of his Crucifixion, and the ledge on which he rests his right hand may be intended to indicate that he is in his tomb, but in another sense this is evidently a timeless representation. A blood-red fringed gothic arch shape frames him, beyond which is a decorated gold leaf ground.

A dating around 1494, close to the Louvre *Self-Portrait*, has been proposed, and both works demonstrate the artist's precocity in his early to mid-twenties. The same goes for the early *St Jerome in the Wilderness* (illus. 35).[39] The story of this work's rediscovery and attribution is so extraordinary that it merits a slight digression, not least because it has all too often in effect been suppressed.[40] Until its reappearance and publication in 1957, it was traditionally given to the Veronese artist Giovan Francesco Caroto, and in consequence a photograph of it was located under his name in the Witt Library at the Courtauld Institute of Art. David Carritt, one of the greatest 'eyes' of the twentieth or any other century, recognized its authorship from the image, not least because of its association with a highly finished coloured drawing. That work, which is on parchment, is monogrammed and dated 1494, and portrays a lion standing against a landscape background.[41] The Witt photograph provided the name and address of the owner, and – luckily for all concerned – the panel was still in the possession of Lieutenant-Colonel Sir Edmund Bacon, Bart, at Raveningham Hall in Norfolk, and direct inspection of the original confirmed Dürer's authorship.[42] By concealing the lion's hindquarters behind the half-kneeling aged saint, the artist was able to redeploy the drawing of the standing lion for a reclining one. It may also be that a year or two intervened between the execution of the drawing and the painting, and it is clear that the former was not made as a preparatory study for the latter.

A now dismembered triptych distinctly uncomfortably combines two full-length standing hermit saints (the Giovanni Bellini-inspired Onophrius and John the Baptist) with a half-length *Salvator Mundi*. There is no record of the elements being together, but all three share the same dimensions and unfinished state. Having been separated in the aftermath of the Second World War, the saints are now reunited in Bremen, while the *Christ* is in New York.[43] The ensemble must date from a couple of years before the artist's second journey to Italy, around the same time as the *Adoration of the Magi* of 1504 (illus. 36).[44]

At over a metre in height, the *Adoration* is not exactly small, but at the same time not big enough to qualify as an altarpiece. Its setting is robustly classical, with the remains of various round-arched structures, mostly on the left, set against a quintessentially northern mountainous prospect over to the right. The figure composition is arranged symmetrically, so that two of the Magi – the older one kneeling and the middle one standing behind him – are in the centre, while their younger black companion and the Virgin and Child are to the sides (the ox and the ass are behind their mistress, but unusually Joseph is nowhere to be seen). Its assurance eloquently proves that Dürer was already a fully mature artist before his second Italian journey of 1506, which has been extensively explored in the previous chapter, and was to yield the artist's only narrative half-length, his ominously claustrophobic *Christ among the Doctors*, which brilliantly contrasts the twelve-year-old Saviour with the often – but not invariably – grotesque elders who press in upon him from all sides.[45]

A whole decade later, in 1516, Dürer monogrammed and dated his *St Philip* and *St James*. Executed on *Tüchlein* (fine canvas) and excellently preserved, they give a vivid sense of how exquisitely the artist could paint in this medium. Better yet, the images are confined to psychologically troubled heads, which in a sense foreshadow the *Four Apostles* of the next decade.[46] In terms of their iconography, there is an undeniable anomaly that may in fact be a simple error: the saints Philip and James the Less share a feast day, and therefore form a natural pair (for all that some commentators have speculated that the plan was to produce a set of all twelve Apostles), but the James represented here has to be James the Greater, one of the two sons of Zebedee and the brother of John, because he wears a cockleshell (his customary attribute and that of all pilgrims) on his red drapery.

Frustratingly, Dürer's *Praying Virgin* must originally have been the right half of a diptych, serving as a pendant to an image of her

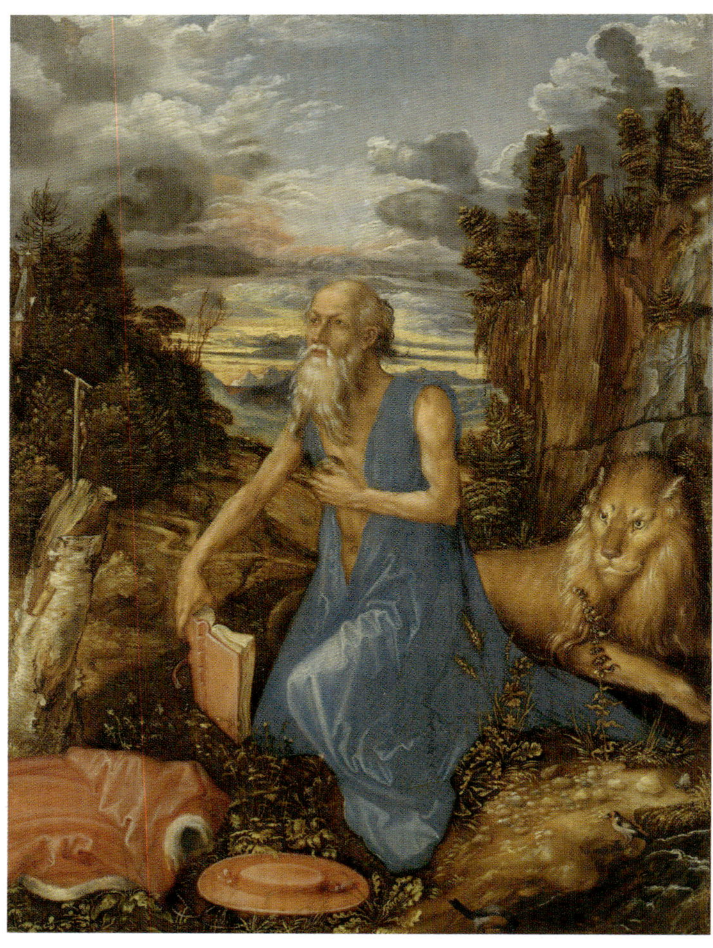

Son, logically depicted as the Man of Sorrows. There is a candidate in the form of a copy for the missing work, but no certainty.[47] Happily, his *St Jerome* of 1521 in Lisbon is in generally good condition.[48] It represents a telling example of Dürer's genius for exploiting studies taken from life for another purpose, since we know he made three drawings of a 93-year-old man – and two

35 Albrecht Dürer, *St Jerome in the Wilderness*, *c.* 1494, oil on pearwood panel.

others, respectively of Jerome's skull and of his books and lectern – during his journey to the Netherlands.[49] Having said that, they work so perfectly that it seems hard to doubt that Dürer controlled the apparently effortlessly natural pose adopted by the man with the thought of such a painting in mind from the outset.

The number of extant mythological and allegorical paintings by Dürer is extremely limited, and nothing suggests that all sorts of others once existed but are irretrievably lost. In spite of the very small size of this group of paintings, the whole area clearly gripped him. Necessity decreed that his engagement with it was in the main confined to the related worlds of prints and drawings, where he was free to do as he pleased both when it came to the choice of subject-matter and, arguably even more crucially, in its

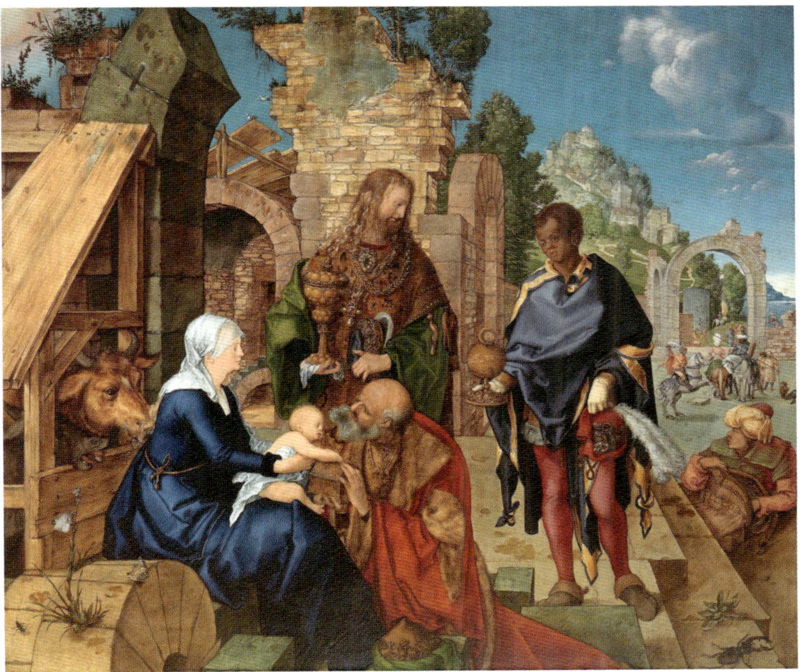

36 Albrecht Dürer, *Adoration of the Magi*, 1504, oil on panel.

interpretation. It is unlikely to be a mere coincidence that his paintings of both *Hercules* and *Lucretia* are essentially straightforward in their iconography, whereas a number of the prints are sufficiently recondite to have baffled the urge of scholars to give them entirely satisfactory titles.

The earlier of the two, a severely compromised canvas titled *Hercules and the Stymphalian Birds*, bears Dürer's monogram and the year 1500: these may not be original, but were certainly visible at a relatively early date, since they appear identically on a copy.[50] In any event, such a dating is not implausible, since the work in question gives every indication of reflecting the artist's awareness of the art of the Pollaiuolo brothers, and specifically his dependence on the pose of the hero in their *Hercules, Nessus and Deianira*, which he must have seen on his presumed first Italian journey of around 1495.[51] At the same time, as was pointed out by Erwin Panofsky, the attitude of the god in a woodcut of Apollo and Daphne in the 1502 edition of the *Quatuor libri amorum* by Dürer's close friend Konrad Celtis is in effect a frontal translation of the figure of Hercules in the picture, which must therefore precede it.[52]

In 1497 Celtis had also published an edition of Seneca's *Hercules Furens* with an accompanying *epistola*, which has in the past been associated with this commission, but that text does not refer to this particular Labour of Hercules. A more plausible context is Frederick the Wise's Schloss at Wittenberg, which in 1507 was recorded by Andreas Meinhard as having had an *aestuarium* (a place where fresh and salt water are mixed) on the ground floor containing four representations of stories of Hercules. Meinhard further noted that one of them showed him killing the Stymphalian harpies ('Er tödtet mit dem Bogen die Stymphalischen Harpyen'). This reference has been plausibly linked with Dürer's canvas, but more might have been made of the fact that the creatures are described as harpies: this is indeed how they are depicted here, but making them half-human is absolutely not sanctioned by classical sources such as Pausanias.[53] Two additional factors support the connection: one is the exceptional rarity of the subject in Renaissance painting, and the other is that the existing canvas is blatantly a fragment of what was once a larger – very possibly arched – whole, as is most plainly demonstrated by the savage truncation of the harpy above Hercules. Given the work's present state, it is only possible to imagine rather than fully experience the muscular energy of the demigod and the combined fury and terror of the recoiling birds.

Happily, the condition of the *Suicide of Lucretia* (illus. 37), which is monogrammed and dated 1518 on the box at bottom left, is generally excellent.[54] The only oddity is that the two connected drawings for the panel date from a decade earlier. Both employ the same technique of black and grey brush with white heightening on greenish prepared paper.[55] The first is a full-length study for the figure, which is monogrammed and dated 1508 on the front edge of the plinth on which she is shown standing before a dark niche. The differences between the figure in the drawing and the painting are not only minimal, but already anticipated in the second sheet, which focuses on Lucretia's now raised right forearm and hand, showing the stiletto entering her breast from above rather than below, and dispenses with her drapery curled around her arm. This detailed study is undated, but must belong to the same moment rather than a decade later, above all because it is a virtual stylistic twin (and indeed mirror image) of a dated study of 1507 for his painting of Eve of the same year.[56] The only other change of plan is that in the painting Lucretia is backed by a radically foreshortened but immediately identifiable bed, which serves as a reminder of the reason for her suicide, namely her rape by Tarquin.[57]

Some Renaissance artists were notoriously slow to complete and deliver paintings, but as a rule Dürer was not of their number. It has sometimes been suggested that he must have started to

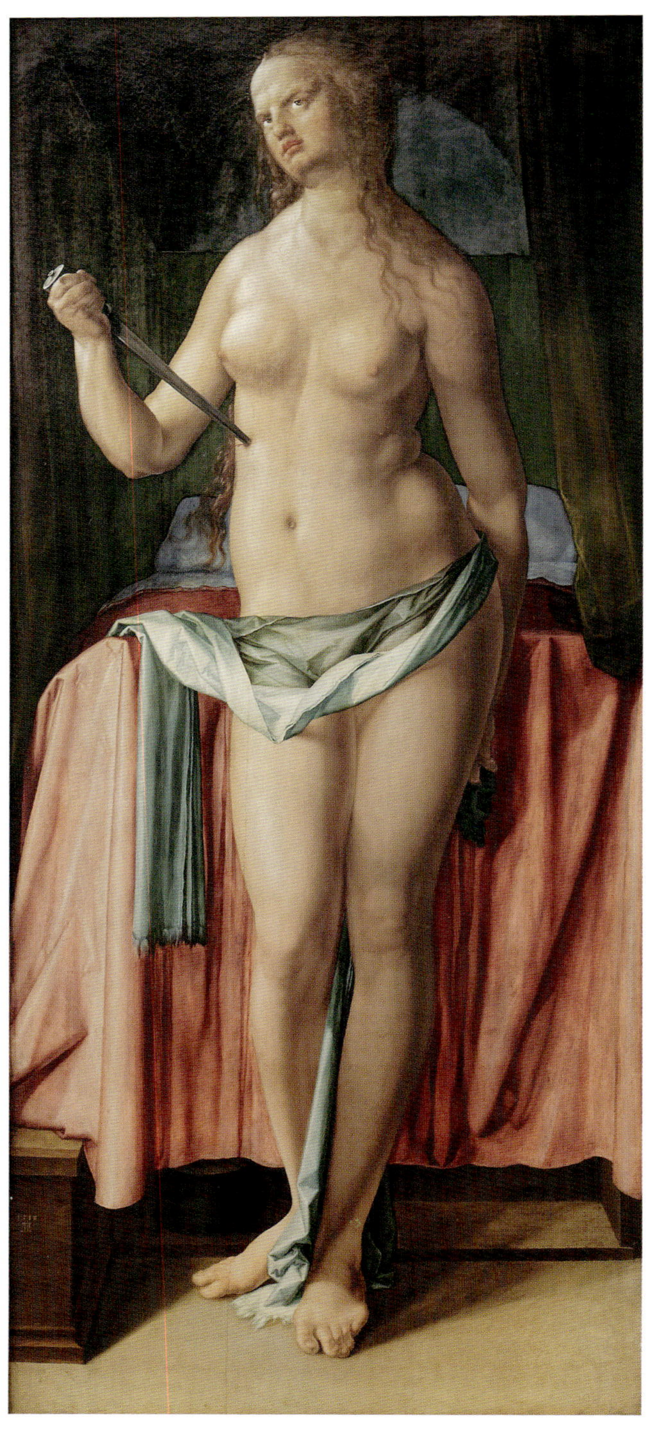

paint the *Lucretia* around 1508, straight after he executed the drawings for it, and then abandoned it, but this seems incredibly unlikely,
not least in view of the uniformity of its handling. However, it
has to be admitted that nothing is known concerning either why
he planned such a work in 1508, or why he produced a more or
less life-size picture on the theme in 1518, and who its original
owner may have been (it is first recorded in Munich in 1598).

In Renaissance Germany the iconography was without precedent, and no doubt Dürer's austere presentation of the single
nude figure in isolation, whose pose may well have been inspired,
at least loosely, by some kind of classical statue of the Venus
Pudica type, would have appeared faithfully Italianate.[58] Nevertheless, to a modern eye it looks profoundly un-Italian, and
Dürer certainly resisted any temptation to take Marcantonio
Raimondi's *Lucretia* after Raphael as his model, as Hans Sebald
Beham was to do in his engraving of the subject the year after,
where the upper body is virtually identical, albeit in reverse.[59] Moreover, the heroine's tormented heavenward gaze is arguably equally
unclassical, although it is marginally less extreme in the painting
than in the drawing.

To these mythologies, there should be added Dürer's only
allegory (illus. 38), a work whose actual meaning is much debated,
and which is painted on the reverse of the monogrammed and
dated *Portrait of a Young Man* of 1507, the sitter of which has been
convincingly identified as Matthäus Landauer's son-in-law,
Wilhelm Haller.[60] Anzelewsky guardedly designates it as an *Old
Woman with a Money-Bag* but then goes on to explain why its traditional association with Avarice – who would not be so open-handed
with money – makes no sense, before suggesting that notions of
the transience of human life must be at its core, also implausibly
citing Giorgione's *Col Tempo* as some sort of parallel.[61]

Whatever the work's precise meaning, and regardless of whether
Dürer was actually inspired by the *Col Tempo*, this comparison is

37 Albrecht Dürer, *Suicide of Lucretia*, 1518, oil on limewood panel.

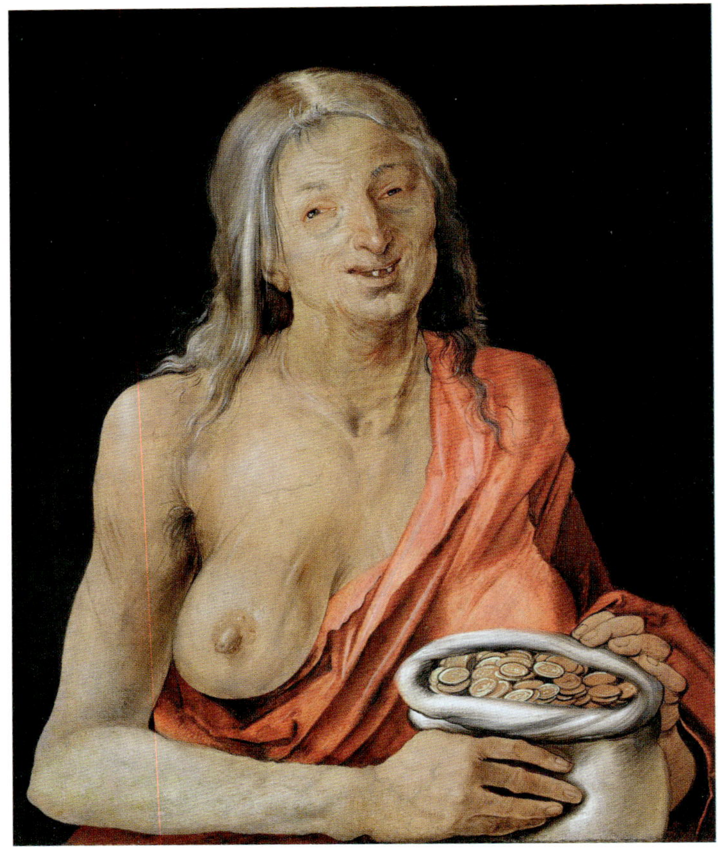

an instructive one, if only for helping to underline the contrast between the poignant sadness of Giorgione's image and the gleeful cruelty of Dürer's. Dürer is encouraging us either to recoil from or to laugh at this hideous distortion of a young seductress, who flashes her gap-toothed grin and wrinkled breast at her intended male victim, and it should not be forgotten that in the period unbound hair – like nudity – was a signifier of sexual licence. However, the most compellingly transgressive touch in the whole

38 Albrecht Dürer, *Allegory of Avarice*, 1507, oil on limewood panel.

image is surely the glimpse of abundant tufts of hair sprouting from under the old crone's right armpit. It would be impossible to attempt anything even approximating to a comprehensive survey, but I would be surprised if one did not have to wait until the twentieth century to find another European painting in which female armpit hair is shown (Frida Kahlo positively delighted in representing her own). Quite how this loosely painted vision was intended to relate to the portrait on the other side remains a mystery, but the notion that the *Young Man* was originally one half of a diptych in company with his wife is an appealing one, in which case the reverse of her likeness would have gone on the right, and would presumably have consisted of a male figure that explained the meaning of both.

Turning, finally, to Dürer's portraits, they unarguably bring out the best of him as a painter, and continue to be immensely powerful right up to the end of his career. Here, the emphasis will above all be upon those of people who were not his intimates, since the portraits of his family and close friends were the focus in the Introduction. Particular attention will also be paid to those select cases where it is possible, thanks to the survival of preparatory drawings or variant likenesses in the form of prints, to explore the ways in which he went about bringing his sitters to life.

Given Dürer's very considerable standing in his own lifetime, and moreover not just in his later years, it is arguably surprising quite how few individuals of real importance he painted. As early as 1496 he executed a portrait on canvas of Frederick the Wise, the Elector of Saxony (1463–1525). The sitter was in Nuremberg that year (14–18 April), which must be when his likeness was taken, although it was presumably worked up at leisure. The artist presents his subject from a sufficient distance to include both of his hands folded one across the other on a table in front of him, but the elector's penetrating gaze makes him feel very close.[62]

Much later, when an older and wearier Frederick stayed in Nuremberg from November 1522 to February 1523, Dürer drew a life study of him, and subsequently elaborated it in an engraving which is dated 1524.[63]

In the case of Emperor Maximilian I, there are two painted portraits – one on canvas and another on panel – and a related but possibly not autograph woodcut, but they all go back to the same source.[64] This is a black chalk study of the head and shoulders of the emperor drawn by Dürer at the Diet of Augsburg in 1518, which he supplemented the year after with a close-up of two hands holding a pomegranate.[65] The hands, which were not included in the woodcut, were precisely replicated in the canvas, but only the left one was repeated in the panel, where it was joined by a new right hand. Conversely, the head is unchanged throughout, and the way the sitter fails to engage our gaze and instead looks away to one side is indeed his preferred formula, although there are a select few exceptions. Where it arguably differs most from Dürer's norm is in the reflective, almost withdrawn, expression.

When it came to spiritual as opposed to secular leaders, the handful of portraits Dürer made are all engravings, naturally enough on the basis of drawings, which have mostly survived and are in the main faithfully adhered to. Two are of Cardinal Albrecht of Brandenburg, who is shown looking away to his left in the smaller one of 1519 and then in pure profile in the slightly larger one of 1523. Intriguingly, this latter represents the one exception in terms of its departure from the eyewitness record, and blatantly softens the unflinching realism of the original silverpoint study.[66] When it comes to Philip Melanchthon, on the other hand, they could hardly be more like in character, although the print is notably more resolved than the pen drawing, and for example accentuates the bulging veins on his temples.[67] Only in the case of Erasmus, where the engraving is dated 1526, is there no extant related drawing, but we know – as an inscription on it boasts – that it was based upon drawings from life made some years before, when they met in the Netherlands in 1520. In his diary Dürer implies there was more than one sitting, while Erasmus refers to an unfinished drawing in his correspondence with Pirckheimer, no doubt the sheet dated 1520, which Dürer evidently kept.[68] In the print, which, however, is not directly based upon that study, Erasmus is presented as a species of modern St Jerome, surrounded by scholarly paraphernalia – and some flowers in a ewer – holding a quill in his right hand and a tiny inkpot in his left one.

The engraving of Melanchthon bears a Latin text, which translates as 'Dürer was able to picture the features of the living Philip, but his skilled hand was unable to picture his mind,' and begs the question as to whether that was genuinely the artist's ambition. It seems altogether more likely that as a rule he sought to represent what he saw in terms of both appearances and personality, but that he was frankly less curious about anything that might lie below the surface.

The overwhelming majority of Dürer's painted portraits are of men, but there are exceptions. Two of the most striking are of otherwise unidentified members of the Fürleger family of Nuremberg, and must date from around 1497–8. Their technique, dimensions and history all prove that they originally formed some sort of diptych, and only went their separate ways in 1830. Yet they make for an odd pair, since the one that must have been on the left sets the figure against a uniform background, and presents her almost – but for her abundant cascade of curly hair – in the guise of the Annunciate Virgin, with her eyes downcast and her hands joined in prayer, whereas her presumptive sister rests her crossed hands on a ledge beside a window onto a distant landscape, and fixes us with a distinctly unimpressed gaze.[69]

Two of the four other women Dürer painted once formed the right halves of a pair of husband-and-wife diptychs of members of another Nuremberg family, the Tuchers, but only three of the panels still exist. In one instance, Hans Tucher, who holds out a ring, looks across at his wife, Felicitas, while she looks out at us, and both a window ledge and the continuous landscape beyond it unite them. In the other, whose format and intimate scale were identical, both Nicolaus and Elsbeth looked inwards and were backed by similar stretches of landscape, but he is lost, and only known in the form of a miniature, whose reliability appears to be confirmed by the likeness of his consort in it. They all have what are presumed to be later but basically reliable inscriptions, which name them, give their ages, and add the common date of 1499, which seems entirely plausible on stylistic grounds.[70]

As their costume indicates, Dürer's two other female portraits were presumably both executed in Venice, and are broadly similar in their small scale, their concentration on the head and the way both women look away to their right. What appears to be the earlier of the two bears the date 1505 and places the freely painted sitter against a black background of the kind that had been standard for Venetian portraits since Antonello da Messina's time there in the 1470s.[71] The other one has a blue backdrop, presumably intended for the sky, and is even looser in handling.[72] Both are best understood as likenesses of *belle* ('beauties'), and were no doubt produced at speed – various passages in Dürer's diary of his journey to the Netherlands underline the amazing speed at which he could paint as well as draw. In view of the penetrating understanding of the likenesses of women in the silverpoint sketchbook executed at that time, the lack of more painted equivalents can only be a source of regret.[73]

Turning to the remainder of the male portraits, the degree to which Dürer was content to stick to two very simple formulae is incredibly striking. One solution involves showing the sitter lit from the left, slightly turned to his right and invariably looking in that same direction. This applies, in chronological order, to *Burkhard von Speyer*, the *Portrait of a Clergyman (Johann Dorsch?)*, *Jakob Fugger*, *Rodrigo da Almada*, *Bernhard von Reesen*, the *Man in a Beret*, *Jakob Muffel* and *Johannes Kleberger*.[74] Of these eight, three include one or both hands – in two cases holding letters – while five do not. They significantly outnumber the three portraits, respectively *Oswald Krell* (the only one of this group with hands), *Unidentified Young Man* and *Hieronymus Holzschuher*, which – although lit and turned the same way – represent their subjects looking directly out at the viewer.[75] In terms of picture format, with one exception they are all conventionally rectangular and upright, the odd man out being *Johannes Kleberger*, who is represented on a square panel but within a circular field, which may indicate some sort of loose inspiration from the art of the medal.

It might be objected that, thus dissected, Dürer's repertoire sounds painfully limited, but that is to misunderstand the context in which they were created, which, after all, was a world without retrospective exhibitions and *catalogues raisonnés*. Nobody would have conceived of these pictures lined up – even virtually – in a row, and the approach adopted meant the artist could devote all his time and attention to two crucial tasks. The first was the mapping of their faces, and the second was the capturing of their moods. Seen in those terms, they do not split up into those who are looking at us and those who are looking away from us, but rather into the knotted brows and passionate intensity of Krell, the unidentified man in a beret, Holzschuher and Kleberger, and the more reflective and even occasionally almost dreamily melancholy rest. What is more, when Dürer actually knew – as he did in the case of Muffel and Holzschuher (illus. 39 and 40) – that they were to be displayed together, he carefully ensured that one would be pensive and look to the side, while the other would stare directly out and all but terrify us. As will be explored in Chapter Five, the individual compositions in his print sequences

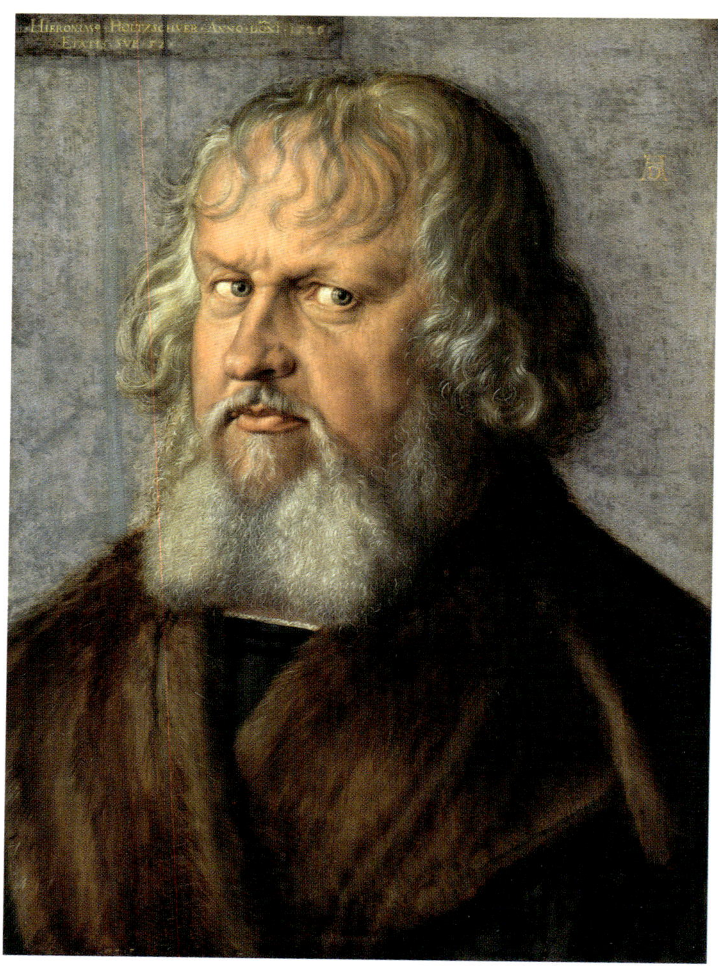

are likewise invariably designed to steer clear of the least hint of
monotony.

Dürer's last, but perhaps most powerful, quality as a portraitist
is his ability to capture a person's body and, in spite of the
Melanchthon inscription, soul. Of course, we have no way of

39 Albrecht Dürer, *Hieronymus Holzschuher*, 1526, oil on limewood panel.

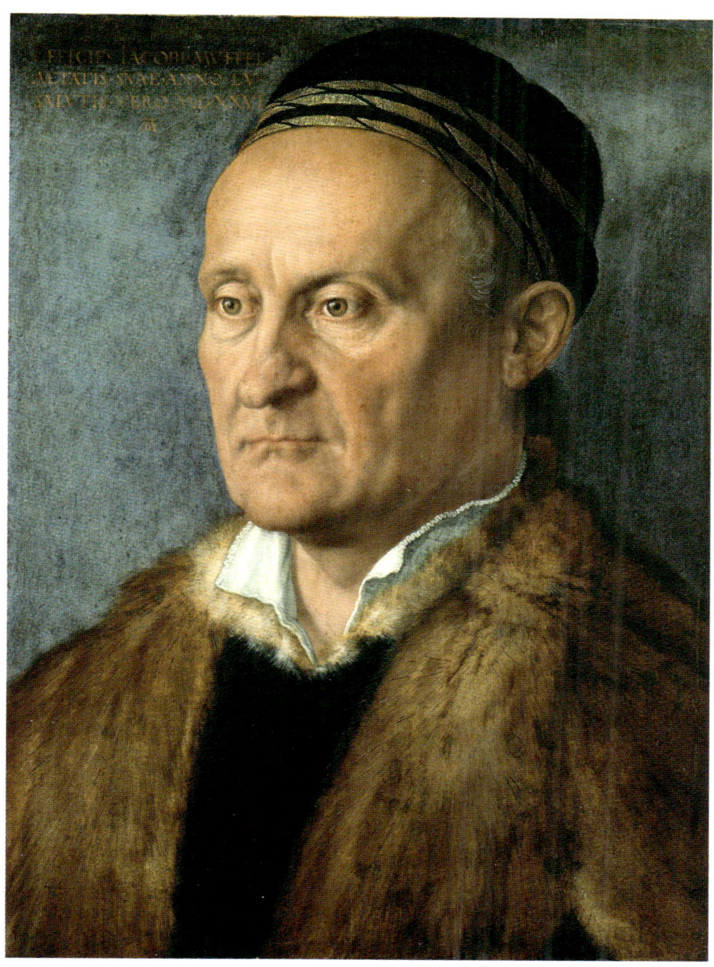

knowing what these people actually looked like, far less what it would have been like to spend time with them, but we believe in their reality. They can never walk into the room, but – on another level – we would not be at all surprised if they did.[76]

40 Albrecht Dürer, *Jakob Muffel*, 1526, oil on canvas, transferred from panel.

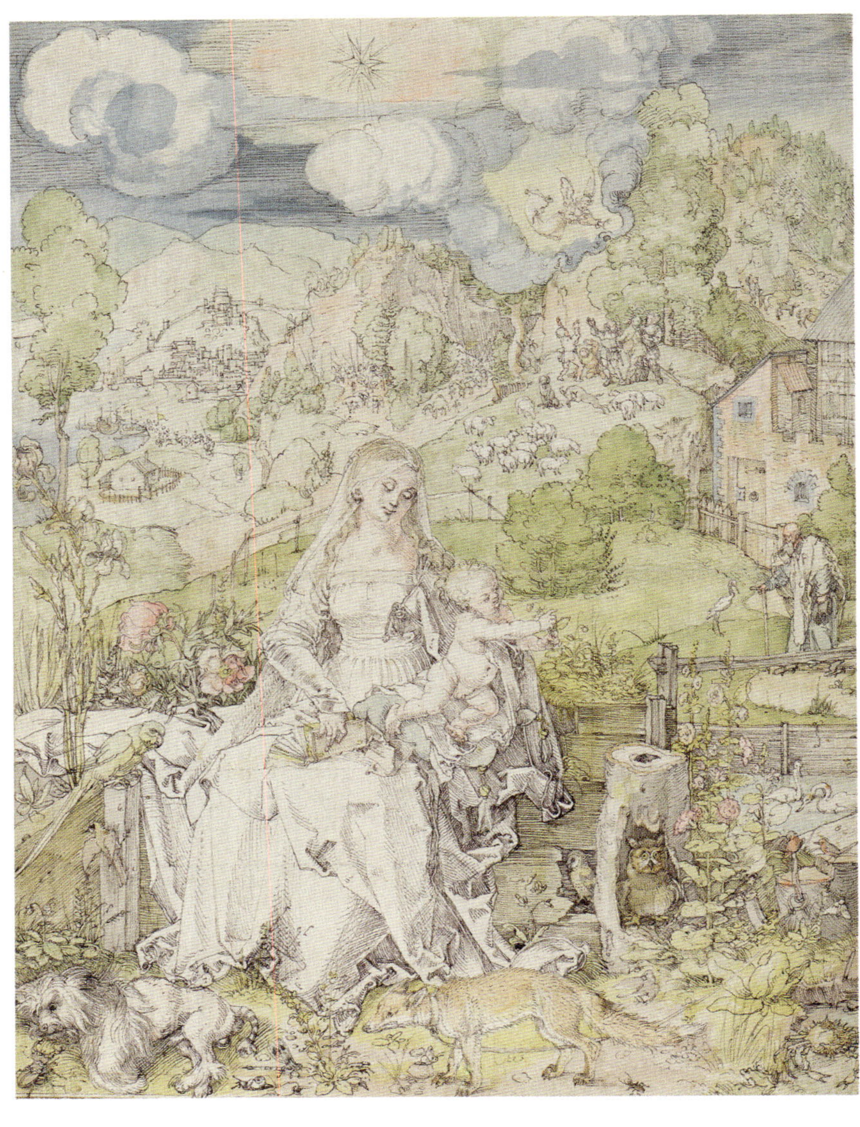

FOUR

Drawings

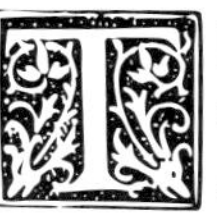Thus far nobody has attempted to write anything even vaguely approximating a full-blown study of Dürer's drawn oeuvre (catalogues are another matter, but end up saying depressingly little about individual sheets). It is to be hoped that the greatest living authority on the subject, Christof Metzger, will manage it one day, but it is not imminent.[1] At best, a chapter on the subject can only hope to scratch the surface, and here the ambition will be to pay close attention to a select few sheets rather than skim pointlessly over the surface of a fractionally more extensive selection.

Dürer's earliest surviving drawing, the *Self-Portrait* in silverpoint in the Albertina, which was made when he was thirteen years old, has already been examined in the Introduction.[2] From then on, he never stopped drawing, and what remains from all that ceaseless activity is an astounding treasure trove of sheets in a whole array of techniques.[3] A number have already been discussed in previous chapters, often from different perspectives. However, before continuing to explore this material, both in general and in detail, two things need to be explained.

The first is that in Dürer's day, drawings – with very rare exceptions – were regarded as a means to an end rather than ends in themselves. They were made almost exclusively in order to create other works of art, and above all paintings (the entirely different role of copy drawings in the context of artistic self-education has

41 Albrecht Dürer, *Virgin and Child with a Multitude of Animals*, c. 1503, pen and blackish-brown ink and watercolour.

already been explored in Chapter Two). After the invention of printmaking, they could equally serve to prepare woodcuts, engravings and etchings, but were also used to create designs for three-dimensional works of art such as sculptures and metalwork. Indeed, Dürer engaged in making all these kinds of drawings. The best drawings scholarship tends to be admirably attentive to examining the differences in appearance between drawings and the works they prepare, but it is my deep conviction that artists were at least as interested in employing them to explore the content of works of art as their form, and in what follows the intention will be to devote equal attention to both aspects.

It is clear that even before Dürer's time drawings were often lovingly preserved within workshops, and handed down to the next generation of artists, but they were neither more nor less than tools of the trade, and painting was indeed still a trade. However, and perhaps especially in certain enlightened circles in Italy, attitudes were beginning to change, and the idea of drawings being thought of as works of art, and therefore as being worth collecting, was afoot. Dürer's own drawings give various indications of his parallel sense of the dignity of the practice of drawing, and he unarguably played a vital role within what amounts to a sea change in their appreciation beyond the world of the artist's workshop.

The second and related point to make is that Dürer's drawings must always have been unprecedented in their range, precisely because they were not all means to an end. Dürer regularly drew the people and the world around him, by no means invariably as part of the preliminary work towards a commission. To give a specific example, the watercolour study *Stag Beetle* (illus. 16), even if it were not to be accepted as an autograph production, must at the very least be a record of a lost sheet by him.[4] The invention also features in two works that have both already been discussed, namely in the highly worked coloured drawing known as the *Virgin and Child with a Multitude of Animals* (illus. 41) and in the artist's painting of the *Adoration of the Magi* (illus. 36).[5] However, nothing suggests that Dürer's initial motivation for immortalizing it was to add a grace note to either of these other projects. The precise dating of all three works is much debated, but it seems hard to doubt that the *Stag Beetle* preceded the two others. In any event, there are plenty of other instances in Dürer's practice where drawings were ultimately employed only years later in paintings, which is a completely different situation from the traditional way in which drawings had previously been used to prepare them.[6] Exactly the same method was applied in relation to prints, as will be explored in the next chapter. As a result, the uniqueness of Dürer's drawings as a body of work is not merely a question of their having survived when so much else has been lost.

The reasons why this must be the case also need to be explained. One of them is that Dürer was the master of an unusual range of drawing media. They tend to serve different purposes, which means their various functions within the creative process must be described. Even allowing for the fact that there are inevitably gaps and unevennesses in terms of what has survived, it does seem broadly possible to give a general account both of the different media Dürer used to draw and of the purposes they served within his creative process. At the same time, it will be important to consider the extent to which his use of materials and way of drawing does or does not change over time. Dürer's was not an especially long life, but he was almost uniquely precocious, which means we can follow his creative journey – admittedly, at times more and at times less fully – for no fewer than 44 years.

The early *Self-Portrait* is executed in silverpoint, and this medium – or metalpoint more generally – remains a constant throughout Dürer's artistic career. A whole sequence of drawings made on his Netherlandish journey in 1521 prove that he continued to employ it into his final decade.[7] The fact that it effectively did not allow for correction meant it placed exceptional demands upon the artist, but also made it a natural choice for highly worked studies. At other times, however, Dürer employed pen and wash or even black chalk on naturally coloured or prepared papers, often combined with white heightening, in order to achieve similar levels of finish.[8]

At the other end of the creative process, first thoughts – where speed was often of the essence – were almost invariably set down in pen and ink.[9] Dürer was demonstrably already producing such drawings in his teens, and over time began to combine wash with the pen line.[10] Having said that, pen offers an extraordinary range of possibilities, and could also be used for immaculately finished solutions. What is more, in comparison to the 'brainstorming' approach adopted by some of his Italian contemporaries such as Leonardo da Vinci, Michelangelo and Raphael, Dürer's drawings are invariably entirely legible, even when he is starting to plan designs.[11] Moreover, although he very occasionally combines a number of options for a single motif on the same sheet of paper, in such cases the individual studies are all neat and tidy, as for instance in the early drawing *Six Cushions*, dated 1493 (illus. 42) or another, much later one of 1521 with nine variations on the theme of St Christopher.[12]

Four other media play a central role in Dürer's technical armoury. The first two are watercolour and body colour. He was already using the former on its own in the 1490s, and invariably employs it in effect to colour in very finished drawings with consistently pale washes. When it comes to those sheets that combine both media, there is no Renaissance artist north or south of the Alps by whom so many such sheets survive. The vast majority are either topographical studies – ranging in scale from landscapes and townscapes to records of individual trees or buildings – or studies of a vast array of members of the animal kingdom. The last two media, which are far from easy to tell apart, are charcoal

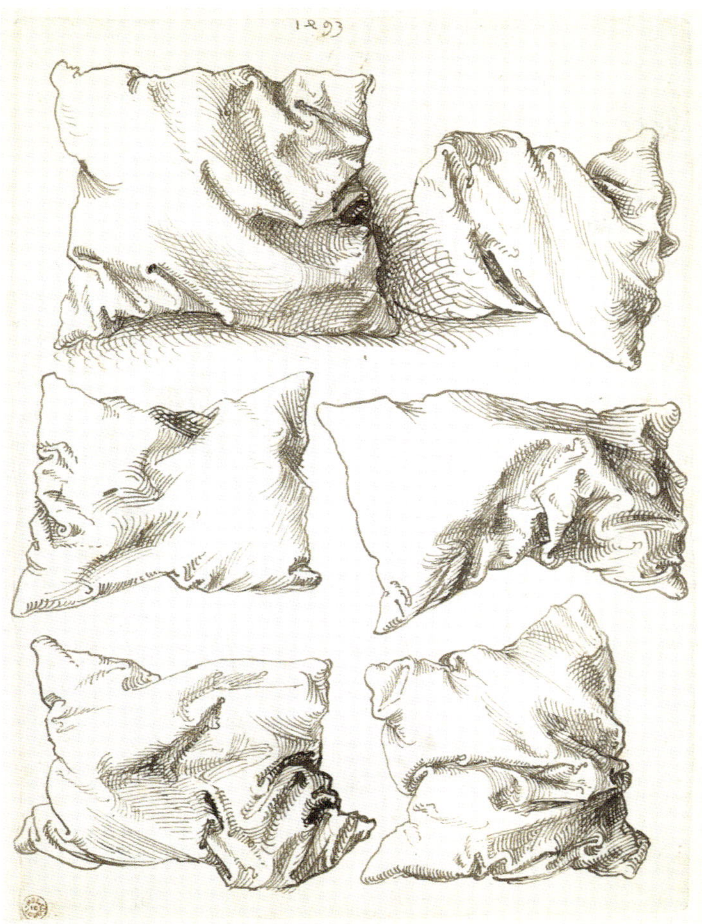

and black chalk: he was already a master of the former well before his second visit to Venice, but the latter, which he employed with notable freedom for portrait heads, was a late addition to his repertory in 1520–21. Conversely, and in spite of the fact that by 1515 he owned a stunning red chalk drawing by Raphael, oddly there is basically no evidence that he tried it out himself,

42 Albrecht Dürer, *Six Cushions*, 1493, pen and brown ink.

except very occasionally as an enhancement in order to give the flesh tones of portrait heads a rosy tint.[13]

Strictly speaking, lack of evidence does not amount to proof, so there can be no certainty that earlier northern European artists were not equally wide-ranging in the ways in which they drew, but everything points to the fact that in all sorts of ways Dürer's drawing practice represented a new departure. Our knowledge of the drawn oeuvres of German or indeed Netherlandish artists before Dürer is almost non-existent, for the simple reason that a heartbreakingly tiny number of sheets by them have survived. However, the explanation for this state of affairs is definitely not that they did not draw at all, and there are ways of in effect proving this. If we take Jan van Eyck as an example, there exists only a single preparatory drawing from his hand, the study in silverpoint for his painting of *Cardinal Niccolò Albergati*.[14] Nevertheless, it is hard to believe that this portrait was the only work by Van Eyck for which he made some kind of preparatory drawing. Indeed, there also exists a panel with a highly elaborate drawing of *St Barbara*, where the intention appears to have been to colour the design in, but only a start has been made on that process.[15] What is more, modern scientific technology, above all in the form of X-ray examination and infrared reflectography, has revealed that Van Eyck routinely executed elaborate underdrawings on his panels, which it has to be assumed were based in their turn on independent preliminary studies by the artist. The most striking case in point is probably the *Arnolfini Wedding*, but it is by no means unique.[16]

Given how few fifteenth-century northern European drawings have come down to us and the corresponding lack of documentary evidence concerning what might once have existed, it makes sense to look to Italy in search of support for the notion that what survives is very much the tip of the iceberg, as I have also endeavoured to show in two earlier publications. In one, archival records from the 1430s and '40s, which is to say long before Dürer's time, are cited in order to reveal extremely obscure provincial artists in the Friuli taking immense trouble in their wills to control the subsequent fate of their drawings, not one of which is known to survive.[17] In the other, it is demonstrated that while the same desire to preserve drawings only grew stronger in Italy throughout the sixteenth century, there could never be any certainty about their longer-term survival. Characteristically, the drawings listed in the post-mortem inventory of Federico Barocci, who died in 1612, far outnumber the current corpus of works on paper by him, for all that it is exceptionally substantial.[18]

In this connection, it is no less plain that even the abundance of drawings by Dürer that still exist, which amounts to in excess of a thousand drawings even excluding the studies in manuscripts (the precise total necessarily depends upon scholarly judgements concerning Dürer's authorship of a number of borderline cases among individual sheets), can only represent a mere fraction of his entire production. The easiest way to demonstrate this is to examine the character of the surviving drawings connected with particular works, and here the artist's *Christ among the Doctors* may serve as an exemplary case study.[19] There exist four meticulously finished drawings that are unproblematically connected with the work. All of them are executed in pen and ink on blue Venetian paper, heightened with white, and comprise a single head study – for Christ – and three studies of hands (one of which includes a pair of hands holding a book that in the end were not used).[20] In consequence, there are six heads and one pair of hands within the painting for which no studies are known, but it would be per-verse to doubt that such drawings once existed. Given the example of the hand study that did not reach the panel, it is not unreason-able to suppose there may have been other comparable trial runs, and that is before one begins to allow for the possibility of alto-gether sketchier first thoughts. If, and there is no reason why not, the same logic is applied to other paintings by the artist, without even mentioning prints, it is not hard to see that what remains to us can only represent a distinctly fragmentary survival. The fact that – by the standards of the time – his drawn oeuvre is exceptionally substantial does not alter this state of affairs.

In much of what follows, the overwhelming impression – and rightly so – will be of Dürer's singularity. However, certain media are all but inevitably better suited to different stages in the creative process. As a result, and not just in the Renaissance, pen and ink have tended to be employed for first ideas, for what might be described as thinking out loud on paper, as well as for more finished studies. Conversely, both metalpoint, where self-correction is virtually impossible, and indeed chalk tend to be reserved for the later stages in the evolution of designs. This was certainly Dürer's way, and it was one he shared with almost all his contemporaries.

If Dürer's drawings range from swiftly executed scribbles to the most exquisitely finished of studies, the extent to which the former are undoubtedly in the minority is nevertheless striking. In theory, this might simply be a consequence of the fact that he did not make many such drawings, but it seems altogether more likely that their rarity is a result of their not being systematically kept. It is impossible to be absolutely certain how their destruction occurred, but it seems plausible that it was the artist himself who deemed them unworthy of preservation, rather than that it was the relative indifference of posterity that led to their disappearance. The reason for saying this is that the handful of survivors are almost invariably either on the versos of more finished designs, or form minor parts of larger wholes, but virtually never survive in isolation.[21]

More generally, Dürer gives all sorts of indications of having cared about his drawings. One way in which he reveals his reverence towards drawings is in his careful preservation of them, and another pointer is his habit of adorning them with his famous

'AD' monogram and often with – usually very brief – explanatory texts. For whose benefit were they added? Neither Dürer himself, nor, for that matter, his immediate dependents, needed to be told that they were the works of his hand, and by no means infrequently the inscriptions that inform us that we are looking at a 'quarry' or a 'pond house' are distinctly superfluous.[22] A different way of thinking about them is to see them as looking to the future, but also as seeking to establish and entrench the status of these kinds of productions as – to drive the point home – works of art. This is arguably particularly true of inscriptions and dates added at a later date, although it is not always easy to know which category any given text falls into.

Crucially, the sheets Dürer preserved are not exclusively confined to his more finished efforts on paper or vellum: the *Pond in the Woods* (illus. 43), for instance, for all its magically atmospheric beauty, is blatantly unfinished, even on its own terms.[23] Unlike their counterparts on the right, the distinctly forlorn tree trunks over to the left are not topped by leaves, presumably because Dürer ran out of time as the sun went down (at which point he started another study of the view on the back of the paper), but he fully grasped the value of keeping the sheet.

In the context of Dürer's drawings (and indeed prints) his habit of adding the monogram has proved incredibly useful in establishing a secure body of work, but his datings of drawings after the event are altogether less reliable. Having said that, it is important to repeat that by no means every monogram or date is authentically Dürer's, and a considerable measure of caution has to be exercised, since such inscriptions cannot invariably be taken at face value. A perfect example is a sheet in the British Museum that combines a group of the Virgin and Child with a supplementary study of the Virgin's drapery. Universally agreed to be an early work, both on grounds of style and because of its connection with his engraving known as the *Virgin and Child with a Dragonfly*, it

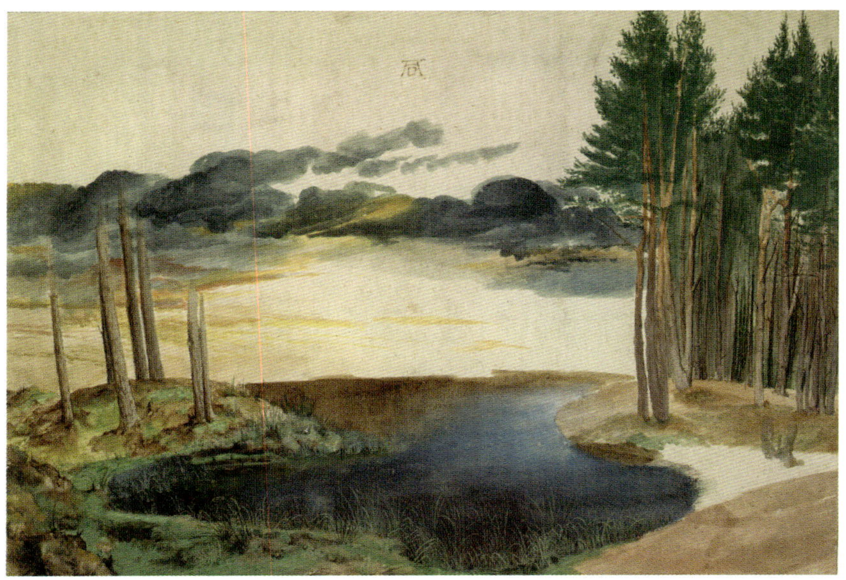

not only bears false Dürer monograms on both recto and verso but is dated 1519 on the recto, which would place it within the final decade of the artist's life.[24] Another early sheet of a *Youth Kneeling before an Executioner*, again in the British Museum, is undated but has an added monogram.[25] Even more obviously, anyone making a faithful copy of an original sheet will almost invariably also copy the monogram and date, as in the case of a close copy of the *Portrait of a Woman from Kärnten* in the British Museum.[26] On the other hand, such copies may have an altogether different value, in preserving inventions where the original is irretrievably lost. As has already been argued in Chapter One in connection with Dürer's once much-loved *Squirrels*, which is now recognized as the work of his later imitator, Hans Hoffmann, it may nevertheless be the case that his sheet is not a clever counterfeit but rather the echo of an original – and now lost – invention by Dürer himself.[27]

43 Albrecht Dürer, *Pond in the Woods*, c. 1497, watercolour and body colour.

To return to the select number of first ideas by Dürer, it is not hard to demonstrate that at least some of them include either one or both of his monogram and a date. What seems to be the first example with both, the *Two Venetian Women* of 1495, combines one highly finished study with the barest of outlines.[28] In the nature of things, most of them – like the sheet in question – are in pen and ink, but there are exceptions. One such is a charcoal drawing of *Death Riding a Horse*, which is dated 1505.[29] In this connection, it is an intriguing paradox that Dürer first added dates as well as monograms to at least some of his drawings a decade or so before he adopted the practice in the context of prints, where the earliest dated engraving is the *Virgin and Child* of 1503, and the earliest dated woodcut is the *Meeting at the Golden Gate* of 1504 from the *Marienleben*.[30]

When it came to large-scale public paintings such as altarpieces, the basic subject-matter would as a rule have been determined by the patrons, sometimes with guidance from the relevant ecclesiastical authorities, but artists probably enjoyed rather more flexibility than is sometimes supposed. In the specific case of Dürer, it is in effect impossible to be completely sure in the absence of contracts or agreements, and above all because so few first ideas for projects of this kind have come down to us. When it comes to such major undertakings as the *Feast of the Rose-Garlands* and the *Heller Altarpiece*, which will both be returned to in due course, a reasonable body of material still exists; however, it all relates to the individual figures and such details as their heads and hands, whereas nothing remains that can offer any understanding of Dürer's initial creative process in relation to the development of the respective compositions. It is true that the *Feast of the Rose-Garlands* is severely compromised, and of course that the *Heller Altarpiece* is only known in the form of a perfectly reliable later copy, but in both instances we are still able to compare the drawings with the end product and determine what, if anything, has changed.

Almost precisely the opposite problem arises in the case of the *Virgin and Child with Saints* of 1521–2 (the evidence for the dating derives from a number of sheets inscribed with these years by Dürer himself). Six first ideas for the invention are known (one of them is preserved in the form of two identical and evidently entirely reliable copies of a now lost original).[31] A number of highly resolved studies for individual figures have likewise been plausibly associated with the commission, but the painting was evidently never completed (and even if one were to believe it had been, it would have to be admitted that no record of its appearance survives).[32] In consequence, the only way to arrive at a full understanding of how Dürer worked is by artfully picking and choosing less and more finished sheets from different projects in order to assemble a composite picture of the ways in which he progressed from first ideas to final thoughts.

The whole *Virgin and Child with Saints* enterprise has very recently been carefully studied by Stijn Alsteens, but will nevertheless be analysed anew here.[33] The first point to be made is that the dramatis personae do not remain the same throughout the evolution of the various designs, but they must nevertheless all be for the same project, and there can be no doubt that this was intended from the outset to be a highly ambitious public commission. It should also be added that over time the format of the composition was modified, so that an initially horizontal conception of 1521, very much along the same broad lines as the *Feast of the Rose-Garlands*, gave way to a vertical arrangement in 1522. This solution would have resulted in an altarpiece altogether more in conformity with what had become the standard Venetian type from the creation of Antonello da Messina's now fragmentary *San Cassiano Altarpiece* of 1475 onwards.[34] Intriguingly, as was observed in Chapter Two, Dürer seems to have deliberately rejected that generic model in the altarpiece he executed in Venice in 1506, but in this instance was belatedly willing to follow its example.

To return to the sheets that adopt a horizontal format, what has long been agreed to be the earliest of the surviving drawings is a sheet in pen and ink in Chantilly.[35] In fact, it and the afore-mentioned copy drawings are not only extensively hatched but considerably more resolved than all the others. It makes sense to presume that they must have been preceded by scribbly outline drawings, just as the others must have been followed by elaborated solutions along the same lines as them. Be that as it may, in this sheet the basic notion – with a central Virgin and Child accompanied by male saints standing on the same level as the Virgin (John the Evangelist and his brother James the Greater, admittedly with a heavily subordinated Joseph further back), female ones lower down (Catherine) and musician angels – is already established.

If the radical asymmetry of the saints in this conception was fully intentional, as opposed to a species of intermediate stage actually destined to lead to a more balanced resolution, it was soon abandoned. In the two copy drawings, whose original must surely have come next, it is true that there are only two saints to the Virgin's proper right as against three to her left, but for the rest – and hereafter – the arrangement of the attendant figures to either side matches up.[36] The standing male saint on the left of the Virgin and Child is definitely Sebastian, who is shown half-naked, with his hands joined in prayer, and with a single arrow transfixing his forehead. His companion is presumably James the Greater, who was already present in the previous sheet, but is here represented without his identifying cockleshell and with an unusually long beard, which might almost make one wonder if he might not be Anthony Abbot, in which case he would make a natural companion for his fellow plague-saint on the other side. When it comes to the female saints, Catherine is again present, but her profile attitude has been given to Agnes with her lamb, and Dorothy, who is identified by the flowers in her hair, has been added on the other side. They are all joined by musician angels on either flank as before, but their number has been increased from two to four.

The next drawing in the sequence is a highly schematic presentation of a notably enlarged cast of characters, and must above all have been produced in order to allow Dürer to continue to organize the figures around the Virgin and Child, but – in terms of the work's iconography – includes some distinctly unresolved aspects.[37] He has labelled those in attendance on the upper register with their names, which should mean their identities are entirely uncontroversial, were it not for the erroneous identification of a bearded man as Elisabeth. Regardless of whether this figure was actually intended to be male or female, they make for an odd grouping, not least because either one or two women are combined with either seven or six men. As a rule, in altarpieces of this kind it was standard practice to pair figures off across the divide, with those nearest to the centre being the most privileged. However, here the holy personages to the proper right (moving inwards from the margins) are James, Joseph, Joachim and Zacharias, while they are balanced (again moving inwards from the margins) by Anna, Elisabeth (or an unidentified elderly male), King David (with his harp) and John the Evangelist. In consequence, and following the guidance of the inscriptions, James and John, Joachim and Anna and Zacharias and Elisabeth would all form couples, but not in terms of their precise locations, and it is as if Joseph and David are simply there to make up the numbers. On the lower level, and following the same system of moving inwards, standing figures of Dorothy, an unidentified female martyr (holding a palm) and Barbara (with a chalice and the host) are matched by Agnes, Apollonia and another unidentified female martyr. The kneeling figure of Catherine looking up in supplication has switched sides, and been replaced by a kneeling elderly female donor in pure profile, and there is now a single angel playing a lute at the base of the throne – very much in the Venetian mode.

In a closely related study, which is if anything even more freely rendered, Dürer has reverted to a solution with musician angels to the sides, but for the rest has slightly reduced the number of figures in attendance on the Virgin and Child.[38] As a result, both the unidentified female martyrs and Zacharias and Elisabeth have disappeared, while the survivors are all in the same positions as before. The one difference is that what appear to be a cat and a fox – they are extremely summarily drawn, but the latter has already appeared in the *Virgin with a Multitude of Animals* – now inhabit the space beneath the Virgin's throne.

At the same time, and for all that these last two sheets are both distinctly schematic renditions, it seems hard to doubt that the latter one must have led to an altogether more fully worked-up but essentially faithful version of the same composition. The reason for saying so, which will be returned to in due course, is that there are a number of highly finished bust-length and head studies that in essence correspond to the related figures here. Nevertheless, before exploring them in greater detail it is necessary to follow Dürer's example and go beyond them.

The reason is that, as explained above, there are two further drawings of vertical format for the altarpiece to be considered. It is far from easy to determine which came first, but on balance it seems logical to suppose that the one to retain seated female saints is more likely to follow on immediately from the horizontal sheet which shares that feature.[39] In any event, they both include an identical cast of characters in very similar sequences. In the former, the male saints (reading from left to right) are James, John the Baptist, Joseph and Joachim, as against John the Baptist, James, Joseph and Joachim, while their female counterparts are Catherine, Margaret (newly introduced at this juncture and accompanied by a 'dragon' derived from Dürer's drawing of a walrus), Agnes and Barbara, as against Margaret, Catherine, Barbara and – by a process of elimination, since she is uniquely attributeless – Agnes. Once again, these are strikingly schematic drawings, but both have intermittent inscriptions denoting the colours of the figures' draperies.

Everything indicates that Dürer executed a considerable number of detailed studies for individual figures in connection with the last redaction of the horizontal solution. In particular, four stunning sheets all correspond perfectly to the presentation of Sts Barbara, Joseph, Anna and Apollonia in the aforementioned drawing.[40] Be that as it may, when the artist subsequently determined on a vertical format for the altarpiece, he does not appear to have tried to retain their attitudes, and it has to be assumed that all his hard work was in effect wasted. Naturally, he may have hoped to find some use for them at a later date, as he did with a study for the Christ Child in the *Feast of the Rose-Garlands*, which was effectively recycled in his *Madonna of the Pear* of 1512, but there cannot have been any guarantees that he would manage to do so.[41] As a matter of fact, however, he may have been more resigned to this state of affairs than we might imagine, since there were almost inevitably countless such dead ends in the careers of busy artists, and disappointments of this kind were simply part of the deal.

One final curiosity needs to be underlined, again since hitherto it appears to have been overlooked. It concerns the direction of light in the various drawings. As has been explained, in spite of speculations concerning the possible patronage of the altarpiece and the identity of the female donor represented in a couple of the drawings, nothing is known concerning its planned destination. However, the lighting in altarpieces invariably had to respond to the principal light source where they were to be installed. Often chapels had a single or dominant window to one side or the other, and there was also a convention that designated the west door of the church in question as the notional principal light source, which meant that altarpieces for chapels on the right side of the church were lit from the right, and altarpieces for chapels on the left side of the church were lit from the left. There are also records of artists who had not seen the destinations of altarpieces asking to be informed about the direction of the light, precisely in order to make sure they got it right.[42] In the case of the purely linear composition studies for the work, it is impossible to draw any conclusions, but both the initial invention and the faithful copies are lit from the left, whereas all the head studies – and indeed a group of drapery studies of the same date plausibly believed to be connected with the project – are lit from the right. There is no way of knowing why this should be so, but the basically consistent identities of the holy personages make it inconceivable that these drawings are not all for a single work.

To all intents and purposes, the finished studies for this altarpiece perform the same function within Dürer's planning of the commission from first ideas to the completed painting as those for the *Christ among the Doctors* referred to above. However, he did not employ the same technique for both works, which is not especially surprising in view of the fact that they date from fifteen years apart, with black and white chalk or occasionally metalpoint on green grounded paper replacing brush and grey wash heightened with white on blue paper.

Conversely, this same combination of media is also found in virtually all the known drawings connected with three religious paintings that are approximately contemporary with the *Christ among the Doctors*, namely the *Madonna of the Siskin*, the *Feast of the Rose-Garlands* and the slightly later *Heller Altarpiece*, which was being worked on by 1508 and was dated 1509.[43] As has been explained above, the six studies for the *Virgin and Child with Saints* are unique in the insight they afford us into how Dürer went about inventing an ambitious composition, but the surviving studies for these three works do further underline his almost obsessive perfectionism.

In the case of the *Madonna of the Siskin*, a number of sheets seem to be connected with the panel, but only two are unquestionably preparatory for it. One is a drawing of the Christ Child (illus. 44) where the broad lines of the pose are basically the same, but various aspects would nevertheless subsequently be carefully modified.[44] In particular, in the painting the left leg is less vertical, the left forearm is horizontal as opposed to vertical and the Child holds a rattle and not a small cross in his right hand. Altogether more tellingly, in the drawing the whole setting is completely different: there is a brocade hanging behind the baby, and he is sitting on a tasselled cushion that rests upon a little seat instead of in his mother's lap. It therefore has to be assumed that the whole conception was radically altered between this drawing and the painting, but there is no way of knowing how many supplementary drawings Dürer made in order to arrive at the final resolution, and especially whether he felt the need to restudy the Child or settled for tweaking the present sheet, either in some kind of cartoon or on the panel. What is clear, at any event, is the fact that a second drawing, a drapery study for part of the Child's shirt, can only have been made after the change of plan, and even it is not precisely replicated on the panel.[45]

With the altogether more ambitious *Feast of the Rose-Garlands*, a similar situation regarding the preparatory drawings is in evidence. All the studies for individual figures or their heads reveal this, but the most striking self-correction occurs in connection with the architect holding a set square at the right margin: in essence his features and pose remain unmodified, but the dishevelled hair recorded in the study for him – which must be a life drawing, or at the very least based upon one – has been carefully tidied up.[46] No less tellingly, the three known hand studies for the altarpiece, which are exceptionally meticulously finished, have also been deemed to require emendation – moreover, in the case of Maximilan's hands, they are both shown separately

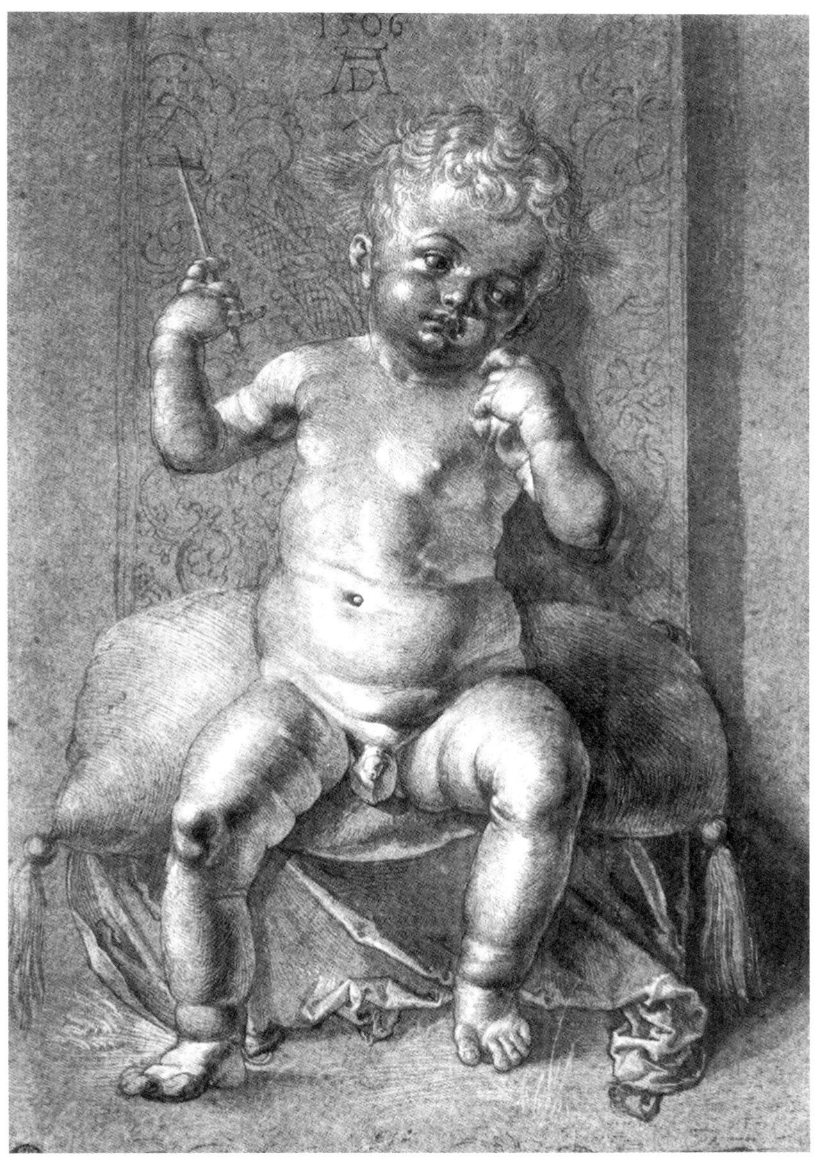

44 Albrecht Dürer, *Study for the Christ Child in the Madonna of the Siskin*, 1506, pen and brush and black ink, heightened with white, on faded blue-grey paper.

in the drawing, but the right one is partially concealed by the left one in the finished work.[47]

In addition to all these drawings on blue paper for particular figures, their heads and their hands, there also exists a gorgeous violet and gold watercolour for the pope's damask mantle (illus. 45).[48] No doubt the artist would not have felt any need to devote such poetic attention to ordinary draperies, but all the same this sheet is a very precious survivor, a type of study whose existence we could otherwise never have surmised, and in that sense a powerful reminder of what I have previously termed the tip-of-the-iceberg nature of Renaissance drawings. As is well known, and has already been discussed, the *Feast of the Rose-Garlands* is a tragic shadow of its former self, but enough remains to leave no doubt that this scintillating evocation of papal splendour suffered the fate of so many other first ideas, and was not translated into paint.

Turning, finally, to the *Heller Altarpiece*, very much the same sorts of detailed studies exist as in the previous instances, with the addition of a superb drawing for the bare feet of the kneeling Apostle in the right foreground of the composition, which are accorded exactly the same painstaking attention as the hands of some of his fellows.[49] In the case of at least one drawing for the *Christ among the Doctors*, two studies of hands were paired on a single folio, while here some heads and hands were combined on a single sheet/opening, but were split in two long ago. In the case of the celebrated *Praying Hands* (illus. 46), their separation from the head study for the same Apostle that originally formed the left half of the same sheet has had the unforeseen consequence of turning the former into a species of cherished icon.[50]

When it came to translating drawings into paint, Dürer's unflinching self-criticism persisted until the very end. It is true that both the technique and above all the handling of the three head studies we possess for the *Four Apostles* of 1526 are novel (they are executed in metalpoint on brown prepared paper, and are more freely and boldly worked), but he still appears to have felt the need to make changes.[51] Each one of the three could be analysed in these terms, but the most blatantly different one is the study for St Peter, above all because of the great bald dome of a head he displays in the painting, but there are also countless other less obvious adjustments.[52]

Dürer's prints are the subject of the next chapter, but it makes sense to examine at least some of the drawings for them here, not least in order to underline the fact that, unsurprisingly, they at times obliged the artist to face all sorts of challenges that the paintings did not, the most straightforward of which resulted from the need to think about compositions – and indeed their lighting – both forwards and backwards, given the way the design on the woodblock or copper plate to be engraved had to be in reverse.

Dürer's more and less rapid pen sketches for his prints represent a particularly interesting group of studies, not least for the ways in which they reveal him thinking both about form and about content. Thus when it comes to his treatment of mythological subjects, it seems clear that on occasion he exploited the complete iconographic freedom the print medium allowed him to change his mind. The connection between a pen drawing of a *Centaur Family* and the engraving of a *Satyr Family* is plain enough, above all because of the attitude that the mother with her child in both share, albeit in reverse, but so is the fact that the male protagonist is an entirely different species of creature.[53] Other differences are also worth noting: in the drawing, the female figure has horns, which associate her with her husband, whereas in the engraving she is straightforwardly human. Moreover, in the print the satyr is ithyphallic, which makes it indecent – if only somewhat playfully so.

In the case of the etching of 1516 often misleadingly referred to as the *Abduction of Proserpina on a Unicorn* (illus. 47), the differences between the print and the pen and ink drawing (again in reverse)

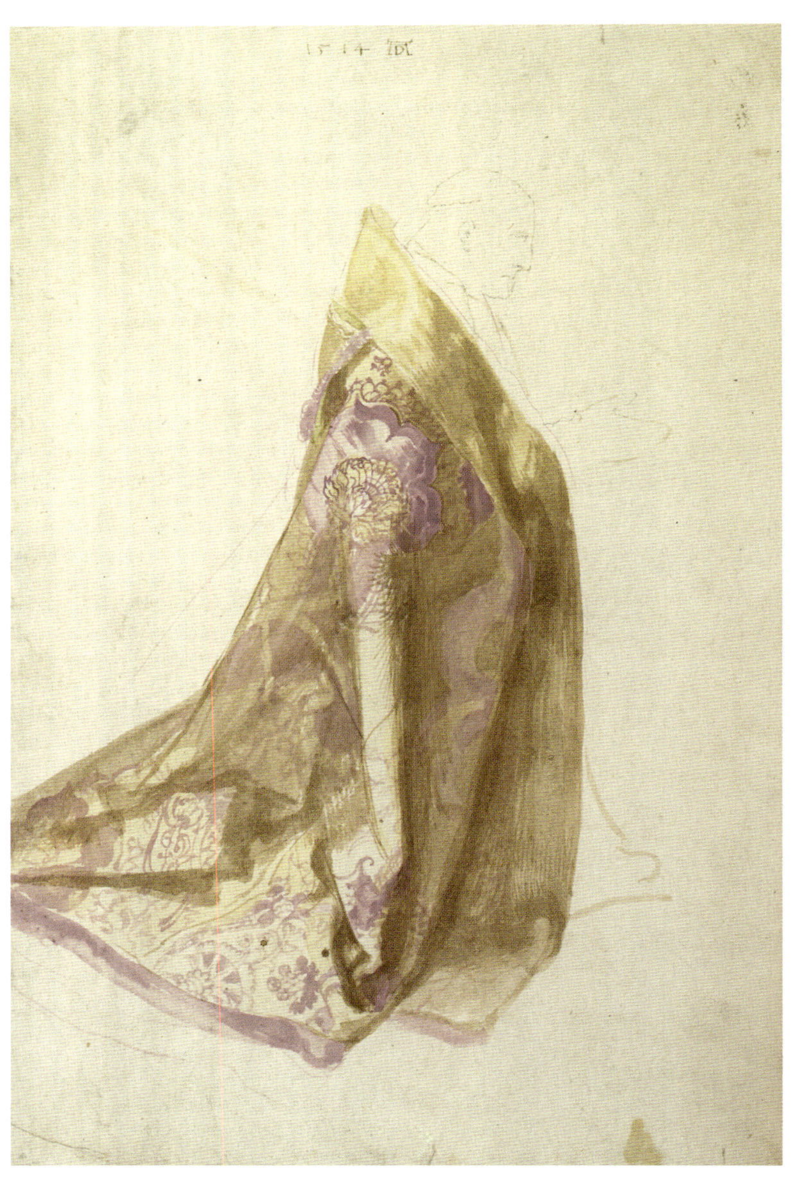

45 Albrecht Dürer, *Study for the Pope's Mantle in the Feast of the Rose-Garlands,*
c. 1506, watercolour.

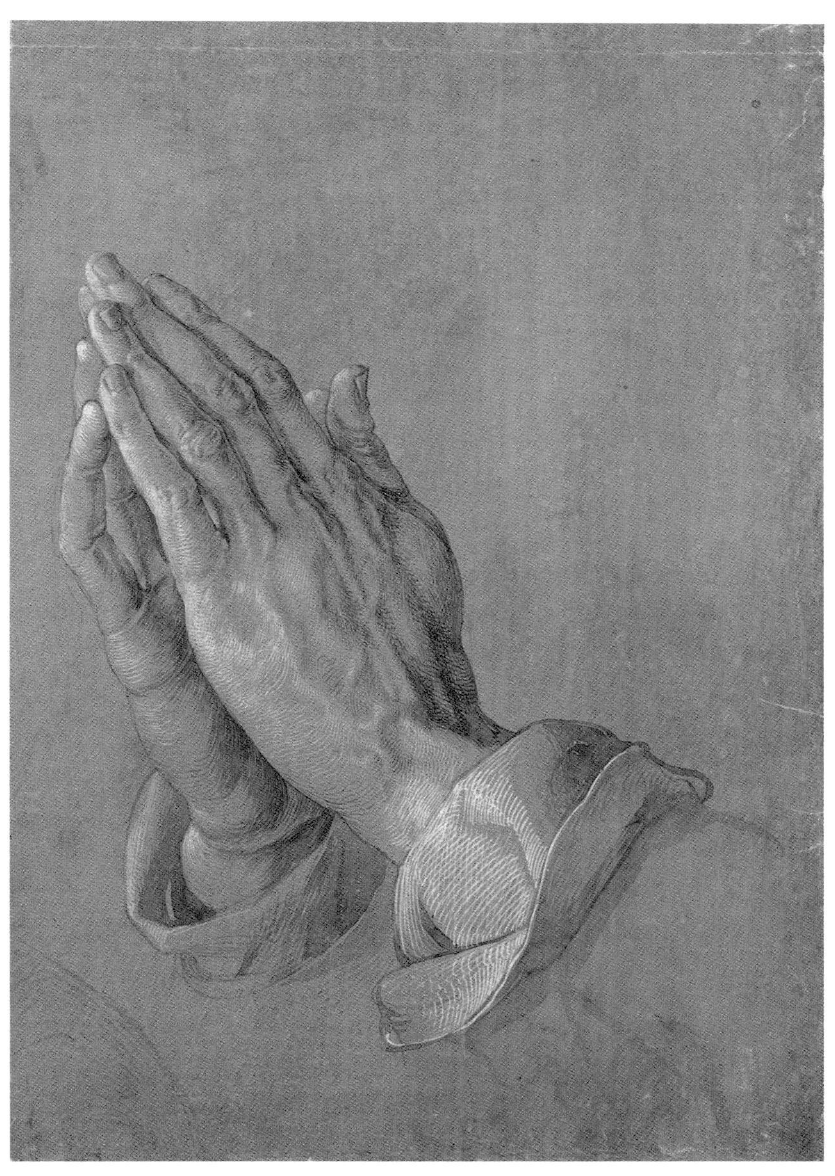

46 Albrecht Dürer, *Praying Hands*, 1508, brush and black and grey ink,
grey wash, heightened with white, on blue prepared paper.

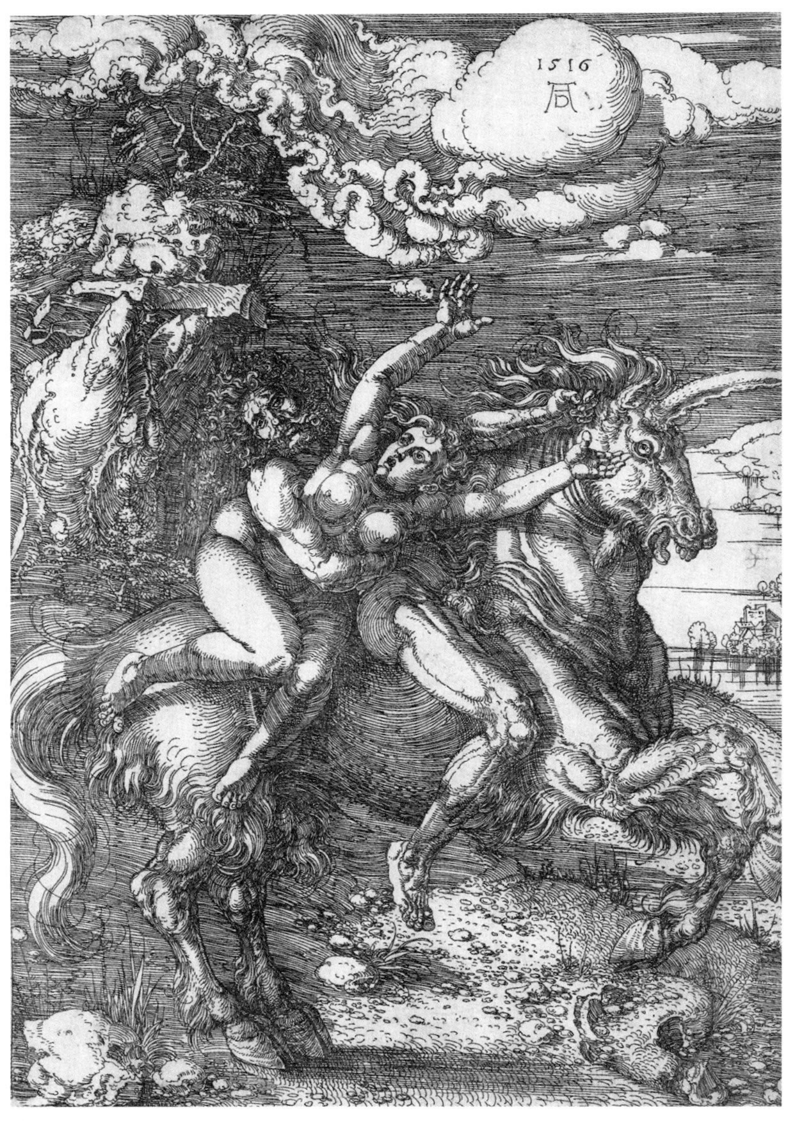

47 Albrecht Dürer, *Abduction of Proserpina on a Unicorn*, 1516, etching.

for the work only serve to increase the improbability of the customary identification of the subject.[54] In terms of the general disposition of the couple, and indeed the horse, nothing separates the preliminary idea from the finished work, but in the former there is no landscape setting, and more tellingly the base of the composition is formed by a confused heap of nude male and female bodies that includes a severed head. In terms of additions in the etching, the backdrop is included, the mount is much shaggier and it vitally has also been given the frankly baffling horn that turns it into a unicorn, but is no part of the myth of Pluto and Proserpina.[55]

With religious subjects, on the other hand, Dürer was almost bound to adopt more conventional solutions. It might also be presumed that he would modify them less radically between the preparatory sketches and the prints, but this does not invariably turn out to be what happens. In the case of two drawings of *St Jerome in His Study*, one undated and the other dated 1511, there has been a good deal of resistance to accepting that they may both be first ideas for what became the famous engraving of the same subject (illus. 52), which is dated 1514 and to which I will return in the next chapter.[56] However, if they have nothing to do with that work, then it might reasonably be wondered not only what purpose they served but why they are so similarly concerned with capturing the combination of solitary calm and scholarly clutter that is such a memorable feature of the print. Conversely, if they are indeed forerunners of it, however distant, then it is the differences as well as any similarities between all three that need to be considered.

In the first, which gives every indication of having been cropped, Jerome's scanty attire designates him as a holy hermit, and he is shown in pensive contemplation of the skull and crucifix on his simple wooden desk. It is true that a sheet of paper and a circular inkwell with a quill are also resting upon it, but he has turned away from them. In terms of the setting, it has various features in common with the engraving, notably the bottle-glass window over to the left, the perspectival flight of the wooden beams of the ceiling and the variety of objects that are distributed along the back wall of the chamber, including a rosary. Hardly surprisingly, there are also differences: some relate to the absences of the lion, the fox and the artist's 'AD' monogram, while others concern the precise choice of still-life elements, and in particular the quirky detail of the saint's drinking vessels impaled on a rack in the top right-hand corner of the composition.

Both the lion and the monogram – not to mention the date – do appear in the second drawing, and there are other correspondences, such as the inclusion of an hourglass beyond the saint, who is represented in cardinal's vestments with his hat roped down his back and is bowed intently over a book. On the other hand, all in all the setting is less similar, mainly because it is less enclosed, and instead offers glimpses of a door over to the right and a grand second room beyond.

Dürer must have created at the very least one complete compositional study not only for each of the woodcuts in the *Marienleben* but for all his other narrative prints (and indeed every print he ever made), yet only four of them – the *Birth of the Virgin*, the *Annunciation*, the *Visitation* and the *Adoration of the Magi* – have survived.[57] As a group, they are exceptionally illuminating concerning his approach to devising religious narratives for the print medium.

The first two things to note about all four is that they are on much the same scale and in reverse to the woodcuts, and therefore the same way round as the designs that were to be cut on the woodblocks. As a rule, it does not make sense to speak of there being a 'right' way round for the representation of a particular subject, but there were two simple conventions that were almost unfailingly observed by artists during the Renaissance. The first results from the universal Christian privileging of the right hand and the right-hand side, and the consequent denigration of the left (which explains the modern meaning of the word 'sinister', which is the Latin for 'left'). The second concerns the widespread habit of organizing narratives so that the action proceeds from left to right, which is doubtless a natural consequence of our reading from left to right. Bearing both these factors in mind, it becomes clear that the alignment of the back-to-front *Annunciation* has been constructed with its ultimate reversal in mind.[58] What is more, in the woodcuts Dürer arranged for a number of gestures – such as the pointing hand of the Angel here and the salutation of the Christ Child in the *Adoration of the Magi* – to be right-handed, but it has to be admitted that their counterparts in the preliminary drawings are rather ambiguous.[59]

Examining all four in chronological order, it emerges that the nature of their relationships with the prints they prepare is far from uniform. In the *Birth of the Virgin* both versions (illus. 48 and 49) have three main episodic details – the bringing of food to the Virgin's mother, St Anne; the baby's bath; and the comic vignette of one of the women in attendance quaffing (presumably beer) – but in each case they are differently managed.[60] As in the drawing, in the woodcut St Anne within her canopied bed is offered a bowl of food with a spoon in it, but a second maid is shown in the act of pouring a visible jet of water into a cup or glass. In the drawing, moreover, the baby's bath is right next to her mother's bed and a stream of water is being poured into it by one of the pair of women looking after her, whereas in the print she has already been removed from it and is being cradled by a single nurse in isolation. Conversely, whereas the beer drinker in the drawing is standing up all on her own and tipping her head back, her counterpart in the woodcut is seated and is part of a whole gaggle of women – the grand total is a round dozen as opposed to the mere five of the sketch, which of course means

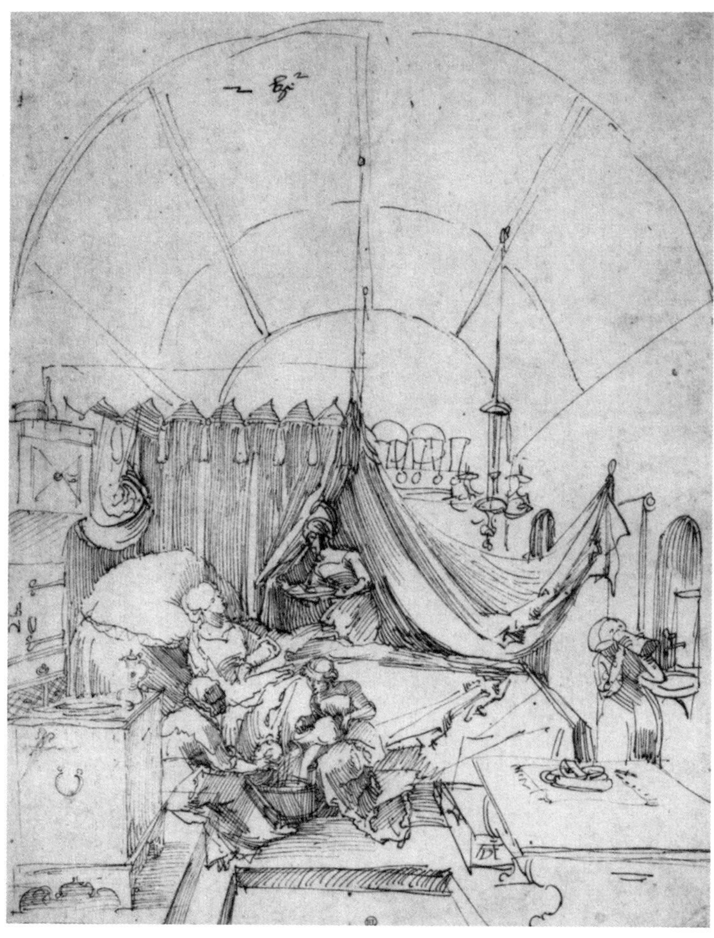

the entire composition is considerably more crowded. The space
is also completely differently arranged, as are all the pieces of
furniture and objects within it. Last but not least, a major iconographic embellishment has been added. A single angel wielding
a censer fills the centre of the upper zone, and is surrounded by a
celestial cloud that conceals part of the bed hangings. Cumulatively,

48 Albrecht Dürer, *Birth of the Virgin*, c. 1503, pen and black ink.

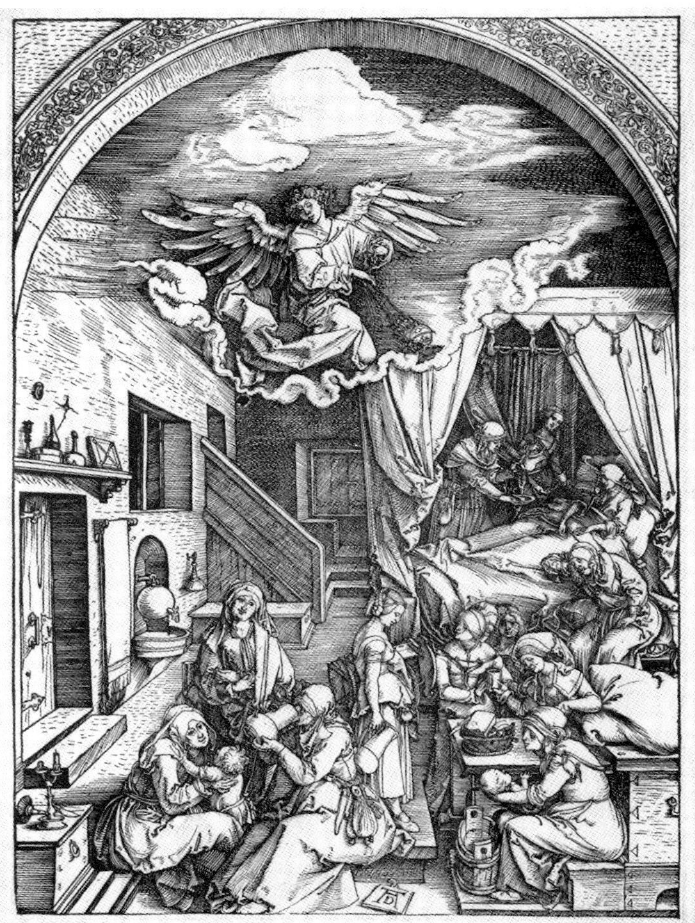

all these changes of plan make it almost impossible to imagine
that Dürer did not require at least one subsequent overall compositional study in order to arrive at his definitive solution.

Moving on to the *Annunciation*, which is the only one of the
four to include pale coloured washes as well as pen and ink, the
template found in the drawing is altogether more faithfully adhered

49 Albrecht Dürer, *Birth of the Virgin*, c. 1503, woodcut.

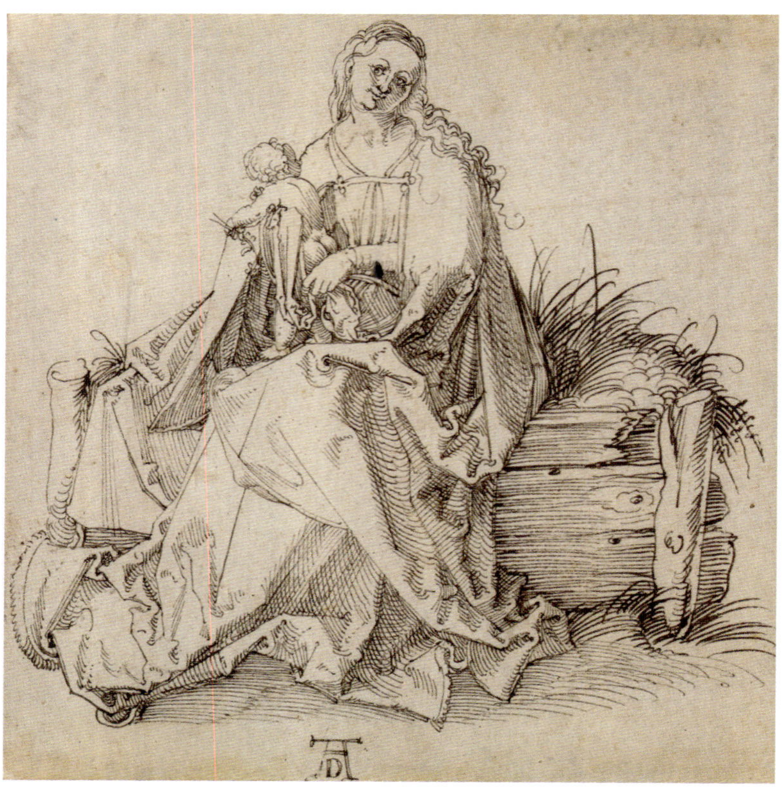

to, although there are all sorts of minor adjustments, which tend to involve addition as opposed to subtraction. Thus in the print a diminutive half-length God the Father holding an orb in his left hand and a book in his right is added, as are a decorative sculptural roundel representing Judith (one of the antetypes of the Virgin) with the severed head of Holofernes just under the vault, and a vase of lilies in the foreground. Virtually the only removal is of a ring in the subsequently omitted wooden ceiling shown in the drawing, which would presumably have served to open and close it.

50 Albrecht Dürer, *Virgin and Child*, c. 1503, pen and black ink.

The drawings for the *Visitation* and the *Adoration of the Magi* are both much more tentative in their pen line and reduce hatching to a minimum, but paradoxically they match the end results even more closely.[61] This is true not only of the main lines of their compositions, but of all sorts of details, so that the inclusion of dogs in the respective foregrounds is foreseen. Remarkably, in the case of the *Visitation*, the exact pose and breed are already established, but the seated hound with the Magi will be replaced by a walking one at the edge of the composition, whose daring cropping is a virtual signature for Dürer. Where more work needed to be done was in relation to such elements as the background landscape in the former and the finer points of the ruined stable architecture – and indeed the disposition of the heavenly choir – in the latter. In both instances, what is put down is a species of shorthand, a sort of visual equivalent of 'and so on and so forth'.

Taking a parallel case that is not connected with a print, the two versions of the *Virgin with a Multitude of Animals* seem to reveal the degree to which Dürer could, at least sometimes, 'nail' nearly every detail of an immensely elaborate composition in an almost clumsily exploratory sketch.[62] Even here, however, a very recently rediscovered pen drawing of the *Virgin and Child* (illus. 50) may well be a far from identical first idea for the project.[63] On other occasions, even he no doubt found himself tearing his hair out, although it has to be admitted that the visual record, as it has come down to us, gives little indication of such fallibility.

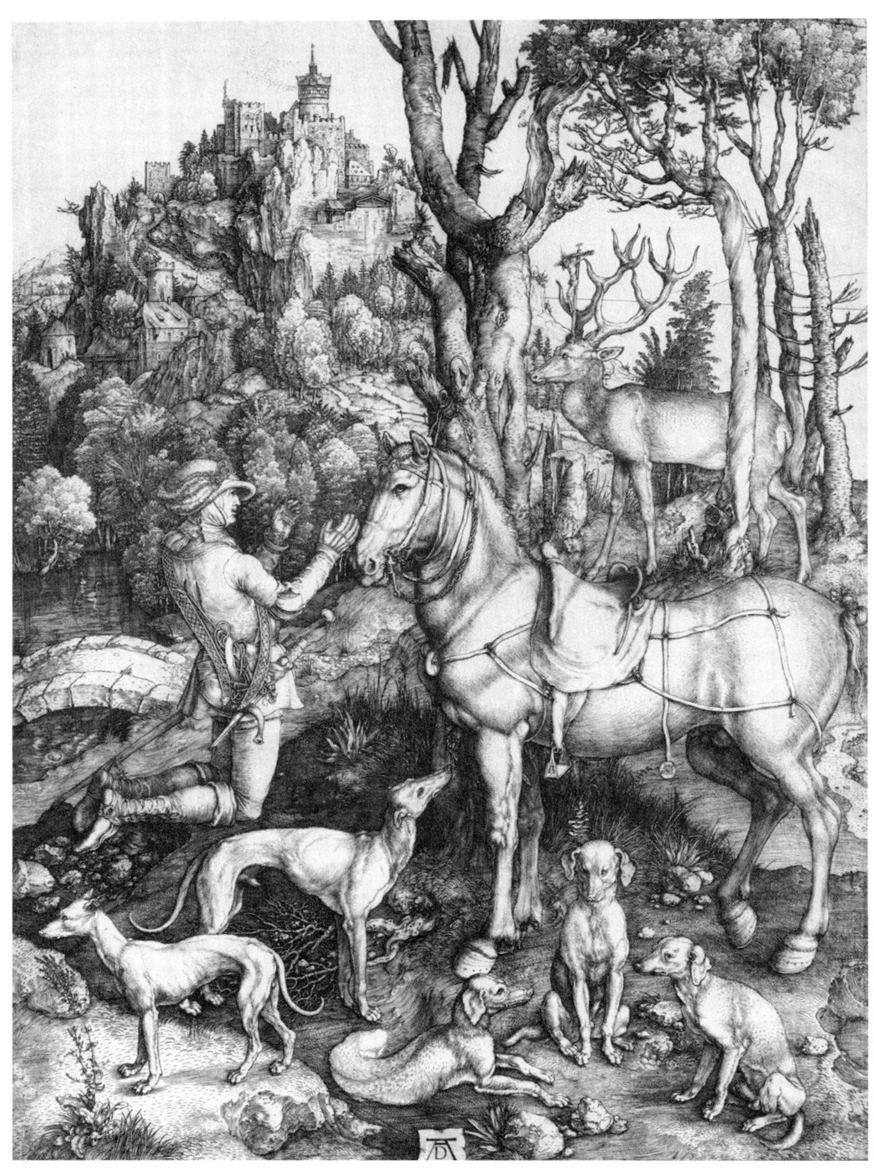

FIVE

Prints

It would be hard to exaggerate the importance of the role prints played both in relation to Dürer's professional career and indeed in establishing his reputation during his lifetime and thereafter. No previous artist either north or south of the Alps had devoted so much energy and sheer invention to the comparatively new medium of printmaking, and the resulting body of work is remarkable not only for its range, but for its originality.

There are at least three fundamental respects in which prints would inevitably have been seen as differing from paintings (the status of drawings as independent works of art – as opposed to as means to an end – was in its infancy).

One obvious way in which prints differed from paintings was that in the main they were monochrome as opposed to coloured, and the existence neither of hand-coloured prints nor indeed of grisaille paintings profoundly modified this more general state of affairs, for the simple reason that both were always in the minority.[1] Dürer understood that this could be a positive advantage and that prints must not be regarded – negatively – as devoid of colour, but instead as offering spectacular opportunities for chiaroscuro. Even telling stories in monochrome need not be a particular drawback: in the case of the *Meeting at the Golden Gate* from the *Marienleben*, for instance, the opulent elaboration of the carved decoration on the Golden Gate itself, which serves as a

51 Albrecht Dürer, *St Eustace*, *c.* 1500, engraving.

frame for the scene of Joachim and Anna tenderly embracing, makes it abundantly plain that this is not just any old archway, and contrasts starkly with the singularly decayed architecture of the interior of the Temple at Jerusalem in the opening scene of the sequence showing the *Rejection of Joachim's Offering*.[2]

A second crucial difference was that prints were multiples: this was one of their appeals, because it meant the same invention could be seen by a whole host of people to a far greater extent than had previously been possible, even acknowledging the practice of disseminating visual ideas through copy drawings.[3] At the same time, both their mode of production and the fact that they were multiples combined forces to ensure that prints by a revered master such as Dürer were within the financial reach of individuals who lacked the means to aspire to own a painting by him. In the diary of his journey to the Netherlands in 1520–21, Dürer records that he gave and also sold considerable numbers of sets of his own prints to all sorts of different kinds of people, in effect using them as a form of currency, and on at least one occasion states that he gave two examples of the same engraving, his *St Jerome*, to Jacopo de' Barbari.[4]

Third, their presence in people's homes meant that they could be looked at repeatedly, and at least some of the time Dürer gives every indication of having borne this in mind in the sheer level of detail he included within them. It is true that Martin Schongauer led the way – but only very occasionally, as in the *Entombment* from his *Small Passion*, where a tiny, half-lowered cross propped up by a ladder is visible on the hill of Calvary – but Dürer went much further in this direction.[5] Instances of his exploitation of the potential appeal of such details will be returned to in what follows.

Last but by no means least, while the subject-matter of many of Dürer's prints was in essence no different in kind from that of his paintings, if more wide-ranging in extent, he did also frequently explore themes that would have been inconceivable in his day for pictures. To begin with, therefore, it seems to make sense to give a brief account of the different categories of prints into which Dürer's production may usefully be divided. Before doing so, however, it is crucial to add that Dürer was a master not only of the woodcut on the one hand, but of the related techniques of engraving, etching and drypoint on the other. Amusingly, if wrongheadedly, Vasari imagined that Dürer started out by making engravings and only subsequently moved on to woodcuts, explaining that he was motivated by two entirely different considerations: one was a combination of the amount of time it took to produce engravings and the number of inventions he had created which were waiting to be turned into prints, while the other related to the fact that in woodcuts artists 'che hanno maggior disegno, hanno più largo campo da poter mostrare la loro perfezione' ('who are more gifted in design, have greater opportunities to demonstrate their prowess').[6] Vasari further erred in supposing that towards the end of his career Dürer reverted to engraving, and one can only presume that this reflected his partial knowledge of his oeuvre.[7] In truth, of course, and apart from various early book illustrations in woodcut, such as those for an edition of the *Comedies* of Terence around 1492–3, always assuming his association with the project is accepted, he appears to have engaged with both techniques at much the same time (etchings and drypoints did admittedly come later).[8] Instead, the differences between his approaches to the two media across his career, and the extent to which he may have favoured one over the other in response to particular subject categories, will be explored.

In the case of Dürer's woodcuts, a not inconsiderable number of the original woodblocks for them still exist, including no fewer than 35 for the *Small Woodcut Passion*, which are all in the British Museum, but their survival has not led to a consensus in relation to the crucial question of who was responsible for their manufacture.[9] As a rule, in Germany in this period woodcuts were made on planks of hard woods such as pearwood, with the inventor of the design drawing it on the surface, which had often previously been prepared with a white ground to allow for greater legibility.[10] Some scholars have argued that at least some of them were then cut by Dürer himself, while others are at least equally convinced that he must have followed the standard practice of the day and delegated this task to professional block-cutters.[11] In either scenario, he would first have become acquainted with the requisite techniques by following the guidance of his godfather, the printer Anton Koberger, and his first teacher, Michael Wolgemut, who was celebrated for his woodcut book illustrations.

When it came to engraving, he would not even have needed to leave home to receive instruction, since goldsmiths like his father were routinely accustomed to incise designs on their productions, the only real difference being that printmakers would of course have been obliged to engrave their inventions onto copper plates, and then print them on good-quality paper.[12] When this process is compared with that involved in making woodcuts, even if they were to be cut by their designer, there is a crucial sense in which the artist has more absolute control over the end product.

Unlike Dürer's all but lifelong involvement with woodcut and engraving, both drypoint and etching were only destined to engage his interest for brief periods. The former, which employed copper plates and differed from etching by virtue of not involving acid, seems to have occupied him in or around 1512, at which time he produced three of them.[13] Two — the *Man of Sorrows* and the *St Jerome* — are indeed dated 1512, while the style of the third, a *Holy Family*, supports the notion that it is their contemporary. Not long after, he explored etching, which would have required him to obtain iron plates and use acid to cut the design into the surface, producing six prints between 1515 and 1518, including such ambitious works as the so-called *Abduction of Proserpina* and the *Landscape with Cannon*.[14]

The other crucial observation to make in connection with Dürer's practice in all these different print media is that, notably in terms of sheer technical virtuosity, he went far beyond any of his predecessors and in effect established a new art form of the greatest distinction. After Dürer, prints may still have had their detractors, but in truth nobody who took the trouble to look at them seriously should have had the audacity to regard their most monumental and sophisticated achievements as poor relations of any other art forms. What is more, the ubiquitous influence of Dürer's prints represents an eloquent tribute to the fascination they exercised on his contemporaries, and have continued to exercise down the centuries.

Understandably, in the context of prints – as equally with his paintings – religious iconography predominates, perhaps especially when it comes to woodcuts, but what Dürer chooses to represent, and how often he returns to a particular subject, tend to be far from predictable. In this respect, his print series are clearly distinct from the rest of his print production, and consideration of them will follow that of his single prints. The largest category of religious art comprises the dozen woodcuts and sixteen engravings either of the Virgin and Child, with or without additional figures, or of isolated episodes from her life. The next-largest group is of episodes from the Old and New Testaments, with the latter hugely predominating (there are a mere three woodcuts and a single engraving of stories from the Old Testament), closely followed by iconic depictions of saints and scenes from their lives.

In the case of the representations of the Madonna, Dürer takes advantage of his absolute freedom to determine both the scale and the complexity of the image to arrive at a species of graphic equivalent of the range of possibilities offered by more and less intimate paintings of the Virgin and Child. However, it is crucial to add that there are profound differences in his approach to the challenges offered by this still relatively new medium. One concerns the fact that he never explores half-length solutions in his prints, whereas they are standard in such panels as the *Haller Madonna* and the *Virgin of the Siskin*, and instead achieves variety in other ways.[15] Another is a consequence of the general diffusion of prints, which explains the absence of assemblies of particular attendant saints beyond the members of the extended Holy Family. The sole exception is the *Madonna of the Carthusians* of 1515, a species of Madonna della Misericordia, in which the Virgin's mantle is held up by Sts John the Baptist and Bruno (thus identified by his name on a book he holds), and extended in protection over a host of kneeling Carthusian monks and one who is lying stretched out full-length under her feet.[16] Instead, there are some prints of singleton saints, represented both iconically and narratively, which tend to feature either such old standbys as Sebastian and George, or local favourites such as Sebaldus, the patron saint of Nuremberg. To these should be added two woodcuts of groups of threes, and of the patron saints of Austria.[17]

A number of Dürer's prints of the Virgin and Child explore the intimate relationship between the new mother and her baby in ways that are virtually unparalleled in paintings of the period, whether north or south of the Alps. Two adopt the by this time standard Italian iconography of the *Madonna del Latte*, in which Mary is shown suckling her son, but do so in a wonderfully naturalistic fashion. Respectively dated 1503 and 1519, they also serve to underline an aspect of Dürer's art that runs the risk of getting lost in a relentlessly evolutionary conception of his work, which will tend to emphasize differences over time, namely the underlying consistency of his vision.[18] Even more remarkable is the *Madonna with the Swaddled Infant* of 1520, where we almost feel as if we run the risk of waking the sleeping Child, whose mother

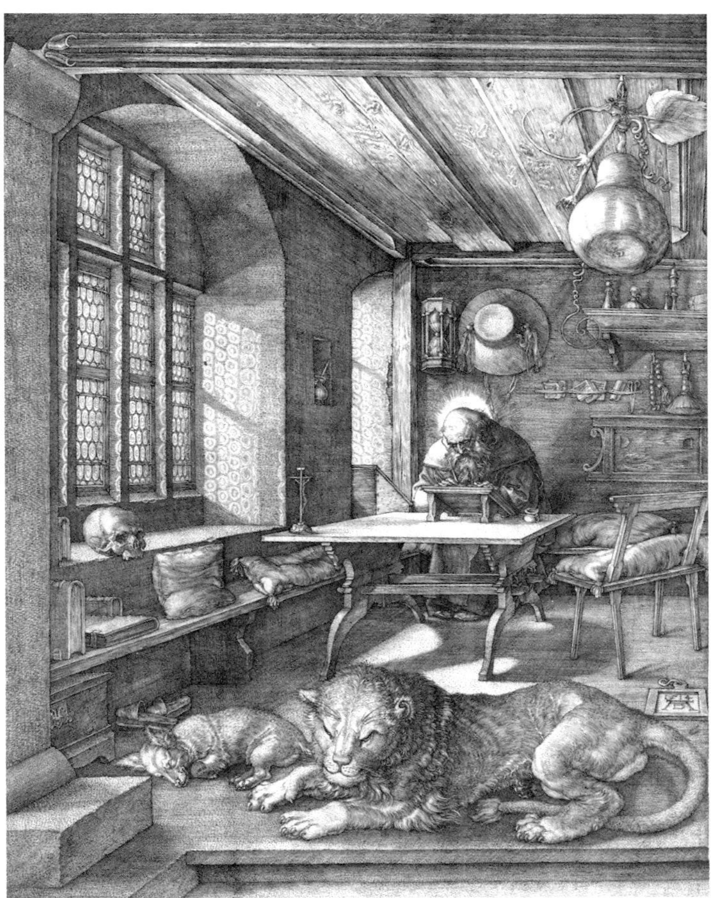

has eyes only for him.[19] Her anxiety is palpable, however, and is shared by her counterpart in the *Madonna Crowned by Two Angels*, who meets our gaze.[20] For the rest, the Virgin tends to look down at her Son.

As is well known, two of Dürer's most ambitious prints, both engravings, are of Sts Eustace and Jerome (illus. 51 and 52), and respectively show off his extraordinary and contrasting gifts as

52 Albrecht Dürer, *St Jerome in His Study*, 1514, engraving.

a poet of wide-open spaces and intimate interiors. *St Eustace* is undated, but is universally agreed to have been executed around 1500, and tellingly demonstrates quite how extraordinarily technically accomplished an engraver Dürer was relatively early on, not just because of the sheer physical scale of the plate, but above all because of its irresistible evocation of a romantic northern landscape.[21] Crucially, Dürer was the first printmaker who made panoramic landscapes a feature of his works, in some instances in the form of uninterrupted prospects at the base of the compositions, and in others, as with the *St Eustace*, with figures inhabiting the settings. He begins to experiment with both approaches in a comparatively simplified form in some of the woodcuts of the *Apocalypse*, and they then play a major part in a select number of his subsequent large-scale productions, such as the *Sea-Monster*, *Hercules at the Crossroads* and *Nemesis*.[22]

In the *St Eustace*, Dürer evidently decided that the major compositional risk was that the scene, in which the human and animal actors need to blend into the landscape but must not be overwhelmed by it, would lack a clear structure. In consequence, he positioned a clump of dead trees in the centre, and thus arranged for the space to be divided by a strong vertical accent. To its left is the kneeling figure of St Eustace, who has dismounted and fallen to his knees in wonder at the vision of a stag in the middle ground, which displays a radiant crucifix between its antlers. This detail features in the story as it is recounted in the *Golden Legend*, where it is further related that Christ speaks to him either through the crucifix or out of the mouth of the stag, and he is converted.[23] The figure of the saint is set against a deep landscape prospect to the left, whereas the right half of the print is more closed off, with any possibility of seeing into the distance blocked by the stag and the trees. At the same time, Eustace is deliberately isolated on a kind of curved hillock, together with his horse and five hunting dogs, who wait patiently for further instructions.

Behind and beyond him, at the left margin of the print, Dürer has represented the arch of a rustic bridge over a river, and two swans swimming on its mirror-calm surface. These kinds of minute details are a recurring feature of his prints, and may well be intended to compel the viewer to scan the entire surface of the scene slowly and carefully. The castle in the far left background here, and indeed the murmuration of starlings wheeling round the topmost tower on the upper horizon, are surely intended to serve a similar purpose. The chamois peering over a precipice in the top right corner of the engraving *Adam and Eve* is just such a grace note, and cannot conceivably serve any iconographic purpose.[24]

In Dürer's day there were two main ways of representing St Jerome: either celebrating him as a holy hermit and setting him in a wilderness landscape, or focusing on his scholarly achievements – famously, he was the author of the Vulgate, the translation of the Bible into Latin – and showing him in his study.[25] Both types are found among Dürer's prints, but it is an example of the latter type, the engraving of 1514, that stands out.[26] The identity of the aged saint, bowed over his lectern and writing, is not in doubt, since his standard attributes – the smiling pussycat of a lion in the foreground and the cardinal's hat hanging on the wall behind him, not forgetting the skull on the window ledge and the miniature crucifix on his desk – are all present and correct, and yet it does not seem anachronistic to sense that the religious theme is little more than a pretext. The true purpose of this engraving is to pay homage to the wonder of home, which is why it arguably represents the birth of genre painting. The Netherlandish tradition of the fifteenth century had of course already placed figures both sacred and secular in lifelike and humble domestic interiors, but these were receptacles for the protagonists, whereas here it almost seems to be the other way round.[27] The saint is nearly lost in the midst of a whole host of meticulously recorded objects – books, cushions, a pair of slippers, an aspergillum, an hourglass, letters and a pair of scissors on a rack, candlesticks, a rosary, a giant gourd dangling from the ceiling and other things – that reveal what a masterly still-life artist Dürer would have been at a later date. Yet even all these particulars are overpowered by the observation of the grain of the wood of the ceiling, and the play of light and shadow, and above all by the reflections of the bottle glass of the windows on the decaying walls of the room. It is no wonder that in the next century Adriaen van Ostade should have replicated this interior in his *Painter in His Workshop*, or indeed that Vermeer should more than once have employed a similar window arrangement and perspective to bring his rooms to life.[28]

Turning to non-religious themes, these are altogether less straightforwardly divided up into distinct types. The three woodcut and six engraved portraits are uncomplicated enough, but drawing a useful dividing line between mythologies and secular scenes is far harder. What is more, scenes of a secular nature include moments from everyday life, but also other less easily defined subjects.

A case in point is the engraving known as the *Promenade*, whose foreground action shows a finely dressed young couple set against an extensive landscape. However, it does not take long to recognize that their walk in the countryside is no idyll: at the right margin, only half-hidden behind a twisting tree trunk, is the skeletal figure of Death gleefully balancing an hourglass on his head, and thus signalling that soon enough their time will be up.[29] The same basic concern is also found in a number of Dürer's drawings.[30] One or two of them may even have been sketches for projected prints, and indeed it is tempting to suppose that a sheet in which a young woman is shown complacently smiling, unaware that Death is holding up her train, is an, admittedly far from identical, first idea for the *Promenade* itself, since both women are shown in profile, hold their crossed hands in front of their waists and wear similarly curved hats.[31]

The *Promenade* is one of Dürer's earliest engravings, and is comparatively modest both in its dimensions and in the degree to which the plate is covered with lines. Conversely, and although it is only somewhat larger (19.2 × 12 cm versus 25 × 19 cm), another engraving whose theme is a form of memento mori is unquestionably among the most ambitious and haunting of all Dürer's prints. Monogrammed and dated 1513 on a classicizing *tabula ansata* in the bottom left corner, lazily propped up against a tree stump crowned by a skull missing its lower jaw, it is universally known as the *Knight, Death and the Devil* (illus. 53).[32] In the diary of his journey to the Netherlands, Dürer himself referred to it as the 'Reuter' ('rider'), but this is no more than a convenient shorthand, and totally fails to disclose the work's iconographic complexities.[33]

The subject-matter of the engraving is the very opposite of straightforward, not least because it is entirely unprecedented. It is true that the basic identities of the three figures are reasonably clear, but the work's precise meaning is altogether less obvious. The knight in armour rides steadfastly forward, loyally accompanied by his dog, and gives every indication of having left the monstrous figure of the Devil behind him. The latter is a virtual repetition of his counterpart in the woodcut of the *Descent into Limbo* of 1510 from the *Large Passion*, and his identity is therefore not in doubt.[34] At the same time, the knight ignores the attentions of the mounted figure of Death, here (as earlier in the *Promenade*) brandishing an hourglass, this time accompanied by a clock face, and equally steers clear of the aforementioned skull at his feet. The general notion is evidently that the knight can resist the snares of the Devil and that Death will have to wait to take him (the hourglass is only half empty), but the identity of the knight himself is more mysterious. There have been attempts to argue that he is a specific individual – in the nineteenth century Joseph Heller proposed that he might be Franz von Sickingen – but they seem far-fetched, not least since the print would have been

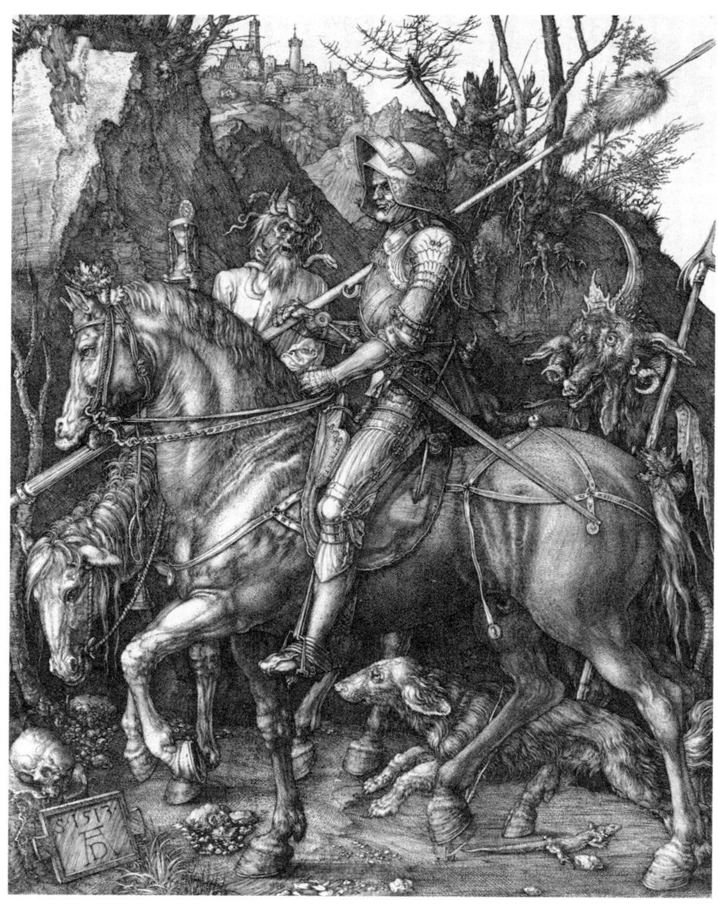

intended for all sorts of audiences.[35] Similar objections mean it is hard to accept a direct association with Erasmus's *Enchiridion militis christiani* of 1503, which enjoins all Christians to be soldiers in the service of God, for all that the print and the text certainly share the general idea of never looking back.[36] Yet Dürer's horseman entirely lacks Christian symbols, which could easily have been introduced to make the point, although Joachim Sandrart

53 Albrecht Dürer, *Knight, Death and the Devil*, 1513, engraving.

may well have been thinking of Erasmus's work when in the next century he described the horseman as 'the Great Christian Knight'.[37]

As already discussed in the previous chapter, it is reasonably clear that Dürer not only possessed what was in effect an archive of his own drawings from across his entire career, which must have been a standard procedure among artists north – and even more south – of the Alps by the end of the fifteenth century, but happily raided it by exploiting old sheets for new projects. This modus operandi did not just apply to paintings; it extended to prints. As a result, in the specific case of the *Knight, Death and the Devil*, drawings made for it not only exist but are complemented by sheets used in it.

The most notable instance of the second category is a watercolour, which is monogrammed and dated 1498 – in other words fifteen years earlier – at the bottom of the page, and inscribed at the top in the artist's hand with the words 'Dz ist dy rustung Zw der czeit/ Im tewtzschlant gewest' ('This is the armour that was [worn] in Germany at this time').[38] Both the time lag and its significantly larger scale make it plain that this sheet was not made for the 'Reuter', but equally that when it was drawn, it cannot have been intended for a print at all, as has sometimes been suggested, since there would have been no point in troubling to colour it in so meticulously. In a way, the most striking thing about its relationship with the final work is how painstakingly Dürer revised his original conception. Naturally, the change from a standing to a walking horse would have been required by the new context, as arguably would the alteration of the rider's physiognomy: in the drawing, the helmet is adorned with the initials 'W. A.', which may well be those of the moustachioed rider, since it is not hard to believe that this is the likeness of an actual individual. However, various other modifications were deemed to be required, and underline the artist's tireless attention to getting every detail right.

To begin with the rider's armour and weapons, it is plain that the basic arrangement is the same and that almost every minute detail has been tweaked. The helmet is more horizontal and the curve of the visor has been altered. The forms of the armour, especially around the elbow and knee, have been carefully emended. The hilt of the dagger is smaller and its point is now almost invisible against the extended right arm of the Devil. The angle of the sword has been rendered less upright and even the circular pommel at its end is differently aligned. Intriguingly, Dürer retained the oak leaves around the top of the horse's tail in the drawing, but complemented them with a second cluster behind its ears. Perhaps most tellingly of all, the dangling element of the horse's harness just behind the saddle is no longer motionlessly vertical, but is instead responsive to the forward walking pace of the engraving. Many more such alterations could be listed, but it is to be hoped that the point has been made.

There also exist three earlier drawings that were employed to set both horse and rider in motion. The first, a monogrammed and dated pen drawing of 1502, represents a very differently clad rider, whose left leg is bent at the knee, but whose sword and lance are already angled at identical diagonals. His mount's head is raised, and the other major difference concerns its equally raised rear hind hoof, which will end up touching the ground in the engraving.[39] It was followed in 1503 by two further dated studies of the horse in isolation, which both make it plain that it is a stallion. One is executed in pen alone, and in essence replicates the pose of the horse in the previous study, but lowers its head, while the other adds some wash and sets it against a black background, but also already endows the steed with a fully classical head.[40]

All these revisions are incorporated in a double-sided sheet where the recto is squared and executed in pen and wash over traces of a preliminary sketch in silverpoint, while the verso, which has been traced through and consequently reversed, is in simple pen and wash, and again against a dark ground.[41] It is on the same scale as the print and is evidently made with it in mind, and yet this is very much a working drawing. The precise details of the armour and weaponry remain to be defined, and the recto tries out a major pentimento in order to lower and adjust the position of the horse's right rear leg. In this respect, it is a revision that emends the previous studies of the walking horse, and fore-shadows the engraving, but it is not followed on the verso. Most striking of all is the addition there of the bounding dog, who is conceived of as being in mid-air (this is surely also the intention in the finished work, but is far more apparent against the backdrop of the dark ground).[42]

Like the knight here, the dog on the sheet's verso is a penultimate thought as opposed to a last word – the overall attitude is the same, but the breed of dog and countless details do not correspond. Remarkably, in this case we also possess the all-but-final stage in the process in the form of a long-lost drawing that was first published as recently as 1961.[43] Here, the flying dog shares the page with a drapery study and three caricatural heads in profile, and comes remarkably close to his appearance in the engraving. However, it is important to add that Dürer evidently decided there was still more work to be done, and very slightly adjusted both the dog's ear and the position of his forelegs.

Before moving on, mention must be made of one more drawing, a landscape detail that relates to five further sheets, three of which Dürer inscribed with the word 'steinpruch' ('quarry'), and which has been associated with the cliffs at the left margin of the engraving.[44] As with the study of the *Knight* dated 1498 examined above, this is a watercolour, and likewise dates from before 1500. What is more, it is altogether less close to the element it appears to be connected with, and at most provided a sort of nudge in the right direction.

A number of scholars have seen a deliberate contrast between the gothic character of the knight and the classical poise of his mount, and various suggestions have been made for its source.[45] As a matter of fact, it and its preliminaries are by no means the first representations of a striding horse in pure profile in Dürer's oeuvre, and in this connection his *Small Horse* engraving of 1505 has often been cited.[46] However, the closest parallel is with the horse in the bronze equestrian statue of *Marcus Aurelius* on the Campidoglio in Rome, and it is tempting to presume that the deep reluctance to allow of the possibility that Dürer ever reached the Eternal City is what has meant the connection has remained hidden in plain sight.[47] Moreover, if Dürer had made a record drawing of it, and then employed it directly on the plate to be engraved, that would explain the only significant difference, namely the reversal of the legs.

The singularity of the subject-matter of the *Knight, Death and the Devil* is by no means an isolated phenomenon among Dürer's prints. The basic meaning of examples such as the *Dream of the Doctor*, the *Sea-Monster* and *Melencolia* (illus. 54) – not least thanks to the inscription – is clear enough, but they are all entirely without real precedents.[48] Moreover, in other instances, the supposed subject is at best uncertain: thus, as discussed in the previous chapter, in the engraving invariably referred to as the *Abduction of Proserpina* nothing actually identifies the protagonists, and the abductor being mounted on a unicorn is wholly unexplained.[49] In the same vein, the fact that the *Young Woman Attacked by Death* offers a straightforward reminder of the brevity of life is easily grasped, but the idea of representing it by depicting a sexual assault is both unique and extremely disturbing.[50]

Within the scenes immortalizing the everyday, a small group involve low-life subjects. In a world where mockery of those less fortunate than us is rightly frowned upon, they are liable to make some people feel distinctly uneasy. Having said that, they are surely

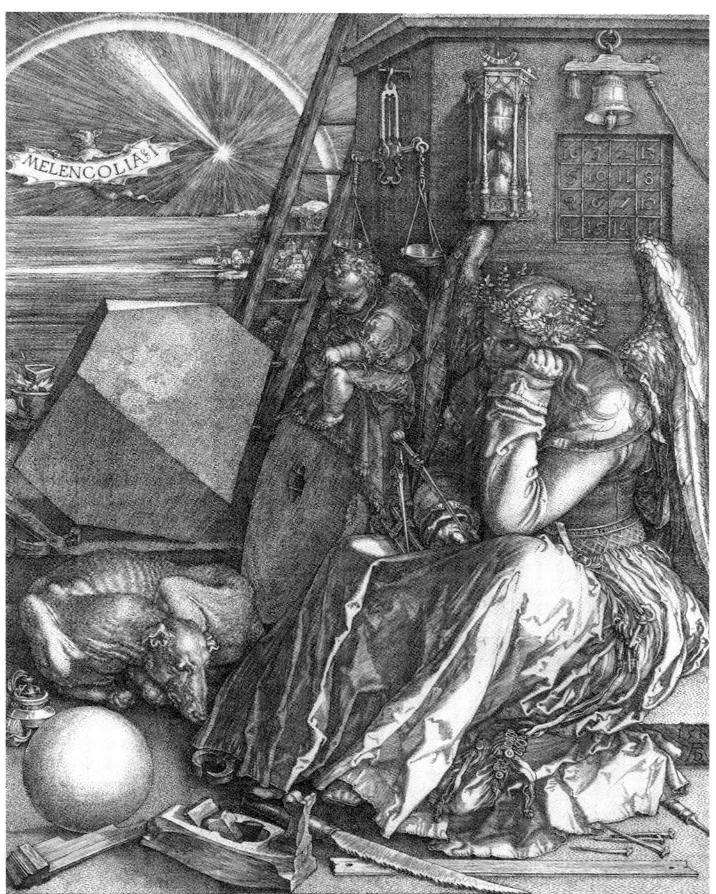

no more suspect than Shakespeare's treatment of the 'rude mechanicals' in *A Midsummer Night's Dream* and other similar characters in his plays.[51] Moreover, it is possibly worth underlining the fact that from a different perspective the notion of granting centre stage to the peasantry may be construed as a bold step in the right direction, only really preceded by Schongauer's *Miller* and *Peasant Couple on Their Way to Market*.[52] A drawing in Berlin combines what

54 Albrecht Dürer, *Melencolia*, 1514, engraving.

appear to be first ideas for two early examples, the *Rustic Couple* and the *Three Peasants in Conversation*, and for all that the sheet in question – as various commentators have argued – is surely not by Dürer, its two vignettes cannot just have been copied from the respective prints.[53] The reason is very simple: even the *Rustic Couple* is not a mere mirror image of the engraving, since details such as the man's coiffure, the position of his dagger and even his gaping expression are not identical. As for the *Three Peasants in Conversation*, the figures are dramatically different in every particular, although the group dynamic and their interaction are much the same. In both the *Rustic Couple* and the *Cook and His Wife*, it is the men – the gormless gesturer and the overweight and bald chef – who come off worst.[54] Perhaps unexpectedly, in the *Oriental Family* of much the same date the figures are altogether more dignified.[55] However, it is only in such later engravings as the *Peasant Couple Dancing* and the *Bagpiper*, both of 1514, and the *Peasant and His Wife at Market* of 1519 that sympathy tempers the mockery.[56]

As stated above, one of the most striking of Dürer's new departures involved the production of a considerable number of print series. It would be wrong to suppose that he was the first artist to devise sequences of prints that are unified by a simple narrative thread – he was preceded in this department, as in so many others, by Martin Schongauer, above all in the latter's own *Passion* – but his approach to the challenges of doing so represents a wholly new endeavour.

Narrative sequences were of course a standard feature of various other artistic genres, and notably of fresco cycles in Italy, of which Giotto's in the Scrovegni Chapel in Padua may serve as a representative example.[57] Given its subject-matter, which involves a combination of the stories of the Virgin's parents, the Virgin and Christ, concluding with the *Last Judgement*, there are numerous scenes within it common both to Dürer's various *Passions* and to his *Marienleben*. The obvious difference, however, is that the space available to Giotto had a determining effect not only upon the physical scale of the individual scenes, some of which had to fit between windows on one of the two side walls of the chapel, but upon their total number and even – given his evident desire to organize the three registers into self-contained groupings, wall by wall – upon the choice of narratives within each subsection. To give perhaps the most blatant examples, once Giotto had decided that the stories of Joachim and Anna, which act as a species of prelude to the life of the Virgin on the upper register of the left wall, should end on a high note with the *Meeting at the Golden Gate* at the end of the sequence, and moreover be balanced by a matching sequence of six scenes beginning with the *Birth of the Virgin* and concluding with her marriage celebrations on the right wall, he had to fill out the narrative on both sides.[58] Conversely, when he decided upon the number of scenes required to cover various stretches of narrative, Dürer was able to do pretty much as he pleased, although it is worth adding that whereas some episodes might be deemed optional extras, others – such as the Crucifixion within any *Passion* – could not conceivably have been omitted. At the beginning of the narrative sequence in the *Marienleben*, for instance, he covered the same narrative ground to which Giotto had devoted a dozen scenes in a mere six.[59]

Such multi-part narrative sequences are also to be found in a variety of other contexts, above all from somewhat earlier periods. On a monumental scale and in addition to frescoes, on occasion extraordinarily ambitious cycles of stained-glass windows were undertaken, arguably the most celebrated example being that at Chartres Cathedral.[60] The fact that it was by no means unique is demonstrated by the profusion of stained glass at Canterbury, but in neither context is there the same sense of a single guiding intelligence, and the work was accomplished over decades or even centuries.[61] The same goes for the most extensive monumental decorations in mosaic, such as those in St Mark's Basilica in Venice.[62]

Therefore, it makes better sense to seek precedents in the form of works on a more comparable scale. Both ivories and enamels were not infrequently organized into elaborate sequences, and at least some of these are relatively similar both in the dimensions of the individual scenes and in their approximate number. Thus, Nicholas of Verdun's *Klosterneuburg Altar* of 1181, which was in fact originally a pulpit, has a grand total of 51 representations, which is considerably more than any of Dürer's print series, but the individual scenes are about 30 centimetres (12 in.) high, and therefore not so different in scale from Dürer's prints.[63]

Turning to the approach adopted in the print sequences, and taking the *Marienleben* as the absolute pinnacle of Dürer's achievement in this field, it seems crucial to begin by stressing the degree to which the artist evidently devised the single woodcuts with an acute sense of the fact that they would be parts of a larger whole. All too often, the scholarly literature on the *Marienleben* seems to get bogged down in issues of chronology, when in truth they should simply be seen as the undeniably necessary preliminaries to a detailed study of the artist's attitude to the potential the medium offered for a whole variety of approaches to issues such as pictorial composition.[64]

It is naturally significant that Dürer's progress on the execution of the work was interrupted by his second journey to Italy, and that the prints of the *Dormition* and *Assumption and Coronation* are dated 1510, whereas most of the rest of the sequence is generally dated around 1503–4, not least on the basis of the date of 1504 inscribed on the *Meeting at the Golden Gate*, with the *Holy Family in Egypt* on occasion being placed earlier, to 1501–2.[65] If such a chronology is broadly accepted, it has consequences for an understanding of the relationship between the narrative order of the various scenes – which was immutable – and the sequence of their execution, above all because the *Holy Family in Egypt* would have been executed before a number of earlier episodes in the

life of the Virgin.[66] On the other hand, it appears unlikely to be
a pure coincidence that the two woodcuts dated 1510 are of the
concluding episodes of the narrative, and they cannot conceivably
have been some sort of afterthought, since they are both essential
components of the story.

The more the prints of the *Marienleben* are examined in their
entirety, the more powerfully it is borne in upon one that Dürer
was determined to exploit the freedom of being in effect his own
patron to make the most of the compositional variety at his dis-
posal. This is particularly strikingly apparent in the simple matter
of figure scale, where most of his precursors (and indeed contemporaries) seem to have felt themselves obliged to maintain a basic
uniformity.[67] Dürer does nothing of the kind, notably by virtue of
extending the action deep into the distance, most straightforwardly
within landscape scenes, but also in interiors.

The *Angel Appearing to Joachim* (illus. 55) is a good example of
this new approach: here the protagonist is uncomplicatedly presented in the foreground with the angel only slightly beyond him,
but the main event is backed up by a mass of ever-diminishing
detail. A sheepdog rests at the left margin of the composition a
little further back, and then come three accompanying shepherds,
whose excited joy at the arrival of the heavenly messenger is plain
to see. In the middle distance, and over to the right – typically
Dürer blocks off the left half of the design and opens out the
right-hand one – is Joachim's flock. Most of the animals are represented as a largely undifferentiated mass, but it is also possible
to pick out a billy goat and a ram clashing horns, and beyond them
another goat standing on its hind legs and browsing from a tree.[68]
In the farthest distance, boats are visible on the sea, birds fly in the
sky and minute buildings (including a windmill on the horizon)
can just be made out.

In the *Marienleben*, Dürer likewise explores depth of field and
radical figural and architectural asymmetry in such interiors as

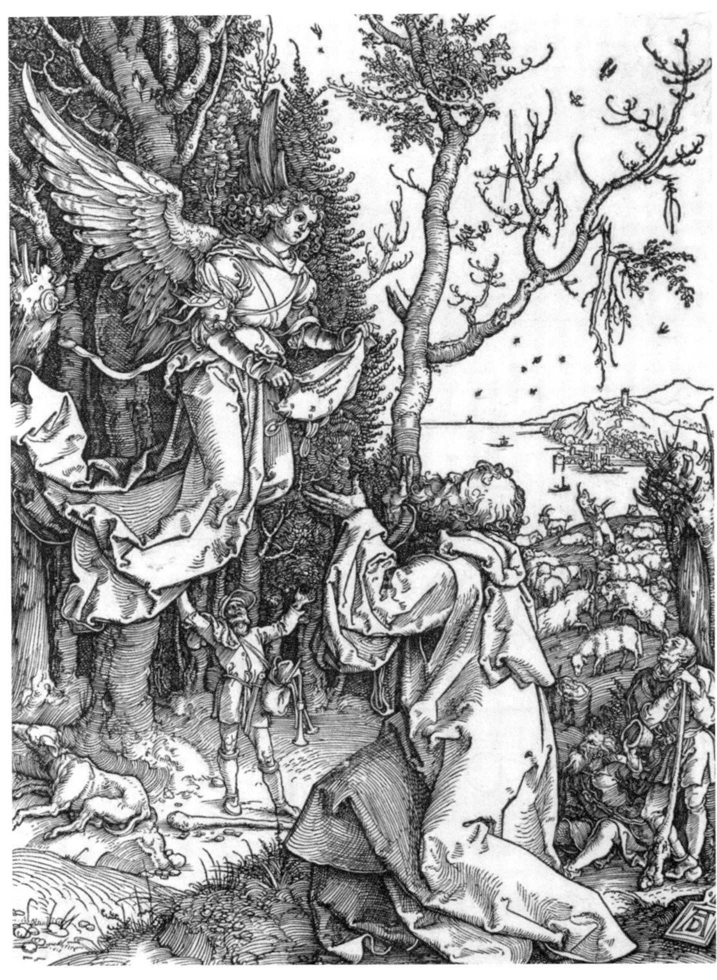

those of the *Purification of the Virgin* (illus. 56) and *Christ among the Doctors*.[69] In the former, the space is divided into three principal zones, so that on the left a heavily draped male figure seen from behind, who wraps his right arm around a colossal column, leads on to the Virgin and Joseph in the centre, who in their turn guide

55 Albrecht Dürer, *Angel Appearing to Joachim, c.* 1503, woodcut.

our gaze towards the Infant Christ – again boldly not showing his face – in the arms of the aged Simeon at the right margin of the plate. Here the principal figures are on a significantly smaller scale than their counterparts elsewhere, and in *Christ among the Doctors* it may take a moment to spot Jesus seated at a species of desk virtually at the back of the space. However, this kind of subordination is by no means invariably Dürer's practice, and in *Christ Taking Leave of His Mother* he brings the protagonists right forward, exploiting the starkly vertical wooden element of the architecture to make manifest the unbridgeable divide that separates mother and son.[70]

At the same time, and by no means just in the *Marienleben*, his iconographic inventions frequently represent highly imaginative variations on established themes. The *Birth of the Virgin* (illus. 49) may serve as a representative example of the way in which Dürer often elects to bring the religious story close to home.[71] St Anne's bedchamber could hardly be less timelessly otherworldly: on the contrary, and even without being especially well informed about the domestic interiors of the Nuremberg of his day, we instinctively sense that he has sought inspiration from a world he knows so well.

A different challenge that Dürer faced in his narrative sequences concerned the need he seems to have felt to avoid routine and monotony. With the exception of the *Apocalypse*, the other cycles – the *Marienleben* and the three *Passions* – inevitably involved a whole host of standard themes, although it was naturally entirely up to Dürer to determine how many scenes each should contain. In this context, a simple comparison of the three *Passions* makes it plain that there is considerable overlap between them, but that there are also episodes which only feature in one or two of them. After all, there are a mere twelve woodcuts in the *Large Passion*, whereas the *Small Passion* runs to no fewer than 37, of which only half a dozen illustrate earlier stages in the narrative, and the *Small Engraved Passion* has sixteen.[72]

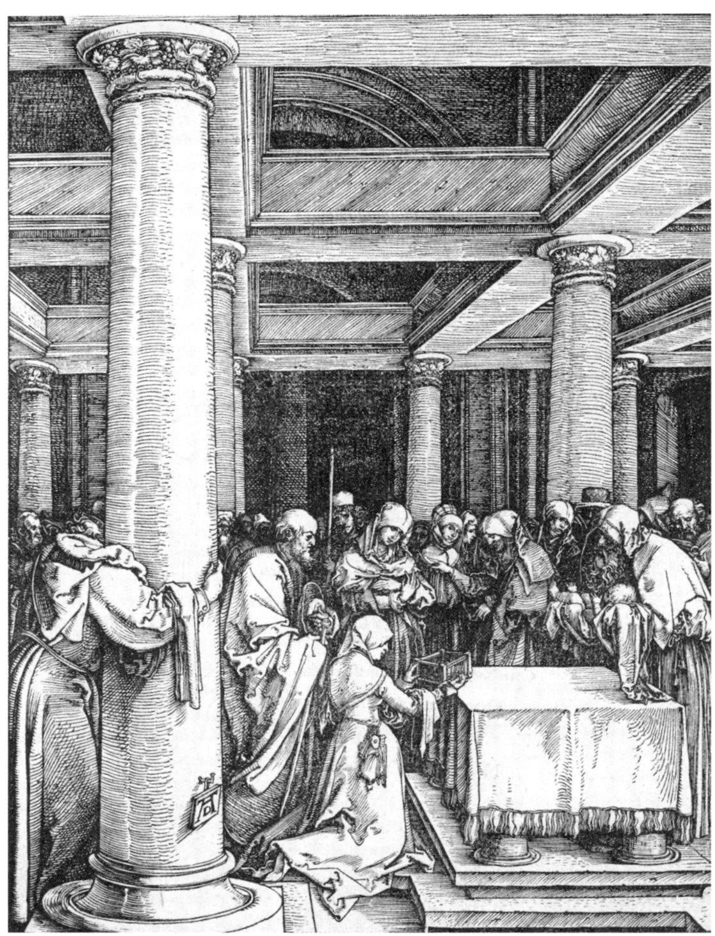

One way of avoiding the danger of stagnation was to aim for variety in the treatment of the most commonly represented subjects, while another was to explore all but unknown episodes within the established Christian narratives. In this connection, it is vital to recall the fact that the visual tradition around the *Marienleben* and the *Passions* involved a combination of events that

56 Albrecht Dürer, *Purification of the Virgin*, c. 1503–4, woodcut.

are recorded in the New Testament and others that are not. At the same time, no single Gospel tells every story that has become standard, nor indeed do all four Gospels invariably tell them identically. One consequence of this state of affairs is that the sequence of a very few scenes is not uniform between the different *Passions*. Thus in the *Small Passion*, the Descent into Limbo comes immediately after the Crucifixion, and therefore precedes the Deposition, the Lamentation and the Entombment, whereas in both the *Large Passion* and the *Small Engraved Passion* it follows the Lamentation and the Entombment, and the Deposition is omitted.[73]

Furthermore, what the Gospels actually relate often needed to be fleshed out considerably. In the case of the accounts of the infancy of Christ, for example, the first point to make is that they only occur in Matthew and Luke, since both Mark and John begin their Gospels with the Baptism of Christ. What is more, within the standard narrative only the Nativity in a stable is common to both, with Matthew telling of the Magi and the Flight into Egypt, and Luke of the Shepherds, the Circumcision, the Purification and Christ among the Doctors. In the case of the episode of the Flight into Egypt, the Gospel According to St Matthew is terse in the extreme, and simply states of Joseph that, after having been told by an angel in a dream to flee with Mary and Jesus, 'When he arose, he took the young child and his mother by night, and departed into Egypt' (Matthew 2:14). In the *Golden Legend* it is related that Joseph brought an ox and an ass to Bethlehem – perhaps to pay the tribute owed with the former and for his wife to be able to ride the latter – and then further explained that both beasts recognized Christ's divinity, but neither detail is to be found in the Gospels.[74]

By the fifteenth century it had long been entirely standard to show Mary on the ass in representations of the Flight into Egypt, but Dürer's treatment – as has been explained, following that of the Master LCz – departs from convention by adding the ox.[75]

At the same time, the inclusion of a vast palm tree at the left margin relates to another apocryphal legend concerning a palm lowering its branches to provide sustenance in the form of dates on the journey. Intriguingly, this motif is found in Schongauer's rendition of the *Rest on the Flight*, but Dürer evidently elected not to follow his example, even though his repetition of what Panofsky correctly identifies as a dragon tree from the same print proves, as one would anyway expect, that he knew it.[76]

An example of the exploration of unfamiliar subject-matter is the decision in the *Marienleben* to add a second scene to the *Flight*, showing the *Holy Family in Egypt* (illus. 57).[77] On the whole, Dürer does not seem to have been particularly gripped by typological connections between the Old and New Testaments, but in this instance the explanation of the activities of Joseph and Mary is that they echo those labours traditionally associated with Adam and Eve after the Fall, and famously celebrated in John Ball's rhyme 'When Adam delved and Eve span . . .'. Be that as it may, it is tempting to claim that, having found his theme, only Dürer would have divided the action between the homely tranquillity of the Virgin taking advantage of her Son's sleep in his crib to get on with her sewing, watched over by solicitous angels, and the hive of activity around Joseph as the shavings produced by his adze are tidied up and stuffed into a wicker basket by a team of industrious winged putti, one of whom is wearing a broad-brimmed straw hat. The setting is an exterior one, with a great diagonal perspective of partially ruined buildings over to the left leading to a round archway. Beyond it is a quintessentially northern hilly landscape dotted with gothic castle-like structures, while in the sky God the Father and the Dove of the Holy Spirit preside over the whole, which is therefore a species of representation of the Trinity.

In terms of the quest to avoid uniformity of approach to established subject-matter, an obvious solution was to vary the moment within a given narrative represented, often by drawing

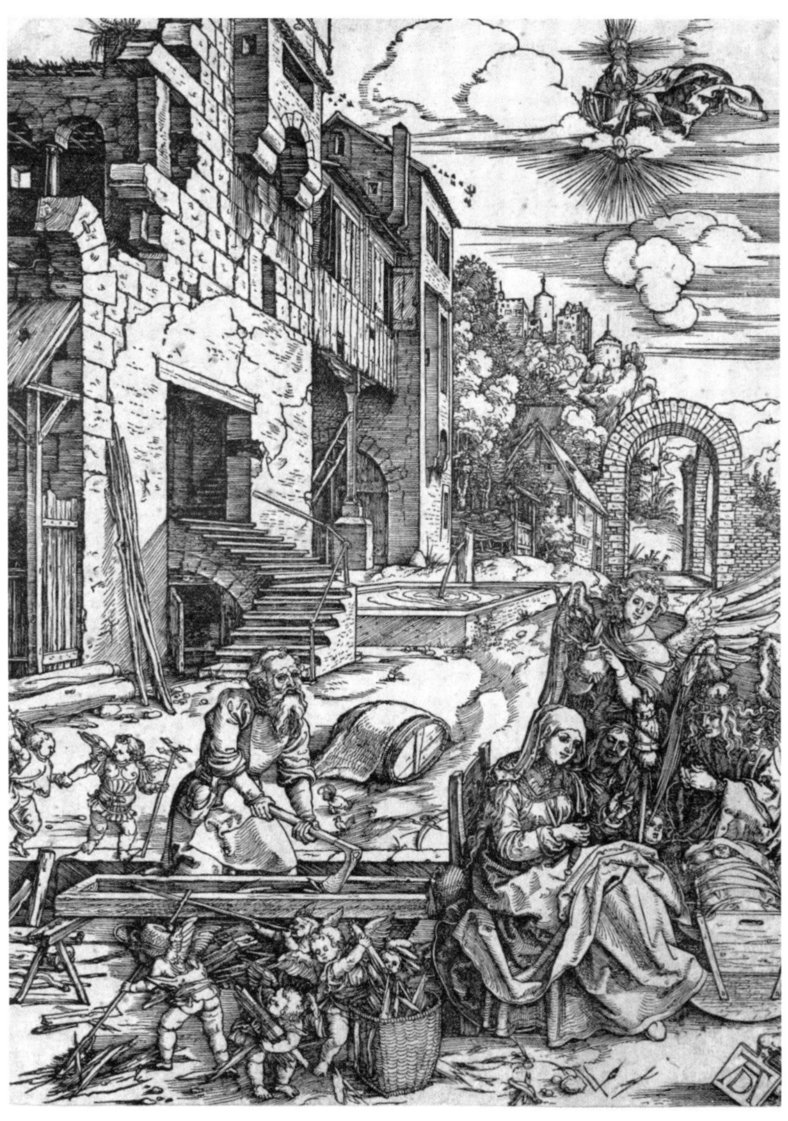

57 Albrecht Dürer, *Holy Family in Egypt*, c. 1501–2, woodcut.

on the different accounts in the four Gospels. A perfect case in point is the way Dürer, almost as if foreshadowing the spirit of the Reformation, confronts the *Agony in the Garden*, which is not only a necessary component of all three *Passions*, but is in addition a subject he returned to in the form of a singleton etching (in this connection, it is important to note that on his trip to the Netherlands Dürer only ever gave complete sets of his narrative cycles as presents, and never extracted individual prints).[78]

In three of the four Gospels the Agony is related in subtly different ways, but it is absent from John's narrative. In all three, the common features are Christ distancing himself from Peter, James and John, who accompany him, in order to pray, and their failure to keep awake after promising to do so, which is thrice-tested in Matthew and Mark, but not in Luke. In terms of other differences, Matthew states that he 'fell on his face', and asked that the cup be taken from him. In Mark, he 'fell on the ground', but there is no mention of the cup. In Luke, the cup is again referred to, but the appearance of an angel to him and his sweating 'as it were great drops of blood to the ground' are also included in the account. As with other crucial episodes in the Gospel narrative, Dürer picks and chooses how to represent the scene.

In the *Large Passion* of around 1497–8, the angel is shown holding the cup, and the hands of the kneeling figure of Christ are shown in the 'orans' position, best known through depictions of St Francis receiving the stigmata. In the foreground, Peter is slightly separated from James and John, and, as always, armed with the sword with which he will soon cut off the ear of Malchus, the servant of the High Priest (the episode is common to all four Gospels, but Peter and Malchus are only named in John's), while Judas and the approaching soldiery are seen in miniature at the gate of the Garden of Gethsemane.[79]

In the *Engraved Passion*, the print is monogrammed and dated 1508, and necessarily bunches all the main figures together. It differs above all in endeavouring to achieve the illusion of night-time, but also in showing the angel holding a cross, and Christ with his arms outstretched above his head.[80] Tantalizingly, the basic compositional idea is anticipated around 1504 in a pen and ink study for the corresponding scene in the *Green Passion*, which is preserved in the form of a reliable copy. Wherever precisely the *Green Passion*, which was slightly over twice the size of the *Engraved Passion*, was meant to lead, it is tempting to suppose that by 1508 Dürer took it for granted that it would have no public existence, and that he could safely re-present the design for its *Agony* with the odd insignificant modification.[81]

In the *Small Woodcut Passion* of around 1510, the angel with the cross is retained, but the character of the presentation of Christ is transformed, with almost theatrical gesticulation being supplanted by a deeply private bowed attitude, which all but conceals his face.[82] In a fascinating and presumably earlier variant, whose identical dimensions leave no doubt that it was originally intended for the *Small Woodcut Passion* but ultimately rejected, the angel with the cross is again present, but Christ is stretched out full-length on the ground with his arms spread.[83]

In 1515 Dürer also executed the aforementioned stand-alone etching of the *Agony*, for which there exist three preparatory drawings.[84] One is a highly polished pen study for the figure of Christ, but differs from the print not only in his more frontal profile, but in representing him with his hands joined in prayer.[85] They are similarly joined in a complete (if unevenly resolved), dated and monogrammed pen sheet, where the angel hovers in the top left corner and a chalice containing a cross rests on a ledge in front of Jesus.[86] In both these respects, the basic conception is already established, but it is only in the third drawing that the sleeping disciples are removed to the middle distance, that the angel is reduced to a disembodied cherub- or seraph-like head, that Jesus' hands are apart, and vitally that he so dramatically fills almost the entire composition. Even in as final a design as this, however, Dürer cannot – as has already been explored in the previous chapter – resist modifying an invention with which almost any other artist would have been satisfied. Specifically, and this is only a selection of the changes he makes, he turns the angel's head out of profile, alters the relationship between his head and the chalice, and elevates its position within the picture field. He also diminishes the extent of Christ's aureole; emends the angle of St Peter's sword, the branches on the tree and its leaves; and adds a second rectangular stone to the one in the bottom right-hand corner of the drawing. It is an almost pathological compulsion: nothing – not even a branch and the leaves on it or a stone – can be left in peace.[87]

Dürer returned to the theme of the Agony in three pen drawings, which all revisit previous solutions. The earliest is a sheet of 1518, which repeats the etching but shows Christ's hands joined in prayer.[88] It was followed in 1520 and 1521 by treatments for the so-called *Oblong Passion* that respectively echo the fallen-on-his-face solution of the rejected print intended for the *Small Woodcut Passion* (admittedly in a more explicitly cruciform configuration and with an empty chalice) and the raised arms and cross of the *Engraved Passion*.[89] Finally, in another horizontal treatment of 1524, the arms are again raised but the angel holds a chalice with a cross in it.[90]

Even a very long monograph exclusively devoted to Dürer as printmaker could not hope to do them all justice, and this is a very different sort of book. It does nevertheless seem important at least to hint at some of what is missing here. A number of individual prints – and categories such as portraits – have admittedly been discussed in previous chapters, but the biggest gap is represented by the *Triumphal Arch of Maximilian I*, which so heroically defeats most of the advantages of prints, since it comprises 36 large sheets of paper and ends up being almost 3.5 metres high.[91] Other oddities include a considerable number of coats of arms, six knots and projections of the earth and the heavens.[92] Still more curious are the illustrations for his treatise on human proportion,[93] as well as the four woodcuts of draughtsmen at work,[94] and notably the woodcut with the reclining female model, which somehow manages to be incomparably more disturbingly indecent than any of the images in Giulio Romano's notorious *Modi*.[95] Were there any need to rub it in, this single image is a haunting reminder of quite what a singular personality Dürer was, no less in his prints than in the incomparably more private universe of his drawings.

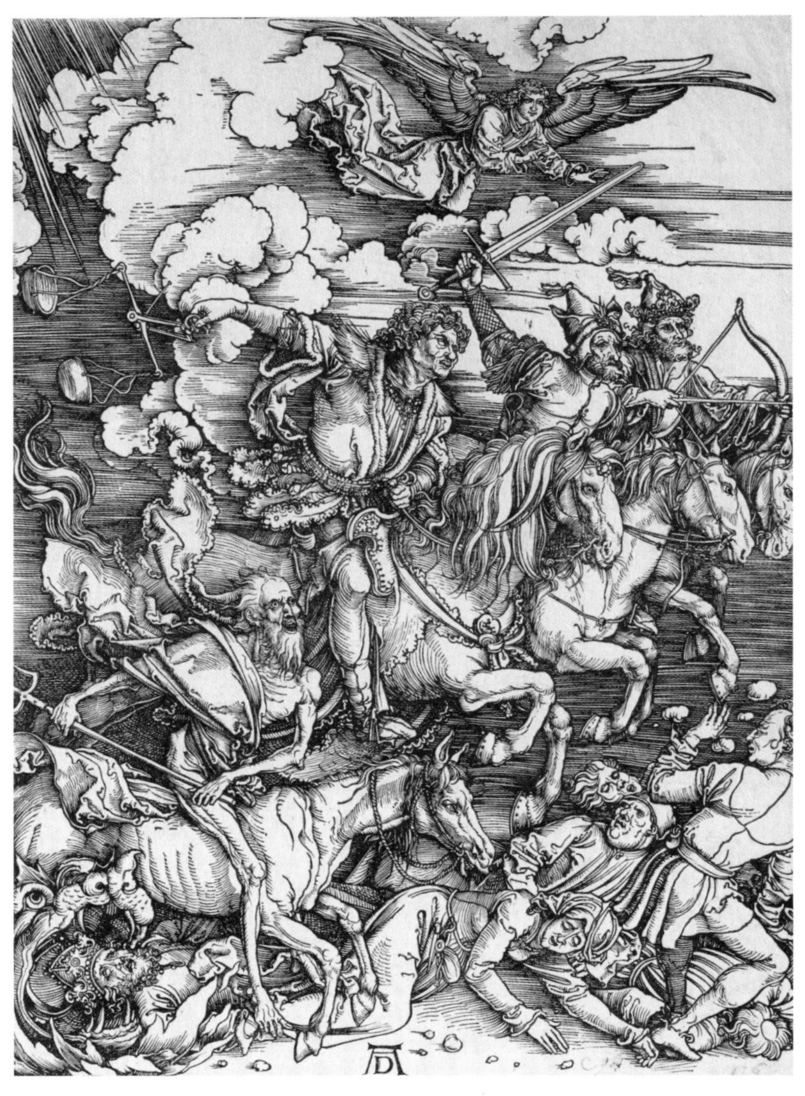

58 Albrecht Dürer, *Four Horsemen of the Apocalypse, c.* 1497–8, woodcut.

Conclusion

short book cannot hope to encompass Dürer's many-sided genius, but in these pages I have endeavoured to give at least a flavour of the singular qualities of his art, and in particular to deal even-handedly with his drawings and prints alongside his paintings. All too often there is a tendency for these aspects of an artist's production to be sidelined in monographs, but that would be especially ill-advised in the case of Dürer. In this respect, as indeed in the intensely personal character of so much of his art, among the Old Masters only his spiritual kinsmen Rembrandt and Goya can really compare with him, but of course Dürer came first. In fact, as has been argued at length in the Introduction, in effect Dürer was the first visual artist in whose oeuvre both art and autobiography are indissolubly linked.

That may indeed be one of the main reasons why he has never lost his appeal. In this concluding chapter, I will be seeking to trace his afterlife, his fame across the centuries, and will be doing so by deliberately selecting a number of overlooked connections alongside the very many immensely familiar ones.

It comes as no surprise that Dürer should have had a dominant effect on all sorts of artists of his immediate circle and his own time. The extent of his influence is such that it does not really need to be explored here, not least since it has inspired a considerable volume of scholarly investigation, including Joseph

Koerner's profound juxtaposition of Dürer and Hans Baldung Grien in his 1993 monograph *The Moment of Self-Portraiture in German Renaissance Art*.[1] Arguably less inevitable was the way limewood sculptors of the period also borrowed from Dürer's prints. Cases in point include the *St John the Baptist Triptych* from Gerolzhofen by Tilman Riemenschneider, which also looks to Schongauer, and an allegory by Peter Dell the Elder, which similarly quotes from Cranach alongside Dürer.[2] What is more, his influence was absolutely not confined to his homeland, and in Chapter Two at least some of the ways in which Italian artists of the sixteenth century responded to his work have been outlined.

By the later years of that century, Dürer was no longer even remotely contemporary, but this did not have the effect of diminishing interest in his creations, which resulted in the artistic phenomenon known as the Dürer Renaissance, which lasted approximately from 1570 to 1630.[3] Its most illustrious representative was Hans Hoffmann, but he was the very opposite of alone in his homage, as the example of Jan Brueghel's *Large Calvary* of 1604, which is an almost pedantically faithful replica of a drawing by Dürer, eloquently demonstrates.[4] In the same spirit, Rudolph II amassed what was almost certainly the largest collection of works by Dürer that has ever been assembled.[5]

It is unquestionably the case that in the seventeenth and eighteenth centuries Dürer's importance for artists gradually diminished, but that is far from meaning that he was forgotten. On the contrary, there are a number of telling indications of the esteem in which he continued to be held. Some of these relate to illustrations of his prints within paintings representing collectors or collections. An Italian example from around 1630 by the Caravaggesque painter Pietro Biancucci shows a young man holding the image of Christ that is the frontispiece to Dürer's *Small Passion*.[6] Unsurprisingly, similar tastes are manifested north of the Alps, as for instance in an anonymous Flemish panel of about 1620 representing *Cognoscenti in a Room Hung with Pictures*, where one of their number has apparently just turned away from intently contemplating an album of prints, open at two pages where no fewer than four of the five items on display are by Dürer.[7]

Intriguing though the abiding interest of collectors is, the homage of great artists is altogether more significant. In the case of Caravaggio's *Taking of Christ* of 1602, Dürer's woodcut of the same subject from the *Small Passion* has previously been proposed as a source for the main group within the composition.[8] As a matter of fact, however, a different woodcut is an even more crucial inspiration, since the attitude of the most prominent of the soldiers is directly borrowed from the figure of the executioner in Dürer's woodcut of the *Beheading of St John the Baptist* of 1510.[9]

When it comes to the greatest Spanish painter of the seventeenth century, and arguably of all time, Diego Velázquez, a debt to one of Dürer's prints is bound to represent even more of a surprise, and is liable to encounter even more resistance. Be that as it may, the pose of the cat sleeping so peacefully in the shadowy centre foreground of *Las Hilanderas* in the Prado is uncannily like – admittedly in reverse – that of his or her counterpart in Dürer's engraving of *Adam and Eve*, and gives every indication of being one great master's homage to another.[10] In this connection, it is tantalizing to note that in his *Arte de la pintura* of 1649 Velázquez's father-in-law, Francisco Pacheco, was only one among many artists and art teachers of the period who encouraged the study of Dürer's works.[11]

It is arguably less of a surprise if Rembrandt was captivated by him. Oddly enough, the 1656 inventory of his possessions only lists (under no. 273) 'Albrecht Dürer's book on proportion with woodcuts', but he was evidently familiar with many of his prints.[12] A telling case in point is the way he adapted a figure in the foreground of the *Ecce Homo* from Dürer's *Large Passion* for the protagonist of his etching of the *Blindness of Tobit*.[13]

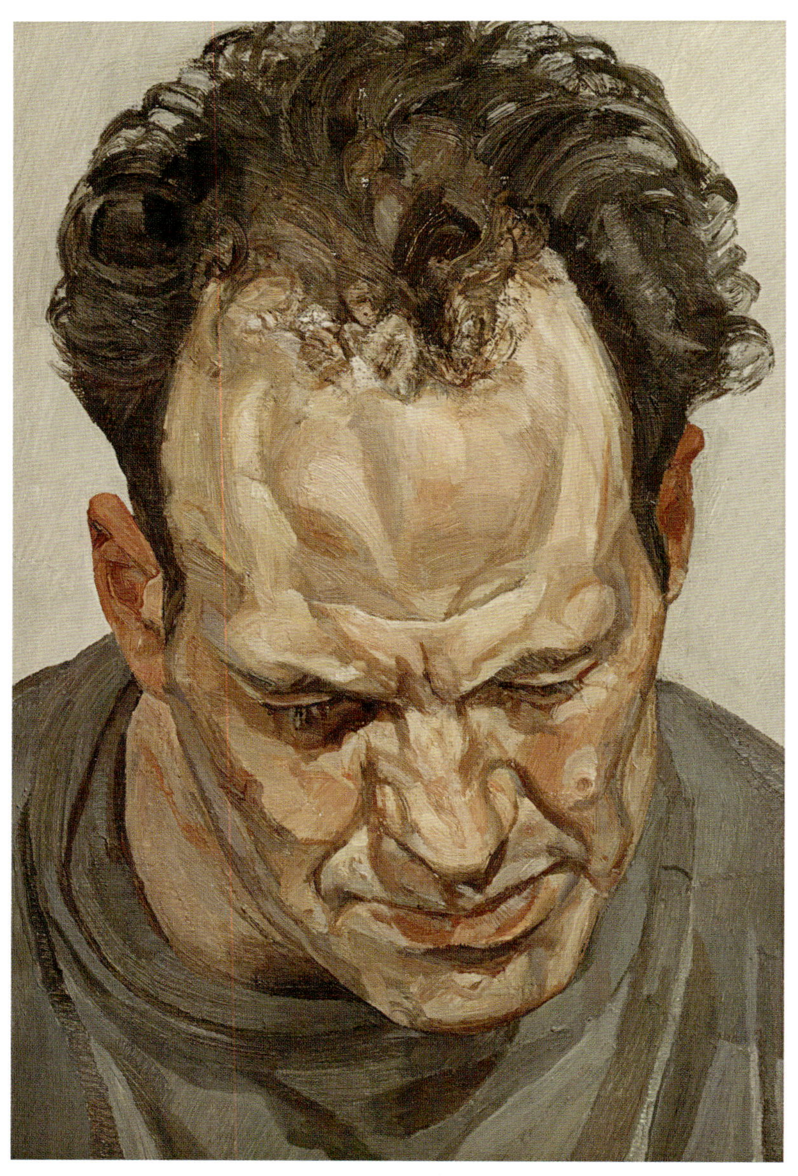

59 Lucian Freud, *Frank Auerbach*, 1975–6, oil on canvas.

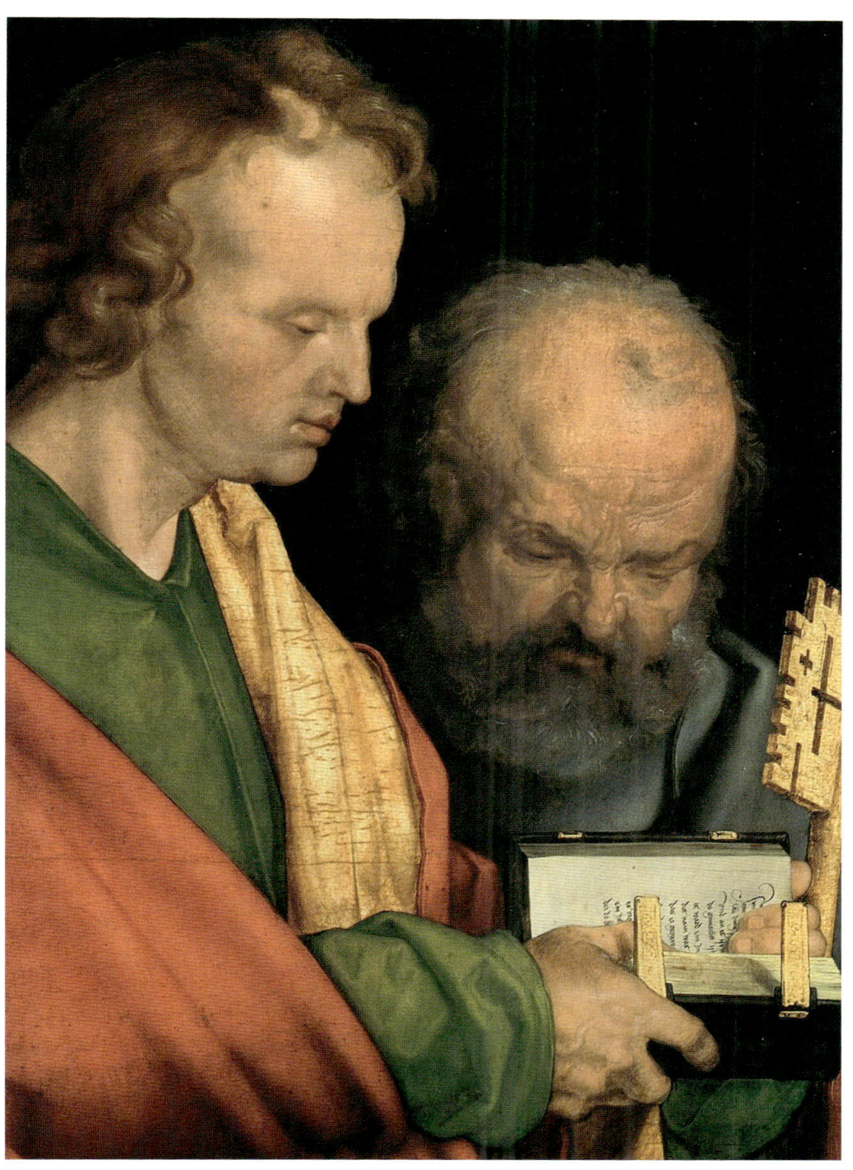

60 Albrecht Dürer, *Four Apostles* (detail of Sts John and Peter), 1526, oil on limewood panel.

In the nineteenth century a very particular species of nationalistic revivalism saw Dürer's star rise even higher, and importantly this adulation was by no means confined to the realm of the visual arts. Tellingly, in Wagner's opera *Die Meistersinger von Nürnberg* of 1868, whose main character is a historical figure who was around a generation younger than Dürer, the poet Hans Sachs (1494–1576), the heroine, Eva, refers to a painting of David by 'Meister Dürer'. No such picture ever existed, but – given the opera's setting – within the fiction it could not conceivably have been painted by anyone else. A different, more hagiographic brand of reverence is enshrined in the reliquary dating from 1871 that contains a lock of Dürer's hair.[14]

In truth, the number of Renaissance artists who are still household names amount to a handful, mostly from Italy as opposed to the Netherlands or Germany, and by the same token the number of their individual works that are instantly recognizable is incredibly few. The *Birth of Venus* and the *Mona Lisa* are both perfect examples of single paintings that enjoy an entirely different status in the popular imagination from all Botticelli and Leonardo's other works. When it comes to Michelangelo, in painting it is his *Creation of Adam* and in sculpture his *David* that stand head and shoulders above the rest. Only with Dürer are there at least half a dozen works that fight it out for the top spot: the *Four Horsemen of the Apocalypse* (illus. 58), the *Hare*, the *Praying Hands*, the *Rhinoceros*, the *Knight, Death and the Devil* and the Alte Pinakothek *Self-Portrait*. Strikingly, they are absolutely not all of a piece, because Dürer is an artist who cannot be summed up in a sentence.

Given his extraordinary range and variety, his appeal for twentieth-century artists predictably took many different forms, perhaps above all within the German tradition. For Otto Dix, when in 1925 he came to paint his *Portrait of the Lawyer Hugo Simons*, it was the gesticulating fingers of one of the self-portrait drawings that captured his imagination.[15] A fascinating example of the perhaps unexpected attraction of his work for a British artist with German roots is to be found in Lucian Freud's celebrated portrait of Frank Auerbach of 1975–6 (illus. 59).[16] Freud's early thraldom to Neue Sachlichkeit is plain to see, but has possibly had the effect of blinding people to this painting's clear, if admittedly far from pedantically literal, dependence upon the great downward-looking domed head of the figure of St Peter in Dürer's so-called *Four Apostles* (illus. 60).[17]

For all that Dix and Freud are artists who go their own very personal ways, both these paintings nevertheless belong to what might be described as the main line of the grand European fig-urative tradition. An altogether less expected admirer of Dürer is represented by Norman Rockwell, an artist whose standing is now – in my opinion, quite rightly – extremely high after decades of unthinking disdain. In his *Triple Self-Portrait* of 1960, the pipe-smoking protagonist seeks inspiration or expresses his admir-ation for four great precursors by virtue of reproductions of self-portraits by them pinned to the top right corner of his canvas. Dürer's Prado *Self-Portrait* is inevitably the earliest of that quartet, and keeps company with examples by Rembrandt, Van Gogh and Picasso.[18]

Dürer has a habit of turning up in the most unexpected con-texts. In Pierre Mac Orlan's popular novel of 1927, *Le Quai des brumes*, which was turned into a memorable film by Marcel Carné in 1938 (it is known in English as *Port of Shadows*), there are two separate references to landscapes that bring Dürer to mind. The novel is not a work of high art, yet the author takes it for granted that his readers will be able to conjure up a mental picture of the sorts of watery landscapes he has in mind.[19] A wholly cinematic invocation occurs in Andrei Tarkovsky's mesmerizing *Ivan's Childhood* of 1962, when the young hero contemplates reproductions of the *Four Horsemen of the Apocalypse*, the *Portrait of Ulrich Varnbüler* and the *Knight, Death and the Devil*. A more predictable genuflection to Dürer's fundamental importance, which consciously seeks to bring out his centrality in the German context, is found in the form of a species of postscript to Günter Grass's novel *Aus dem Tagebuch einer Schnecke* (From the Diary of a Snail) of 1972.[20]

A final example of a bizarre homage to Dürer may be a good way of underlining two important elements of the long shadow it seems certain he will continue to cast. The first is that he is virtually guaranteed to turn up in the most unexpected places, and the second is that the power of his inventions does not need to have anything to do with his being their creator. In Francis Ford Coppola's 1992 gothic horror movie *Bram Stoker's Dracula*, the portrait of Dracula in his sinister castle is to all intents and purposes a perfect replica of Dürer's Alte Pinakothek *Self-Portrait*, the only difference being that the features of Gary Oldman, who plays the part of Count Dracula, are substituted for those of the artist. It may reasonably be surmised that only a happy few of the millions of people who have seen the film are aware of the source of the likeness, but what is hard to doubt is the fact that Hollywood knows a visually arresting image when it sees one. Dürer has never gone away, and happily he is here to stay.

REFERENCES

Introduction: Life and Times

1 Friedrich Winkler, *Die Zeichnungen Albrecht Dürers*, 4 vols (Berlin, 1936–9), vol. I, pp. 7–8, no. I; and Walter L. Strauss, *The Complete Drawings of Albrecht Dürer*, 6 vols and 2 supplements (New York, 1974), vol. I, pp. 4–5, 1484/1.

2 Winkler, *Zeichnungen*, vol. I, pp. 186–7, no. 267; Strauss, *Drawings*, vol. II, pp. 688–9, 1503/18; Joseph Leo Koerner, *The Moment of Self-Portraiture in German Renaissance Art* (Chicago, IL, and London, 1993), pp. 239–46, fig. 120; and Christof Metzger, ed., *Albrecht Dürer*, exh. cat., Albertina, Vienna (2019–20), pp. 70–73, fig. I (commentary by Erwin Pokorny), where it is dated *c.* 1499.

3 Hans Rupprich, ed., *Dürer: Schriftlicher Nachlass*, 3 vols (Berlin, 1956–69); and Jeffrey Ashcroft, *Albrecht Dürer: Documentary Biography*, 2 vols (New Haven, CT, and London, 2017), for all this material; and Peter Strieder, ed., *1471 Albrecht Dürer 1971*, exh. cat., Germanisches Nationalmuseum, Nuremberg (1971), pp. 36–7, no. 22, for an autograph letter.

4 Sebastian Gulden, 'An Ideal Neighbourhood: The Physical Environment of the Early Dürer as a Space of Experience', in *The Early Dürer*, ed. Daniel Hess and Thomas Eser, exh. cat., Germanisches Nationalmuseum, Nuremberg (2012), pp. 29–38.

5 Ibid., p. 29, fig. I, for a pre-war photograph.

6 Jane Campbell Hutchison, *Albrecht Dürer: A Biography* (Princeton, NJ, 1990), pp. 14–15.

7 Rupprich, *Nachlass*, vol. I, p. 31, Ashcroft, *Albrecht Dürer: Documentary Biography*, vol. I, p. 35; and Fedja Anzelewsky, *Dürer: Das malerische Werk*, 2 vols (Berlin, 1991), vol. I, pp. 247–8, nos 131–2, and vol. II, plates 145–6, figs 160–61, for the portrait.

8 Hess and Eser, *Early Dürer*, p. 32, and pp. 398–9, no. 93.

 9 Campbell Hutchison, *Biography*, pp. 46–7.
10 Ashcroft, *Documentary Biography*, vol. I, pp. 64–7, docs 7–8, and
    pp. 90–91, doc. 13, for his employment of Konrad Schweitzer and
    Georg Kohler on 8 and 26 July 1497, and Jakob Arnold in 1500; and
    Rupprich, *Nachlass*, vol. I, p. 244, for Arnolt (*sic*), and vol. III, p. 448,
    for Schweitzer.
11 Johannes Röll, 'Stoss, Veit', in *The Dictionary of Art*, ed. Jane Turner,
    34 vols (London, 1996), vol. XXIX, pp. 726–31; and Rainer Kahsnitz,
    ed., *Veit Stoss in Nürnberg: Werke des Meisters und seiner Schule in Nürnberg und
    Umgebung* (Munich and Berlin, 1983).
12 Herbert Bauer and Georg Stolz, *Engelsgruss und Sakramentshaus in St.
    Lorenz zu Nürnberg* (Königstein im Taunus, 1974), esp. p. 3, for the
    work's patronage.
13 Campbell Hutchison, *Biography*, p. 119.
14 Anzelewsky, *Das malerische Werk*, vol. I, pp. 191–202, no. 93,
    figs 74–84, and vol. II, plates 91–6, figs 104–9.
15 Ibid., vol. I, pp. 78–9, and pp. 212–16, nos 103–4, figs 90–92,
    and vol. II, plates 108–10, figs 121–4; and Campbell Hutchison,
    Biography, p. 97, for documentary evidence of his return.
16 Campbell Hutchison, *Biography*, p. 119.
17 Rupprich, *Nachlass*, vol. I, pp. 146–202; Ashcroft, *Documentary Biography*,
    vol. I, pp. 545–628; Susan Foister and Peter van den Brink, *Dürer's
    Journeys: Travels of a Renaissance Artist*, exh. cat., National Gallery, London
    (2021–2); and Philip Hoare, *Albert and the Whale* (London, 2021).
18 Franz Fuchs, 'Eine neue Notiz zu Dürers Krankheit und Tod',
    Mitteilungen des Vereins für Geschichte der Stadt Nürnberg, CVII (2020),
    pp. 279–88.
19 Rupprich, *Nachlass*, vol. I, pp. 30–31, no. 18; and Ashcroft, *Documentary
    Biography*, vol. I, p. 35.
20 Winkler, *Zeichnungen*, vol. I, pp. 8–9, no. 3; and Strauss, *Drawings*,
    vol. I, pp. 10–11, 1484/4, attribute the sheet to Dürer, but Koerner,
    Moment of Self-Portraiture, pp. 43–4, argues that it is a self-portrait,
    and p. 457, n. 34, lists the different opinions of a variety of scholars.
    See also Metzger, ed., *Dürer*, pp. 77 and 446, no. 3, for a recent
    confirmation of Koerner's attribution.
21 Anzelewsky, *Das malerische Werk*, vol. I, pp. 118–20, nos 2–4.1, fig. 9,
    and vol. II, plates 1–4, figs 1–4.
22 Ibid., vol. I, pp. 151–4, no. 48, figs 37–40, and vol. II, plate 44, fig.
    54; and Foister and Van den Brinck, *Journeys*, p. 62, no. 19, as 'After
    Albrecht Dürer'.

23 Anzelewsky, *Das malerische Werk*, vol. I, p. 152, fig. 38.

24 Winkler, *Zeichnungen*, vol. III, pp. 28–9, no. 559; and Strauss, *Drawings*, vol. III, pp. 1394–5, 1514/1.

25 Rupprich, *Nachlass*, vol. I, p. 31; and Ashcroft, *Documentary Biography*, vol. I, pp. 395–9, nos 92.1 and 92.2.

26 Winkler, *Zeichnungen*, vol. I, p. 101, no. 115; Strauss, *Drawings*, vol. I, pp. 404–5, 1496/6; Stephanie Buck and Stephanie Porras, eds, *The Young Dürer: Drawing the Figure*, exh. cat., Courtauld Gallery, London (2013–14), pp. 151–3, no. 9 (entry by Stephanie Porras); and Metzger, ed., *Dürer*, pp. 109 and 447, no. 21.

27 Winkler, *Zeichnungen*, vol. III, p. 38, no. 574; Strauss, *Drawings*, vol. III, pp. 1764–5, 1519/5; Metzger, ed., *Dürer*, pp. 415 and 463, no. 189, for the drawing; and Anzelewsky, *Das malerische Werk*, vol. I, pp. 259–61, no. 147, figs 135–9, and vol. II, plate 158, fig. 174, for the painting.

28 Winkler, *Zeichnungen*, vol. IV, pp. 36–7, no. 814; Strauss, *Drawings*, vol. IV, pp. 1998–9, 1521/1; and Foister and Van den Brink, *Journeys*, pp. 186–7, fig. 100. See also Winkler, *Zeichnungen*, vol. I, p. 162, no. 232; Strauss, *Drawings*, vol. II, pp. 510–11, 1500/4, for a home-grown costume study generally agreed to represent Agnes.

29 Winkler, *Zeichnungen*, vol. III, pp. 20–21, no. 780; Strauss, *Drawings*, vol. IV, pp. 2096–7, 1521/57; Metzger, ed., *Dürer*, pp. 410, 412 and 463, no. 188; and Foister and Van den Brink, *Journeys*, p. 211, fig. 117.

30 Winkler, *Zeichnungen*, vol. III, p. 28, no. 558; Strauss, *Drawings*, vol. III, pp. 1450–51, 1514/30; and Foister and Van den Brink, *Journeys*, p. 158, fig. 80.

31 Winkler, *Zeichnungen*, vol. III, pp. 27–8, no. 557; and Strauss, *Drawings*, vol. III, pp. 1452–3, 1514/31.

32 Rainer Schoch, Matthias Mende and Anna Scherbaum, *Albrecht Dürer: Das druckgraphische Werk*, 3 vols (Munich, London and New York, 2001–4), vol. I, pp. 198–200, no. 79 (entry by Rainer Schoch); and Metzger, ed., *Dürer*, p. 176, and pp. 243 and 455, no. 102.

33 Winkler, *Zeichnungen*, vol. I, pp. 7–8, no. 1; Strauss, *Drawings*, vol. I, pp. 4–5, 1484/1; and Metzger, ed., *Dürer*, pp. 76, 174, and 446, no. 2.

34 Winkler, *Zeichnungen*, vol. I, p. 25, no. 27; Strauss, *Drawings*, vol. I, pp. 146–7, 1493/6; and Koerner, *Moment of Self-Portraiture*, p. 7, fig. 2.

35 Winkler, *Zeichnungen*, vol. I, p. 25, no. 26; Strauss, *Drawings*, vol. I, pp. 58–9, 1491/9; and Koerner, *Moment of Self-Portraiture*, p. 4, fig. 1.

36 Anzelewsky, *Das malerische Werk*, vol. I, pp. 124–6, no. 10, fig. 14, and vol. II, plate 10, fig. 14.

37 Koerner, *Moment of Self-Portraiture*, p. 31.

38 Winkler, *Zeichnungen*, vol. I, pp. 186–7, no. 267; Strauss, *Drawings*, vol. II, pp. 688–9, 1503/18; Koerner, *Moment of Self-Portraiture*, pp. 239–46, fig. 120; and Metzger, ed., *Dürer*, pp. 70–73, fig. 1 (commentary by Erwin Pokorny).

39 Pietro Aretino, *Dialogues*, trans. Raymond Rosenthal (New York, 1994), p. 207, for a character in the *Ragionamenti* who claims that 'painters and sculptors, except for Baccio Bandinelli's grace, are all voluntary madmen, and you can see this is true by the fact that they take their own privates and bestow them on their paintings and marble statues,' as quoted by Philip Sohm, 'Giving Vasari the Giorgio Treatment', *I Tatti Studies in the Italian Renaissance*, XVIII/1 (2015), pp. 61–111.

40 Winkler, *Zeichnungen*, vol. II, p. 141, no. 482; Strauss, *Drawings*, vol. III, pp. 1758–9, 1519/2; and Koerner, *Moment of Self-Portraiture*, pp. 176–7, fig. 91.

41 Winkler, *Zeichnungen*, vol. IV, pp. 103–4, no. 944; Strauss, *Drawings*, vol. IV, pp. 2280–81, 1525/4; and Klaus Albrecht Schröder and Maria Luise Sternath, *Albrecht Dürer*, exh. cat., Albertina, Vienna (2003), p. 41, fig. 9. See also Rupprich, *Nachlass*, vol. I, pp. 214–15, and Ashcroft, *Documentary Biography*, vol. II, p. 577.

42 Anzelewsky, *Das malerische Werk*, vol. I, pp. 124–6, no. 10, fig. 14, and vol. II, plate 10, fig. 14.

43 Jeroen Stumpel and Jolein van Kregten, 'In the Name of the Thistle: Albrecht Dürer's Self-Portrait of 1493', *Burlington Magazine*, CXLIV/1186 (2002), pp. 14–18, esp. pp. 14–15; and Rupprich, *Nachlass*, vol. I, p. 31.

44 Koerner, *Moment of Self-Portraiture*, p. 31.

45 Stumpel and van Kregten, 'In the Name of the Thistle'; and Schoch, Mende and Scherbaum, *Das druckgraphische Werk*, vol. I, pp. 36–7, no. 5 (entry by Rainer Schoch).

46 Schoch, Mende and Scherbaum, *Das druckgraphische Werk*, vol. I, pp. 27–8, no. 1 (entry by Rainer Schoch).

47 David Ekserdjian, 'The Portrait in Renaissance Italy and Lorenzo Lotto: Past, Present, and Future', in *Los retratos de Lorenzo Lotto*, ed. Enrico Maria Dal Pozzolo (Madrid, 2022), pp. 8–17, especially pp. 12–14, for an overview.

48 Anzelewsky, *Das malerische Werk*, vol. I, pp. 154–6, no. 49, figs 41–3, and vol. II, plate 43, fig. 53, and plates 45–6, figs 55–6.

49 Ibid., vol. I, pp. 166–71, no. 66, figs 52–6, and vol. II, plate 43, fig. 53, and plates 61–2, figs 72–4. See also Philipp Zitzlsperger, *Dürers Pelz*

und das Recht im Bild: Kleiderkunde als Methode der Kunstgeschichte (Berlin, 2008), for a radical redating to circa 1509.

50 Campbell Hutchison, *Biography*, pp. 67–8; and Koerner, *Moment of Self-Portraiture*, pp. 184–5.

51 Rupprich, *Nachlass*, vol. I, pp. 156, 165 and 172; and Ashcroft, *Documentary Biography*, vol. I, pp. 562, 573 and 583, for three *Veronicas* Dürer records himself as having painted on his journey to the Netherlands.

52 Koerner, *Moment of Self-Portraiture*, remains the most profound and also detailed consideration of the work in all its aspects.

53 I owe these observations to François Quiviger.

54 Anzelewsky, *Das malerische Werk*, vol. I, pp. 229–30, no. 117V.

55 Giorgio Vasari, *Le opere di Giorgio Vasari con nuove annotazioni e commenti di Gaetano Milanesi*, 8 vols and index (Florence, 1878–85), vol. V, p. 442.

56 Ibid., vol. IV, pp. 353–4, and vol. V, p. 551.

57 Koerner, *Moment of Self-Portraiture*, p. 112, for the practice, and p. 470, n. 102, for examples and further references. See also Joanna Woods-Marsden, *Renaissance Self-Portraiture: The Visual Construction of Identity and the Social Status of the Artist* (New Haven, CT, and London, 1998), for a more general survey, which, however, all but omits Dürer.

58 Cristina Acidini Luchinat, ed., *The Chapel of the Magi: Benozzo Gozzoli's Frescoes in the Palazzo Medici-Riccardi Florence* (London, 1994), p. 47.

59 Pietro Scarpellini, *Perugino* (Milan, 1984), pp. 74–5, no. 25, p. 144, fig. 27, p. 148, fig. 32, p. 79, no. 33, and p. 156, fig. 48.

60 Ibid., pp. 98–9, no. 98, and p. 222, fig. 166.

61 Anzelewsky, *Das malerische Werk*, vol. I, pp. 178–9, no. 73, and vol. II, plate 72, fig. 84.

62 Ibid., vol. I, pp. 188–9, no. 82, and vol. II, plates 85–6, figs 99–102.

63 Winkler, *Zeichnungen*, vol. IV, p. 70, no. 886; Strauss, *Drawings*, vol. IV, pp. 2194–5, 1522/8. Winkler is against the identification, but Strauss and Koerner, *Moment of Self-Portraiture*, pp. 179–83, fig. 96, are both in favour. See also *West European Drawing of XVI–XX Centuries: Kunsthalle Collection in Bremen: Catalogue* (Moscow, 1992), pp. 134–5, no. 40, for a reproduction in colour.

64 Anzelewsky, *Das malerische Werk*, vol. I, pp. 270–73, no. 170K, figs 145–7.

65 Ibid., vol. I, pp. 191–202, no. 93, figs 74–84, and vol. II, plates 91–6, figs 104–9. Martin Bailey, *Dürer* (London, 1998), p. 90, no. 30, rightly points out that the Feast was not introduced until a later date, but by now the title has established itself as the standard one.

66 Anzelewsky, *Das malerische Werk*, vol. I, p. 201, for various suggestions concerning his identity.

67 Ibid., vol. I, pp. 216–21, no. 105, figs 93–6, and vol. II, plates 111–14, figs 125–8. See also Vittorio Sgarbi, *Carpaccio* (New York, London and Paris, 1995), pp. 182–3, for another treatment of the subject, which, however, cannot have inspired Dürer, since it is dated 1515.

68 Anzelewsky, *Das malerische Werk*, vol. I, pp. 219–20.

69 Ibid., vol. I, pp. 221–8, nos 106–8, figs 97–104, and vol. II, plates 115–20, figs 129–35.

70 Ibid., vol. I, p. 226, fig. 101, for a detail of the self-portrait and the tablet.

71 Ibid., vol. I, pp. 230–33, no. 118, fig. 105, and vol. II, plates 122–30, figs 137–45.

72 Ibid., vol. II, plate 130, fig. 145, for a detail of the self-portrait and the *tabula ansata* in colour.

73 Winkler, *Zeichnungen*, vol. II, pp. 118–19, no. 445; and Strauss, *Drawings*, vol. II, pp. 1060–61, 1508/23.

74 Campbell Hutchison, *Biography*, p. 22.

75 Anzelewsky, *Das malerische Werk*, vol. I, p. 193; and Irving Lavin, 'Divine Grace and the Remedy of the Imperfect: Michelangelo's Signature on the St Peter's Pietà', *Artibus et Historiae*, XXXIV/68 (2013), pp. 277–327, for *faciebat*.

76 Winkler, *Zeichnungen*, vol. III, pp. 77–9, no. 662; Strauss, *Drawings*, vol. III, pp. 1458–9, 1514/34, for *Arion*; and Winkler, *Zeichnungen*, vol. III, pp. 79–80, nos 664–6; Strauss, *Drawings*, vol. III, pp. 1456–7, 1514/33, pp. 1460–63, 1514/35–6, for the other three.

77 Ferruccio Ferri, ed., *Le poesie liriche di Basinio* (Turin, 1925), pp. 77–92, for the 'Cyris', and p. 86, no. VIII, line 1 for Arion.

78 Winkler, *Zeichnungen*, vol. III, p. 79, no. 663; Strauss, *Drawings*, vol. III, pp. 1462–3, 1514/36; and Otto Kurz, 'Huius Nympha Loci: A Pseudo-Classical Inscription and a Drawing by Dürer', *Journal of the Warburg and Courtauld Institutes*, XVI (1953), pp. 171–7.

79 Winkler, *Zeichnungen*, vol. III, p. 80, no. 665; and Strauss, *Drawings*, vol. III, pp. 1456–7, 1514/33.

80 Winkler, *Zeichnungen*, vol. III, pp. 79–80, no. 664; and Strauss, *Drawings*, vol. III, pp. 1460–61, 1514/35. I am extremely grateful to George Lemos for his assistance with the Greek text.

81 Schoch, Mende and Scherbaum, *Das druckgraphische Werk*, vol. I, pp. 65–7, no. 18 (entry by Rainer Schoch).

82 Ibid., pp. 76–8, no. 22 (entry by Rainer Schoch).

83 Ibid., pp. 95–9, no. 33 (entry by Rainer Schoch).

84 Rupprich, *Nachlass*, vol. I, pp. 39–60, nos 1–10; Ashcroft, *Documentary Biography*, vol. I, pp. 133–74, nos 29.1–10, for the ten extant letters; and Metzger, *Dürer*, pp. 250–51 and 455, no. 103, for an autograph letter. See also Campbell Hutchison, *Biography*, pp. 48–56, for an exemplary short account of Pirckheimer and Dürer.

85 Winkler, *Zeichnungen*, vol. II, pp. 6–8, nos 268 and 270; and Strauss, *Drawings*, vol. II, pp. 658–61, 1503/3–4.

86 Schoch, Mende and Scherbaum, *Das druckgraphische Werk*, vol. II, pp. 237–9, no. 99 (entry by Matthias Mende).

1 Man and the Natural World

1 David Ekserdjian and Tom Henry, *Raphael*, exh. cat., National Gallery, London (2022), pp. 268–9, no. 78 (entry by David Ekserdjian).

2 Friedrich Winkler, *Die Zeichnungen Albrecht Dürers*, 4 vols (Berlin, 1936–9), vol. I, p. 26, no. 28; and Walter L. Strauss, *The Complete Drawings of Albrecht Dürer*, 6 vols and 2 supplements (New York, 1974), vol. I, pp. 140–41, 1493/3.

3 Hans Rupprich, ed., *Dürer: Schriftlicher Nachlass*, 3 vols (Berlin, 1956–69), vol. I, pp. 43–5, no. 29.2; and Jeffrey Ashcroft, *Albrecht Dürer: Documentary Biography*, 2 vols (New Haven, CT, and London, 2017), vol. I, pp. 139–42, no. 29.2.

4 Giorgio Vasari, *Lives of the Artists*, intro. and notes by David Ekserdjian, 2 vols (London, 1996), vol. II, pp. 75–6; and Giorgio Vasari, *Le opere di Giorgio Vasari con nuove annotazioni e commenti di Gaetano Milanesi*, 8 vols and index (Florence, 1878–85), vol. V, p. 400, for the original Italian: '. . . volle Alberto mostrare che sapeva fare gl'ignudi.'

> Ma ancora che questi maestri fussero allora in que' paesi lodati, ne' nostri le cose loro sono per la diligenza dell'intaglio comendate; e voglio credere che Alberto non potesse per aventura far meglio, come quello che non avendo commodità d'altri ritraeva, quando aveva a fare ignudi, alcuno de' suoi garzoni che dovevano avere, come hanno per lo più i Tedeschi, cattivo ignudo, se bene vestiti si veggiono molti begli uomini di que' paesi.

As noted in David Ekserdjian, *The Italian Renaissance Altarpiece: Between Icon and Narrative* (New Haven, CT, and London, 2021), p. 391, in

his *Il Figino* of 1591, in much the same vein Gregorio Comanini
condemned Dürer for having represented Jews with German
moustaches and German features.

5 Rainer Schoch, Matthias Mende and Anna Scherbaum, *Albrecht
Dürer: Das druckgraphische Werk*, 3 vols (Munich, London and New
York, 2001–4), vol. II, pp. 52–5, no. 107 (entry by Rainer Schoch).

6 Otto Pächt, *Van Eyck: Die Begründer der altniederländischen Malerei*
(Munich, 1993), plate 25, for Jan van Eyck's representation of Adam
with chest hair.

7 Winkler, *Zeichnungen*, vol. III, p. 73, no. 646; and Strauss, *Drawings*,
vol. II, pp. 1066–7, 1508/26.

8 Anne Röver-Kann, *Albrecht Dürer: Das Frauenbad von 1496*, exh. cat.,
Kunsthalle Bremen (2001).

9 Pächt, *Van Eyck*, plate 26.

10 Kenneth Clark, *The Nude: A Study of Ideal Art* (Harmondsworth, 1960),
pp. 300–334, Chapter Eight, 'The Alternative Convention'.

11 Röver-Kann, *Frauenbad*, pp. 18–20, fig. 5.

12 Winkler, *Zeichnungen*, vol. I, p. 97, no. 148, and pp. 106–7, no. 159;
and Strauss, *Drawings*, vol. I, pp. 444–5, 1498/1, and vol. II, 526–7,
1500/12, for two further overweight female nudes.

13 Joachim Sandrart, *Teutsche Akademie der Bau-, Bild- und Mahlerey-Künste*
(Nuremberg, 1675), p. 222.

14 Schoch, Mende and Scherbaum, *Das druckgraphische Werk*, vol. I,
pp. 61–4, no. 17 (entry by Rainer Schoch); and Bruce Edelstein and
Davide Gasparotto, *Miraculous Encounters: Pontormo from Drawing to Painting*,
exh. cat., Morgan Library and Museum, New York, and J. Paul Getty
Museum, Los Angeles (2018–19), pp. 114–17, no. 5 (entry by Giada
Damen), for its possible inspiration of Pontormo's *Visitation*.

15 Clark, *Nude*, p. 317, for the same point.

16 Schoch, Mende and Scherbaum, *Das druckgraphische Werk*, vol. I,
pp. 110–13, no. 39 (entry by Rainer Schoch).

17 Winkler, *Zeichnungen*, vol. I, pp. 180–84, nos 261–2; and Strauss,
Drawings, vol. II, pp. 580–83, 1501/7–8, for the drawings; and Walter
L. Strauss, ed., *The Complete Engravings, Etchings and Drypoints of Albrecht
Dürer* (New York, 1972), pp. 88–91, no. 42a–b; and Peter Parshall,
Stacey Sell and Judith Brodie, *The Unfinished Print*, exh. cat., National
Gallery of Art, Washington, DC (2001), pp. 14–15, fig. 3, for the trial
impressions.

18 Winkler, *Zeichnungen*, vol. II, p. 57, no. 333; and Strauss, *Drawings*, vol. II,
pp. 760–61, 1504/17.

19 Winkler, *Zeichnungen*, vol. II, pp. 57–8, nos 334–5; Strauss, *Drawings*,
    vol. II, pp. 594–5, 1502/2, and pp. 756–9, 1504/15–16; and Giulia
    Bartrum, *Albrecht Dürer and His Legacy*, exh. cat., British Museum,
    London (2002), pp. 152–3, nos 89–90.
20 Winkler, *Zeichnungen*, vol. II, p. 77, no. 359, and pp. 58–9, no. 336;
    Strauss, *Drawings*, vol. II, pp. 594–5, 1502/2, and pp. 754–5, 1504/13;
    and Bartrum, *Legacy*, pp. 151–3, nos 88 and 91.
21 Winkler, *Zeichnungen*, vol. II, p. 77, no. 359; and Strauss, *Drawings*, vol. II,
    pp. 592–3, 1502/1, identify them as rabbits, but Fritz Koreny, *Albrecht
    Dürer und die Tier- und Pflanzenstudien der Renaissance*, exh. cat., Albertina,
    Vienna (1985), pp. 134–5, no. 42; and Bartrum, *Legacy*, pp. 152–3,
    no. 91, correctly identify them as hares.
22 A. E. Popham, *The Drawings of Leonardo da Vinci* (London, 1946), p. 137,
    no. 185, for an example.
23 Fedja Anzelewsky, *Dürer: Das malerische Werk*, 2 vols (Berlin, 1991),
    vol. I, pp. 78–9, and pp. 212–16, nos 103–4, figs 90–92, and vol. II,
    plates 108–10, figs 121–4; and Norbert Wolf, *Dürer* (Munich, Berlin,
    London and New York, 2010), pp. 259–60, no. 34. See also Christian
    Schoen, *Albrecht Dürer. Adam und Eva: Die Gemälde, ihre Geschichte und
    Rezeption bei Lucas Cranach d. Ä. und Hans Baldung Grien* (Berlin, 2001).
24 Fedja Anzelewsky, *Dürer: His Art and Life* (London, 1980), p. 135; and
    Rupprich, *Nachlass*, vol. I, p. 256, for the letter of 30 July 1511 from
    Thurzo to Wolfgang Hoffmann in which he reports the purchase.
    See also Anzelewsky, *Das malerische Werk*, vol. I, pp. 254–6, no. 143,
    figs 133–4, and vol. II, plate 152, fig. 167, for Dürer's admittedly later
    portrait of *Jakob Fugger*.
25 Winkler, *Zeichnungen*, vol. II, pp. 106–8, nos 421–8, and pp. 112–13,
    no. 434; Strauss, *Drawings*, vol. II, pp. 750–53, 1504/11–12,
    pp. 980–87, 1506/51–5, and pp. 996–7, 1507/1; and Bartrum, *Legacy*,
    p. 163, nos 104–5, for both sheets dated 1506.
26 Winkler, *Zeichnungen*, vol. II, pp. 106–8, nos 422 and 428; and Strauss,
    Drawings, vol. II, pp. 752–3, 1504/12, and pp. 980–81, 1506/51.
27 Winkler, *Zeichnungen*, vol. II, pp. 106–8, nos 423–4 and 426–7; and
    Strauss, *Drawings*, vol. II, pp. 982–7, 1506/52–5.
28 Schoch, Mende and Scherbaum, *Das druckgraphische Werk*, vol. I,
    pp. 319–474, no. 277 (entry by Berthold Hinz); and Bartrum, *Legacy*,
    p. 222, no. 172.
29 Schoch, Mende and Scherbaum, *Das druckgraphische Werk*, vol. I, pp. 43–4,
    no. 8 (entry by Rainer Schoch); Winkler, *Zeichnungen*, vol. III,
    pp. 70–71, no. 645; and Strauss, *Drawings*, vol. III, pp. 1312–13, 1512/8.

30 Winkler, *Zeichnungen*, vol. I, pp. 54–5, nos 69–70, p. 56, no. 75, and
pp. 58–61, nos 78–81; and Strauss, *Drawings*, vol. I, pp. 272–3,
1495/4–6, pp. 284–9, 1495/12–13, 15, p. 292, 1495/17. See also
Christof Metzger, ed., *Albrecht Dürer*, exh. cat., Graphische Sammlung
Albertina, Vienna (2019–20), p. 180, for the important observation
that Dürer knew Venetian women wore *zoccoli* (wooden clogs) and
drew one on Winkler, *Zeichnungen*, vol. I, p. 55, no. 70; and Strauss,
Drawings, vol. I, pp. 270–71, 1495/5; and also for the use he made
of the figure on Winkler, *Zeichnungen*, vol. I, pp. 54–5, no. 69; and
Strauss, *Drawings*, vol. I, pp. 268–9, 1495/4, in his woodcut of the
Whore of Babylon in his *Apocalypse*.

31 Winkler, *Zeichnungen*, vol. IV, pp. 43–4, nos 826–8; Strauss, *Drawings*,
vol. IV, pp. 2066–7, 1521/37–9; and Susan Foister and Peter van den
Brink, *Dürer's Journeys: Travels of a Renaissance Artist*, exh. cat., National
Gallery, London (2021–2), p. 188, no. 74, and p. 189, fig. 101.

32 Cristina Acidini Luchinat, ed., *The Chapel of the Magi: Benozzo Gozzoli's
Frescoes in the Palazzo Medici-Riccardi, Florence* (London, 1994), p. 63, for
this detail. See also David Bindman and Henry Louis Gates Jr, eds,
The Image of the Black in Western Art, vol. II: *The Early Christian Era to the
Age of Discovery*, 2 parts (Cambridge, MA, and London, 2010), for a
magisterial overview of the whole subject, and part II,
pp. 195–6 and 277–9, figs 263–4, for specific references to Dürer.

33 Schoch, Mende and Scherbaum, *Das druckgraphische Werk*, vol. II,
pp. 512–14, no. A14 (entry by Rainer Schoch); Anzelewsky, *Das
malerische Werk*, vol. I, pp. 188–9, no. 82, and vol. II, plates 85–6,
figs 99–102; and Schoch, Mende and Scherbaum, *Das druckgraphische
Werk*, vol. II, pp. 512–14, no. A14 (entry by Rainer Schoch), and
pp. 484–5, no. 258 (entry by Rainer Schoch). See also Jean Devisse
and Michel Mollat, 'The Shield and the Crown', in *The Image of the
Black in Western Art*, vol. II, part II, ed. Bindman and Gates, pp. 31–40,
for the popularity of representations of black people in heraldry.

34 Winkler, *Zeichnungen*, vol. II, pp. 111–12, no. 431; Strauss, *Drawings*,
vol. II, pp. 1062–3, 1508/24; and Klaus Albrecht Schröder and Maria
Luise Sternath, *Albrecht Dürer*, exh. cat., Albertina, Vienna (2003),
pp. 386–7, no. 127 (entry by Maria Luise Sternath).

35 Rupprich, *Nachlass*, vol. I, p. 167; and Ashcroft, *Documentary Biography*,
vol. I, p. 577, for the diary entry.

36 Winkler, *Zeichnungen*, vol. IV, p. 40, no. 818; Strauss, *Drawings*, vol. IV,
pp. 2012–13, 1521/8; and Foister and Van den Brink, *Journeys*,
pp. 204 and 213, fig. 119.

37 Bindman and Gates, eds, *The Image of the Black in Western Art*, vol. II,
    part II, p. xv.
38 Foister and Van den Brink, *Journeys*, p. 213, for this quotation.
39 Winkler, *Zeichnungen*, vol. II, p. 86, no. 375, and pp. 8–9, nos 271–2;
    Strauss, *Drawings*, vol. II, pp. 890–91, 1505/27, and pp. 184–7,
    1503/16–17; and Bartrum, *Legacy*, pp. 156–7, no. 96, and pp. 146–7,
    nos 81–2.
40 Winkler, *Zeichnungen*, vol. II, pp. 110–11, no. 429; Strauss, *Drawings*,
    vol. II, pp. 1064–5, 1508/25; and Bartrum, *Legacy*, p. 165, no. 106.
41 Rupprich, *Nachlass*, vol. I, p. 152; and Ashcroft, *Documentary Biography*,
    vol. I, p. 557.
42 Anzelewsky, *Das malerische Werk*, vol. I, p. 59, and pp. 206–10, no. 98,
    figs 86–9, and vol. II, plate 101, fig. 114; and Isolde Lübbeke,
    The Thyssen-Bornemisza Collection: Early German Painting, 1350–1550
    (London, 1991), pp. 218–41, no. 50.
43 Winkler, *Zeichnungen*, vol. IV, p. 8, no. 749, and p. 40, no. 819; and
    Strauss, *Drawings*, vol. IV, pp. 1922–3, 1520/10, and pp. 1958–9,
    1520/28.
44 Winkler, *Zeichnungen*, vol. II, pp. 6–7, no. 268; Strauss, *Drawings*,
    vol. II, pp. 658–9, 1503/3; and Schoch, Mende and Scherbaum,
    Das druckgraphische Werk, vol. II, pp. 37–9, no. 99 (entry by Matthias
    Mende).
45 Dominique Cordellier and Paola Marini, *Pisanello: Le peintre aux sept
    vertus*, exh. cat., Musée du Louvre, Paris (1996), p. 76, nos 36–7,
    pp. 251–6, nos 155–65, p. 266, nos 168–9, pp. 348–9, nos 230–32,
    and p. 351, nos 233–4, for Pisanello and his circle; and Popham,
    Leonardo, pp. 102–3, nos 9–14, and p. 110, no. 63A, for the cats, and
    p. 112, nos 78–9, for the bear.
46 Koreny, *Tier- und Pflanzenstudien*. See also Colin Eisler, *Dürer's Animals*
    (Washington, DC, and London, 1991), for a comprehensive overview.
47 Metzger, ed., *Dürer*.
48 David Ekserdjian, 'La nascita dell'entomologia e gli inizi della
    natura morta', in *Natura morta: rappresentazione dell'oggetto – oggetto come
    rappresentazione*, ed. Costanza Barbieri and Damiana Frascarelli,
    Convegno internazionale di studi, Napoli, Accademia di Belle Arti,
    11–12 December 2008 (Naples, 2010), pp. 23–8, for an overview of
    the whole subject.
49 Koreny, *Tier- und Pflanzenstudien*, pp. 119–21, no. 36; and Ekserdjian,
    'La nascita dell'entomologia', pp. 23–8, p. 24. See also Marco Rossi,
    Giovannino de Grassi: La corte e la cattedrale (Cinisello Balsamo, 1995),

p. 50, fig. 42, for an earlier – but far less accurate – depiction of a
male stag beetle in flight by Giovannino de Grassi.

50 Winkler, *Zeichnungen*, vol. II, pp. 23–4, no. 296; Strauss, *Drawings*,
vol. II, pp. 696–7, 1503/22; Koreny, *Tier- und Pflanzenstudien*, pp. 114–18,
no. 35; and Schröder and Sternath, *Dürer*, pp. 278–81, no. 75, for the
drawing; and Anzelewsky, *Das malerische Werk*, vol. I, pp. 188–9,
no. 82, and vol. II, plates 85–6, figs 99–102, for the painting.

51 Strauss, *Drawings*, vol. I, pp. 210–11, 1494/8; and Metzger, ed.,
Dürer, pp. 148 and 450, no. 46.

52 Schoch, Mende and Scherbaum, *Das druckgraphische Werk*, vol. I,
pp. 29–31, no. 2 (entry by Rainer Schoch), where it is referred
to as a dragonfly in the title. See also Eisler, *Dürer's Animals*, p. 18,
where it is wrongly identified as a mayfly; and Walter L. Strauss,
ed., *The Complete Engravings, Etchings and Drypoints of Albrecht Dürer*
(New York, 1972), pp. 8–9, no. 4, where he notes, 'The dragonfly
has been variously identified as a grasshopper, a praying mantis and
a butterfly,' but fails to take the next step and acknowledge that it
is none of them. I am extremely grateful to George McGavin for
confirming my suspicions on this point.

53 Winkler, *Zeichnungen*, vol. I, pp. 67–8, no. 92; Strauss, *Drawings*, vol. I,
pp. 302–5, 1495/22; and Koreny, *Tier- und Pflanzenstudien*, p. 22, fig. 22.

54 Schoch, Mende and Scherbaum, *Das druckgraphische Werk*, vol. I,
pp. 73–5, no. 21 (entry by Rainer Schoch); Winkler, *Zeichnungen*,
vol. III, pp. 77–8, no. 662; and Strauss, *Drawings*, vol. III, pp. 1458–9,
1514/34.

55 Anzelewsky, *Das malerische Werk*, vol. I, pp. 188–9, no. 82, and vol. II,
plates 85–6, figs 99–102.

56 Winkler, *Zeichnungen*, vol. III, pp. 60–61, no. 616; Strauss, *Drawings*,
vol. II, pp. 596–7, 1502/3; Koreny, *Tier- und Pflanzenstudien*, pp. 48–9,
no. 7; and Bernard Aikema and Andrew John Martin, *Dürer e il
rinascimento tra Germania e Italia*, exh. cat., Palazzo Reale, Milan (2018),
pp. 249 and 360–61, no. 3/19 (entry by Susanne Christine Martin).

57 Koreny, *Tier- und Pflanzenstudien*, pp. 40–47, no. 6; and David
Ekserdjian, *Still Life before Still Life* (New Haven, CT, and London,
2018), pp. 8–10, fig. 5.

58 Winkler, *Zeichnungen*, vol. III, pp. 59–60, no. 615; Strauss, *Drawings*,
vol. II, pp. 612–13, 1502/11; and Koreny, *Tier- und Pflanzenstudien*,
pp. 54–5, no. 10.

59 Koreny, *Tier- und Pflanzenstudien*, pp. 56–61, nos 11–13.

60 Ibid., p. 70.

61 Winkler, *Zeichnungen*, vol. I, p. 186, no. 266; Strauss, *Drawings*, vol. II,
    pp. 640–41, 1502/25; and Bartrum, *Legacy*, pp. 138–40, nos 72–3.
62 Winkler, *Zeichnungen*, vol. III, pp. 57–8, no. 614; Strauss, *Drawings*,
    vol. II, pp. 610–11, 1502/10; and Koreny, *Tier- und Pflanzenstudien*,
    pp. 70–73 and pp. 84–5, no. 22.
63 Winkler, *Zeichnungen*, vol. I, pp. 166–7, plate XXIII; Strauss, *Drawings*,
    vol. IV, pp. 2072–3, 1521/40; and Koreny, *Tier- und Pflanzenstudien*,
    pp. 80–81, no. 20.
64 Winkler, *Zeichnungen*, vol. I, pp. 168–9, no. 244, and p. 167, no. 240;
    Strauss, *Drawings*, vol. II, pp. 604–5, 1502/7; and Koreny, *Tier- und
    Pflanzenstudien*, p. 20, fig. 14, and p. 117, fig. 35.9. Koreny, *Tier- und
    Pflanzenstudien*, p. 116, for the erroneous claim that the drawing *Stork*
    appears in the engraving *Adam and Eve*.
65 Jane Campbell Hutchison, *Albrecht Dürer: A Biography* (Princeton, NJ,
    1990), p. 73, for this anecdote.
66 Winkler, *Zeichnungen*, vol. I, pp. 167–8, no. 241; Strauss, *Drawings*, vol. II,
    pp. 504–5, 1500/1; and Bartrum, *Legacy*, pp. 140–42, nos 74–5.
67 Winkler, *Zeichnungen*, vol. I, p. 96, no. 145; Strauss, *Drawings*, vol. I,
    pp. 412–13, 1496/11; and Bartrum, *Legacy*, pp. 110–11, nos 41–2.
68 Winkler, *Zeichnungen*, vol. I, pp. 167–8, nos 239 and 242–3, vol. II,
    pp. 78–81, nos 362, 364–7 and 369; Strauss, *Drawings*, vol. I,
    pp. 350–55, 1495/45–7, pp. 410–11, 1496/9, pp. 568–71, 1501/1–2,
    vol. II, pp. 586–9, 1501/10–11, vol. VI, pp. 3022–3, no. XW.369;
    and Bartrum, *Legacy*, pp. 153–5, nos 92–4.
69 Winkler, *Zeichnungen*, vol. I, p. 171, no. 248; Strauss, *Drawings*, vol. II,
    pp. 594–5, 1502/2; and Koreny, *Tier- und Pflanzenstudien*, pp. 136–7,
    no. 43, for the original, and pp. 138–49, nos 44–9, for no fewer than
    six copies.
70 Koreny, *Tier- und Pflanzenstudien*, pp. 96–7, no. 28.
71 Ibid., pp. 166 and 168–9, no. 57; and Foister and Van den Brink,
    Journeys, pp. 197–8, no. 85.
72 Rupprich, *Nachlass*, vol. I, p. 155; *Schriften*, p. 65.
73 Winkler, *Zeichnungen*, vol. IV, pp. 20–21, nos 779 and 781, and pp. 42–3,
    no. 824; Strauss, *Drawings*, vol. IV, pp. 2020–23, 1521/12–13, and vol. VI,
    pp. 3080–81, no. XW.824; and Koreny, *Tier- und Pflanzenstudien*,
    pp. 170–71, nos 58–9, for more lions. See also Rupprich, *Nachlass*,
    vol. I, p. 168; and Ashcroft, *Documentary Biography*, vol. I, p. 578.
74 Philip Hoare, *Albert and the Whale* (London, 2021), for a charmingly
    idiosyncratic account of this quest.
75 Bartrum, *Legacy*, pp. 208–9, no. 153, and pp. 285–7, nos 242–3.

76 Max J. Friedländer, *Landscape – Portrait – Still Life: Their Origin and Development* (Oxford, 1949), for an overview of the rise of landscape and still life in the period.

77 Winkler, *Zeichnungen*, vol. III, pp. 62–3, no. 620; Strauss, *Drawings*, vol. III, pp. 1438–9, 1514/23; and Schoch, Mende and Scherbaum, *Das druckgraphische Werk*, vol. I, pp. 179–85, no. 71 (entry by Matthias Mende).

78 Winkler, *Zeichnungen*, vol. III, pp. 69–70, nos 637–44, and vol. IV, pp. 21–2, nos 783–5; and Strauss, *Drawings*, vol. III, pp. 1084–5, 1509/6–7, pp. 1284–5, 1511/16, pp. 1288–9, 1511/18, pp. 1434–5, 1514/21, pp. 1596–9, 1515/66–8.

79 Pächt, *Van Eyck*, plate 17 and pp. 187–8, fig. 111.

80 Aikema and Martin, *Rinascimento*, pp. 236 and 357, no. 3/12 (entry by A. Polati), for the drawing; and Davide Gasparotto, ed., *Giovanni Bellini: Landscapes of Faith in Renaissance Venice*, exh. cat., J. Paul Getty Museum, Los Angeles (2017–18), pp. 116–25, no. 11 (entry by Antonio Mazzotta), for the painting.

81 Claire Pace, *Lives of Adam Elsheimer* (London, 2006), p. 39.

82 Ibid., pp. 77–80.

83 Winkler, *Zeichnungen*, vol. II, pp. 67–8, no. 346; Strauss, *Drawings*, vol. II, pp. 710–11, 1503/29, for the *Great Piece of Turf*; and Koreny, *Tier- und Pflanzenstudien*, pp. 176–209, nos 61–73, and Metzger, ed., *Dürer*, pp. 146–61, nos 49–55, for two diametrically opposed views of the whole topic.

84 Rupprich, *Nachlass*, vol. I, p. 85–7, no. 32, and Ashcroft, *Documentary Biography*, vol. I, p. 535–9, no. 154, for the letter; and Foister and Van den Brink, *Journeys*, p. 50, for this quotation. See also Rupprich, *Nachlass*, vol. I, pp. 159 and 162; and Ashcroft, *Documentary Biography*, vol. I, pp. 565 and 569, for pairs of spectacles bought on the Netherlandish journey.

85 Christopher Isherwood, *Goodbye to Berlin* [1939] (London, 2003), p. 9, 'I am a camera with its shutter open, quite passive, recording, not thinking.'

86 Winkler, *Zeichnungen*, vol. I, pp. 47–8, nos 63–4, pp. 84–5, no. 112, and p. 89, no. 121, Strauss, *Drawings*, vol. I, pp. 204–7, 1494/5–6, pp. 1396–9, 1496/2–3, for the trees; and Winkler, *Zeichnungen*, vol. I, pp. 80–84, nos 106–11, and Strauss, *Drawings*, vol. I, pp. 236–7, 1494/19, p. 360, 1495/40, pp. 360–67, 1495/50–53, for the quarries.

87 Winkler, *Zeichnungen*, vol. I, pp. 46–7, nos 61–2; Strauss, *Drawings*, vol. I, pp. 200–203, 1496/3–4; and Anzelewsky, *Art*, p. 41, plate 26; *West*

European Drawing of XVI–XX *Centuries: Kunsthalle Collection in Bremen: Catalogue* (Moscow, 1992), pp. 88–9; Metzger, ed., *Dürer*, p. 141, no. 41; and Schröder and Sternath, *Dürer*, p. 185, no. 30, for colour illustrations.

88 Winkler, *Zeichnungen*, vol. I, pp. 52–4, nos 66–8; Strauss, *Drawings*, vol. I, pp. 200–203, 1496/3–4; and Metzger, ed., *Dürer*, pp. 127–9, nos 36–8.

89 Winkler, *Zeichnungen*, vol. I, pp. 73–4, no. 99; Strauss, *Drawings*, vol. I, pp. 334–5, 1495/37; and Metzger, ed., *Dürer*, p. 130, figs 5–6.

90 Foister and Van den Brink, *Journeys*, pp. 147–226, for the whole subject.

91 Winkler, *Zeichnungen*, vol. IV, pp. 41–2, nos 821–2; and Strauss, *Drawings*, vol. IV, pp. 1926–7, 1520/20–21.

92 Winkler, *Zeichnungen*, vol. IV, pp. 14–15, nos 762–4, pp. 17–18, nos 768 and 772; Strauss, *Drawings*, vol. IV, pp. 1942–3, 1520/20, pp. 1496–7, 1520/22, pp. 2100–101, 1521/59, for the former; and Winkler, *Zeichnungen*, vol. IV, pp. 15–17, nos 765 and 769, and pp. 19–20, nos 774 and 778; Strauss, *Drawings*, vol. IV, pp. 1962–3, 1520/30, pp. 1968–9, 1520/33, pp. 1972–3, 1520/35, and pp. 2102–3, 1521/60, for the latter.

93 Foister and Van den Brink, *Journeys*, p. 197, no. 85. See also Franz Unterkircher, *Le Livre du cueur d'amours espris* (London, 1975), fol. 47v, for an incomparably more suggestive rendering of twilight.

94 Jean Lognon, Raymond Cazelles and Millard Meiss, *The 'Très Riches Heures' of Jean, Duke of Berry* (New York, 1969), pp. 107 and 115; Pächt, *Van Eyck*, plate 17 and pp. 185–6, fig. 110; and Unterkircher, *Livre*, fols. 2, 12v, 55.

95 Lorne Campbell, *The Fifteenth Century Netherlandish Schools*, National Gallery Catalogues (New Haven, CT, and London, 1998), pp. 232–9 and 254–9.

96 Joseph Leo Koerner, *Bosch and Bruegel: From Enemy Painting to Everyday Life* (Princeton, NJ, 2017).

2 Study, Travel and Influence

1 Katherine Crawford Luber, *Albrecht Dürer and the Venetian Renaissance* (Cambridge, 2005).

2 Isolde Lübbeke, *The Thyssen-Bornemisza Collection: Early German Painting, 1350–1550* (London, 1991), pp. 218–41, no. 50, for an unusually positive reading.

3 Hans Rupprich, ed., *Dürer: Schriftlicher Nachlass*, 3 vols (Berlin, 1956–69), vol. I, p. 31; and Jeffrey Ashcroft, *Albrecht Dürer: Documentary Biography*, 2 vols (New Haven, CT, and London, 2017), vol. I, p. 35.

4 Lübbeke, *Thyssen-Bornemisza Collection*, pp. 392–5, no. 90.

5 Rupprich, *Schriftlicher Nachlass*, vol. I, p. 31; and Ashcroft, *Albrecht Dürer: Documentary Biography*, vol. I, p. 35.

6 Rupprich, *Schriftlicher Nachlass*, vol. I, p. 31; and Ashcroft, *Albrecht Dürer: Documentary Biography*, vol. I, p. 35.

7 Fedja Anzelewsky, *Dürer: Das malerische Werk*, 2 vols (Berlin, 1991), vol. I, pp. 117–20, nos 2–4, and vol. II, plates 1–4, figs 1–4.

8 Fritz Koreny, 'A Coloured Study by Martin Schongauer and the Development of the Depiction of Nature from Van der Weyden to Dürer', *Burlington Magazine*, CXXXIII/1062 (1991), pp. 588–97, esp. p. 589.

9 Charles Ilsley Minott, *Martin Schongauer* (New York, 1971), pp. 66–7, plate 9, and pp. 100–101, plates 54.1–11.

10 Friedrich Winkler, *Die Zeichnungen Albrecht Dürers*, 4 vols (Berlin, 1936–9), vol. I, pp. 15–17, nos 13–15; and Walter L. Strauss, *The Complete Drawings of Albrecht Dürer*, 6 vols and 2 supplements (New York, 1974), vol. VI, pp. 2898–902, nos XW.13–15.

11 Koreny, *Schongauer*.

12 Winkler, *Zeichnungen*, vol. I, pp. 13–14, no. 9; and Strauss, *Drawings*, vol. II, pp. 478–9, App. I:I, for the drawing; and see also Stephanie Buck and Stephanie Porras, eds, *The Young Dürer: Drawing the Figure*, exh. cat., Courtauld Gallery, London (2013–14), pp. 162–5, no. 12, for a sheet that Dürer inscribed with an attribution to one Anton Peurer and dated 1487.

13 Fedja Anzelewsky, 'Eine Gruppe von Malern und Zeichnern aus Dürers Jugendjahren', *Jahrbuch der Berliner Museen*, XXVII (1985), pp. 35–59; and Lübbeke, *Thyssen-Bornemisza Collection*, pp. 150–55, no. 34.

14 Rainer Schoch, Matthias Mende and Anna Scherbaum, *Albrecht Dürer: Das druckgraphische Werk*, 3 vols (Munich, London and New York, 2001–4), vol. I, pp. 247–8, no. AI (entry by Rainer Schoch).

15 Alan Shestack, *Master LCz and Master WB* (New York, 1971), pp. 20–21, figs 7–8, for the comparison. Both beasts are shown in the background of Hugo van der Goes's *Portinari Altarpiece*, but there they are en route to the Nativity.

16   Julia Zaunbauer, 'Artistic Beginnings on the Upper Rhine',
     in *Albrecht Dürer*, ed. Christof Metzger, exh. cat., Albertina,
     Vienna (2019–20), pp. 85–6; and Schoch, Mende and
     Scherbaum, *Das druckgraphische Werk*, vol. III, pp. 33–6, no. 261
     (entry by Rainer Schoch), and pp. 37–49, no. 262 (entry by
     Rainer Schoch).

17   Jane Campbell Hutchison, *Albrecht Dürer: A Biography* (Princeton,
     NJ, 1990), p. 31, for these sources.

18   Winkler, *Zeichnungen*, vol. I, pp. 90–93, nos 122–41; Strauss,
     Drawings, vol. I, pp. 238–55, 1494/20–29, and pp. 374–89,
     1495/57–64; and Jay A. Levenson, Konrad Oberhuber and
     Jacquelyn L. Sheehan, *Early Italian Engravings from the National Gallery
     of Art*, exh. cat., National Gallery of Art, Washington, DC (1973),
     pp. 81–157, nos 14–66.

19   Levenson, Oberhuber and Sheehan, *Engravings*, pp. 130–31, no. 48;
     Winkler, *Zeichnungen*, vol. I, p. 93, no. 141; and Strauss, *Drawings*,
     vol. I, pp. 222–5, 1494/12–13.

20   F. Carlo Schmid, 'Prints after the Antique up to 1869', *Print
     Quarterly*, XXXVIII/2 (2021), pp. 184–7, figs 129–30, for their
     respective treatments of *Logic*. See also Winkler, *Zeichnungen*, vol. I,
     p. 90, for this connection.

21   Levenson, Oberhuber and Sheehan, *Engravings*, pp. 186–7, no. 74,
     and pp. 188–9, no. 76; Winkler, *Zeichnungen*, vol. I, pp. 45–6,
     nos 59–60; Metzger, ed., *Dürer*, pp. 192–204, nos 73–6; and
     Erika Simon, 'Dürer und Mantegna 1494', *Anzeiger des Germanischen
     Nationalmuseums* (1971–2), pp. 21–40.

22   Metzger, ed., *Dürer*, esp. p. 198.

23   Levenson, Oberhuber and Sheehan, *Engravings*, pp. 182–5, no. 73;
     and Schoch, Mende and Scherbaum, *Das druckgraphische Werk*,
     vol. II, pp. 509–10, no. A12 (entry by Rainer Schoch).

24   David Ekserdjian, 'Mantegna's Lost *Death of Orpheus*', in
     Gedenkschrift für Richard Harprath, ed. Wolfgang Liebenwein and
     Anchise Tempestini (Munich and Berlin, 1998), pp. 144–9.

25   David Landau and Peter Parshall, *The Renaissance Print, 1470–1550*
     (New Haven, CT, and London, 1994), pp. 104–8, figs 92–4.

26   Marzia Faietti, '*Aemulatio versus simulation*: Dürer oltre Mantegna',
     in *Dürer e l'Italia*, ed. Kristina Herrmann Fiore, exh. cat, Scuderie
     del Quirinale, Rome (2007), pp. 81–7, esp. p. 81.

27   Winkler, *Zeichnungen*, vol. I, pp. 61–2, no. 82; Strauss, *Drawings*,
     vol. I, pp. 264–5, 1495/2.

28 Alison Wright, *The Pollaiuolo Brothers: The Arts of Florence and Rome* (New Haven, CT, and London, 2005), pp. 417–18, figs 343–4, for links between the two artists.

29 Winkler, *Zeichnungen*, vol. I, pp. 62–3, no. 84; and Strauss, *Drawings*, vol. I, pp. 266–7, 1495/3, for the drawing; and Gigetta Dalli Regoli, *Lorenzo di Credi* (Cremona, 1966), pp. 159–60, no. 127, fig. 167; and Federico Zeri and Elizabeth Gardner, *A Catalogue of the Collection of the Metropolitan Museum of Art. Italian Paintings: Florentine School* (New York, 1971), p. 69, and plate 91, for the painting.

30 Winkler, *Zeichnungen*, vol. I, pp. 63–4, no. 86; and Walter L. Strauss, *The Complete Drawings of Albrecht Dürer*, 6 vols and 2 supplements (New York, 1974), vol. I, p. 292, no. 1495/17.

31 See https://briquet-online.at/wzrep/stevenson/stevenson67.pdf, under no. 4412. I am immensely grateful to David Landau for pointing this out to me.

32 Giulia Bartrum, *Albrecht Dürer and His Legacy*, exh. cat., British Museum, London (2002), p. 243, no. 194; and Andrew Butterfield, ed., *Verrocchio: Sculptor and Painter of Renaissance Florence*, exh. cat., National Gallery of Art, Washington, DC (2019–20), pp. 10–11, fig. 8. See also Schoch, Mende and Scherbaum, *Das druckgraphische Werk*, vol. I, pp. 71–2, for the connection.

33 Butterfield, *Verrocchio*, pp. 260–65, no. 39 (entry by Lorenza Melli); and Gigetta Dalli Regoli, *Verrocchio, Lorenzo di Credi, Francesco di Simone Ferrucci* (Paris, 2003), pp. 81–2, no. 28. See also David Ekserdjian, 'Dürer and Raphael – Raphael and Dürer', in *Dürer Unseen*, ed. Giulia Bartrum (London, 2022), pp. 95–111, and esp. pp. 99–100, fig. 1; and David Ekserdjian, 'Raphael's Small Madonnas and Holy Families: A Question of Influence', in *Studi raffaelleschi*, I, ed. Barbara Agosti, Anna Maria Ambrosini Massari, Silvia Ginzburg (Urbino, 2022), pp. 10–31, especially p. 15, for the importance of Dürer's print for Raphael's *Terranuova Madonna* in Berlin.

34 Bartrum, *Legacy*, p. 242, no. 193.

35 Winkler, *Zeichnungen*, vol. I, pp. 79–89, nos 106–21; Strauss, *Drawings*, vol. I, pp. 263–4, 1494/19, pp. 340–41, 1495/40, pp. 360–67, 1495/50–53, pp. 394–401, 1496/1–4, pp. 404–7, 1496/6–7, pp. 418–19, 1496/13, vol. II, pp. 520–23, 1500/9–10, vol. VI, pp. 2912–13, no. XW.120; and Metzger, ed., *Dürer*, pp. 140–43, nos 34 and 41.

36 John Shearman, *Raphael in Early Modern Sources, 1483–1602*, 2 vols (New Haven, CT, and London, 2003), vol. I, pp. 86–92, esp. p. 88.

37 David Ekserdjian, 'A Dürer Drawing and a Classical Torso', *Master Drawings*, XXXII/3 (1994), pp. 273–4.

38 David Ekserdjian, 'The Northern Renaissance Response to the Antique before the Sack of Rome', *Colnaghi Studies Journal*, VIII (2021), pp. 14–29.

39 Schoch, Mende and Scherbaum, *Das druckgraphische Werk*, vol. II, pp. 188–93, nos 157–8 (entry by Anke Fröhlich).

40 Phyllis Pray Bober and Ruth Rubinstein, *Renaissance Artists and Antique Sculpture: A Handbook of Sources* (London, 1986), pp. 166–8, no. 132; and Rainald Grosshans, *Maerten van Heemskerck: Die Gemälde* (Berlin, 1980), fig. 186, for a pen drawing of the Belvedere Torso by Heemskerck showing it on the ground.

41 Schoch, Mende and Scherbaum, *Das druckgraphische Werk*, vol. II, pp. 191–3, no. 158 (entry by Anke Fröhlich); and Ekserdjian, 'The Northern Renaissance Response to the Antique', pp. 19–21.

42 Bober and Rubinstein, *Antique Sculpture*, pp. 71–2, no. 28.

43 Winkler, *Zeichnungen*, vol. I, pp. 180–84, nos 262–3, and vol. II, p. 57, no. 333; and Strauss, *Drawings*, vol. II, pp. 582–3, 1501/8, pp. 760–61, 1504/17, and vol. VI, pp. 3008–9, no. XW.263, for the drawings; and Schoch, Mende and Scherbaum, *Das druckgraphische Werk*, vol. I, pp. 110–13, no. 39 (entry by Rainer Schoch), for the print. See also Joseph Leo Koerner, *The Moment of Self-Portraiture in German Renaissance Art* (Chicago, IL, and London, 1993), pp. 192–5, figs 100–101, for the connection.

44 Schoch, Mende and Scherbaum, *Das druckgraphische Werk*, vol. I, pp. 169–73, no. 69 (entry by Matthias Mende), for the print.

45 Winkler, *Zeichnungen*, vol. II, pp. 77–8, no. 361; and Strauss, *Drawings*, vol. II, pp. 708–9, 1503/28.

46 Winkler, *Zeichnungen*, vol. IV, p. 69, no. 884; and Strauss, *Drawings*, vol. IV, pp. 2118–19, 1521/68, for the sheet; and Arnold Nesselrath, 'Albrecht Dürer's Silverpoint Sketchbook', in Susan Foister and Peter van den Brink, *Dürer's Journeys: Travels of a Renaissance Artist*, exh. cat., National Gallery, London (2021), pp. 180–81, fig. 98 and no. 71, for the link.

47 Dominique Cordellier and Bernadette Py, *Musée du Louvre, inventaire général des dessins italiens: Raphaël, son Atelier, ses copistes* (Paris, 1992), pp. 457 and 459, no. 789 recto, for a comparable pose derived from a Roman coin.

48 Anzelewsky, *Das malerische Werk*, vol. I, pp. 189–90, no. 84, and vol. II, plate 87, fig. 99; Anchise Tempestini, *Giovanni Bellini: Catalogo completo*

dei dipinti (Florence, 1992), pp. 150–53, no. 51, for the prototype; and
David Ekserdjian, 'Spigolature intorno al "Catalogo generale dei
dipinti e delle miniature delle collezioni civiche veronesi" (2010)',
Verona illustrata, 28 (2015), pp. 35–9, esp. p. 37, for the date.

49 Michael Levey, *Albrecht Dürer* (London, 1964), p. 26; and Tempestini,
Bellini, pp. 172–7, no. 60.

50 Campbell Hutchison, *Biography*, pp. 71–2.

51 Ernst Ullmann and Elvira Pradel, *Albrecht Dürer: Schriften und Briefe*
(Berlin, 1984), pp. 108–10, letter of 2 April 1506.

52 Peter Humfrey, *The Altarpiece in Renaissance Venice* (New Haven, CT, and
London, 1993), pp. 120–21, and plate 103.

53 Anzelewsky, *Das malerische Werk*, vol. I, pp. 191–202, no. 93, and vol. II,
plates 91–6, figs 104–9, for the *Madonna of the Rose-Garlands;* and
Terisio Pignatti, *Giorgione: Complete Edition* (London, 1971), pp. 102–3,
no. 15, for Giorgione and Titian's work on the Fondaco.

54 Olga Kotková, '"The Feast of the Rose Garlands": What Remains of
Dürer?', *Burlington Magazine*, CXLIV/1186 (2002), pp. 4–13.

55 Bernard Aikema, 'La pala di Cingoli', in *Lorenzo Lotto: Atti del Convegno
Internazionale di Studi per il V Centenario della Nascita (Asolo, 1980)*, ed. Pietro
Zampetti and Vittorio Sgarbi (Venice, 1981), pp. 443–56, esp. p. 444.

56 Anna Padoa Rizzo, 'Firenze e Europa nel Quattrocento: la "Vergine
del Rosario" di Cosimo Rosselli', in *Studi di Storia dell'Arte in onore di
Mina Gregori*, ed. M. Boskovits (Florence, 1994), pp. 64–9, esp. p. 67,
fig. 5, for an example dated 1477.

57 Peter Humfrey, *Lorenzo Lotto* (New Haven, CT, and London, 1997),
p. 131, fig. 132, for an example of circa 1510 by Wolf Traut.

58 John Marciari and Suzanne Boorsch, *Francesco Vanni: Art in Late
Renaissance Siena*, exh. cat., Yale University Art Gallery, New Haven,
CT (2013–14), p. 216, fig. 79a. Anna B. Jameson, *Legends of the Madonna
as Represented in the Fine Arts* (London, 1903), p. 65, for the erroneous
claim that the iconography did not exist in Italy prior to the Battle
of Lepanto in 1571 and the institution of the Feast of the Rosary.

59 Humfrey, *Altarpiece*, pp. 262–6, and plates 252–3.

60 David Ekserdjian, *The Italian Renaissance Altarpiece: Between Icon and
Narrative* (New Haven, CT, and London, 2021), pp. 61–107, for the
whole subject of contracts.

61 Humfrey, *Altarpiece*, p. 92, and plate 80.

62 Ibid., pp. 82–3, and plates 73–4, also illustrating a second example
of the type.

63 Ekserdjian, *Altarpiece*, pp. 110–16, for the *sacra conversazione*.

64 Winkler, *Zeichnungen*, vol. II, pp. 155–6, no. 509; and Strauss, *Drawings*,
    vol. III, pp. 1254–5, 1511/1.

65 Winkler, *Zeichnungen*, vol. II, pp. 89–97, nos 380–401; Strauss,
    Drawings, vol. II, pp. 914–45, 1506/9–30; and Metzger, ed., *Dürer*,
    pp. 272–9 and 456–7, nos 111–18.

66 John Steer, *Alvise Vivarini: His Art and Influence* (Cambridge, 1982),
    pp. 168–9, no. 43, and p. 229, plate 13.

67 Kotková, '"Feast of the Rose Garlands"', p. 4.

68 Ibid., where nothing is made of this.

69 Rupprich, *Nachlass*, vol. I, pp. 54–7, for the letters of 8 and 23
    September 1506.

70 Caroline Campbell, Dagmar Korbacher, Neville Rowley and Sarah
    Vowles, *Mantegna and Bellini*, exh. cat., National Gallery, London, and
    Gemäldegalerie, Staatliche Museen zu Berlin (2018–19), pp. 226–7,
    fig. 220; and Schoch, Mende and Scherbaum, *Das druckgraphische Werk*,
    vol. I, pp. 45–8, no. 9 (entry by Rainer Schoch).

71 Enrico Maria dal Pozzolo, *Giorgione* (Milan, 2009), p. 159, fig. 118,
    and p. 163, fig. 122.

72 Anzelewsky, *Das malerische Werk*, vol. I, pp. 202–3, no. 94, and
    pp. 206–10, no. 98, and vol. II, plates 97–101, figs 110–14.

73 Hans Rupprich, ed., *Dürer: Schriftlicher Nachlass*, 3 vols (Berlin,
    1956–69), vol. I, pp. 56–8, no. 9; and Jeffrey Ashcroft, *Albrecht Dürer:
    Documentary Biography*, 2 vols (New Haven, CT, and London, 2017),
    vol. I, pp. 163–6, no. 29.9, letter of 23 September 1506.

74 Anzelewsky, *Das malerische Werk*, vol. I, pp. 206–8, figs 86–9.
    See also Lübbeke, *Thyssen-Bornemisza Collection*, pp. 218–41, no. 50.

75 Campbell Hutchison, *Biography*, pp. 88–90, for this episode, and
    Rupprich, *Schriftlicher Nachlass*, vol. I, pp. 52–4, no. 7; and Ashcroft,
    Documentary Biography, vol. I, pp. 150–58, no. 29.7.

76 Sixten Ringbom, *Icon to Narrative: The Rise of the Dramatic Close-Up in
    Fifteenth-Century Devotional Painting*, 2nd edn (Doornspijk, 1983); and
    Cristina Quattrini, *Bernardino Luini: Catalogo generale delle opere* (Turin,
    2019), pp. 400–402, no. 163.

77 Eckhart Knab, Erwin Mitsch and Konrad Oberhuber, *Raphael: Die
    Zeichnungen* (Stuttgart, 1983), p. 629, no. 504.

78 Arnold Nesselrath, 'Raphael's Gift to Dürer', *Master Drawings*, XXXI/3
    (1993), pp. 376–89, esp. p. 377.

79 Rolf Quednau, 'Raphael und "alcune stampe di maniera tedesca"',
    Zeitschrift für Kunstgeschichte, XLVI (1983), pp. 129–73, esp. p. 131, figs
    1–2; and Giorgio Vasari, *Le opere di Giorgio Vasari con nuove annotazioni e*

commenti di Gaetano Milanesi, 8 vols and index (Florence, 1878–85),
vol. V, p. 401.

80   Vasari, *Vite*, vol. IV, pp. 353–4, for the quotation, and vol. V, p. 551,
for a second account of the portrait.

81   Vasari, *Vite*, vol. IV, p. 354; and Quednau, 'Raphael und "alcune stampe
di maniera tedesca"', pp. 129–37; David Ekserdjian, 'Establishing a
Norm for the High Renaissance: Raphael and the Dissemination of
a Style', in *Modello, regola, ordine: Parcours normatifs dans l'Italie du
Cinquecento*, ed. Hélène Miesse and Gianluca Valenti (Rennes, 2018),
pp. 217–35, esp. pp. 226–7; Ekserdjian, *Dürer and Raphael – Raphael and
Dürer*, for Raphael and Dürer more generally; and David
Ekserdjian, *Raphael's Small Madonnas and Holy Families* (Urbino, 2022),
p. 17, for this specific connection.

82   Jürg Meyer zur Capellen, *Raphael: The Paintings*, 3 vols (Landshut,
2001–9), vol. II, pp. 227–32, no. 30, for the painting; and Winkler,
Zeichnungen, vol. IV, p. 54, no. 852; Strauss, *Drawings*, vol. IV, pp. 2116–
17, 1521/67; and Peter van den Brink, 'A Tale of Two Drawings:
Albrecht Dürer and Gossart's Lost Middelburg Altarpiece', in
*Ingenium at Labor: Studia ofiarowane Profesorowi Antoniemu Ziembie z okazji 60.
Urodzin* (Warsaw, 2020), pp. 109–17, esp. pp. 112–13, figs 4–5, for
the drawing and its association with Raphael.

83   Winkler, *Zeichnungen*, vol. III, p. 50, no. 594; and Strauss, *Drawings*,
vol. III, pp. 1618–19, 1515/78, for the drawing; and Metzger, ed.,
Dürer, pp. 240–47, for the whole argument, which includes a further
– and in my opinion less convincing – association. See also Winkler,
Zeichnungen, vol. II, pp. 136–7, no. 474; and Strauss, *Drawings*, vol. II,
pp. 1078–9, 1509/3, for another formally related *Dead Christ*.

84   Winkler, *Zeichnungen*, vol. IV, p. 28, no. 796; and Strauss, *Drawings*, vol. IV,
pp. 2028–9, 1521/16, for the drawing; and Meyer zur Capellen,
Raphael, vol. II, pp. 233–46, no. 31, for the *Baglioni Entombment*.

85   Innis H. Shoemaker and Elizabeth Broun, *The Engravings of
Marcantonio Raimondi*, exh. cat., Spencer Museum of Art, Lawrence,
KS, Ackland Art Museum, Chapel Hill, NC, and Wellesley College
Art Museum, Wellesley, MA (1981–2), pp. 88–9, no. 18; and Schoch,
Mende and Scherbaum, *Das druckgraphische Werk*, vol. II, pp. 512–14,
no. A14 (entry by Rainer Schoch). See also Ekserdjian, 'Establishing
a Norm', p. 227, for the connection.

86   Shoemaker and Broun, *Marcantonio*, pp. 94–5, no. 20, for the print;
and David Piper, *Treasures of the Ashmolean Museum: An Illustrated Souvenir
of the Collections* (Oxford, 1995), p. 27, no. 23, for the sculpture.

87 Rupprich, *Schriftlicher Nachlass*, vol. I, p. 158; and Ashcroft, *Documentary Biography*, vol. I, p. 563.

88 Rupprich, *Schriftlicher Nachlass*, vol. I, p. 168; and Ashcroft, *Documentary Biography*, vol. I, p. 578.

89 Rupprich, *Schriftlicher Nachlass*, vol. I, p. 160; and Ashcroft, *Documentary Biography*, vol. I, p. 565.

90 Winkler, *Zeichnungen*, vol. IV, p. 16, no. 766; Strauss, *Drawings*, vol. IV, pp. 1950–51, 1520/24; and Foister and Van den Brink, *Journeys*, p. 174, figs 92–3, for the drawing and the bronze; and Rupprich, *Schriftlicher Nachlass*, vol. I, p. 168; and Ashcroft, *Documentary Biography*, vol. I, p. 577, for Michelangelo.

91 Van den Brink, 'A Tale of Two Drawings'.

92 Rupprich, *Schriftlicher Nachlass*, vol. I, pp. 174 and 154; and Ashcroft, *Documentary Biography*, vol. I, pp. 585 and 565.

93 Rupprich, *Schriftlicher Nachlass*, vol. I, p. 155; and Ashcroft, *Documentary Biography*, vol. I, p. 560.

94 Julius Held, *Dürers Wirkung auf die niederländische Kunst seiner Zeit* (The Hague, 1931); and Fritz Koreny, 'Albrecht Dürer und die Niederlände', in *El siglo de Durero: Problemas historiográficos*, ed. Mar Borobia (Madrid, 2008), pp. 333–44.

95 David Ekserdjian, *Parmigianino* (New Haven, CT, and London, 2006), pp. 25–6, figs 13–14, where further derivations are also given.

96 David Ekserdjian, 'A Print Source for Botticelli: A Devil by the Master E.S.', *Apollo*, CXLVIII/441 (1998), pp. 15–16; Pietro Scarpellini, *Perugino* (Milan, 1984), p. 85, no. 48, and p. 173, fig. 77; and Kim W. Woods, *Making Renaissance Art* (New Haven, CT, and London, 2007), p. 222, plate 6.8, for Perugino's *St Sebastian* and its source.

97 David Ekserdjian, 'Regional Riches', *Apollo* (July–August 2017), pp. 94–5; and Ekserdjian, 'Copying Drawings in the Renaissance: Animal Studies, an Altarpiece by Orazio Gentileschi and a Drawing by Raphael', *Colnaghi Studies Journal*, IX (2021), pp. 31–41, p. 34, fig. 4, and p. 40, n. 14, for the *Peasant Couple*; and Carmen Bambach, *Michelangelo: Divine Draftsman and Designer*, exh. cat., Metropolitan Museum of Art, New York (2017–18), pp. 32–5, nos 2–3, for the *St Anthony*.

98 Quednau, 'Raphael und "alcune stampe di maniera tedesca"', pp. 137–42, for an overview of Dürer's reception in Italy.

99 Giuliano Frabetti, *L'autunno dei manieristi a Ferrara* (Ferrara, 1978), p. 49, and fig. 16.

100 K. T. Parker, *Catalogue of the Collection of Drawings in the Ashmolean Museum*, vol. II: *Italian Schools* (Oxford, 1972), pp. 109–10, no. 229 (as Giovanni Ambrogio Figino), where only some of these sources are identified; and Elena Parma, *Perino del Vaga: tra Raffaello e Michelangelo*, exh. cat., Palazzo Te, Mantua (2001), p. 300, no. 168; and Schoch, Mende and Scherbaum, *Das druckgraphische Werk*, vol. II, pp. 70–72, no. 112 (entry by Peter Krüge), pp. 79–81, no. 116 (entry by Peter Krüge), pp. 82–4, no. 117 (entry by Peter Krüge), pp. 197–9, no. 160 (entry by Anke Fröhlich), and vol. I, pp. 61–4, no. 17 (entry by Rainer Schoch), for the prints.

101 Parma, *Perino del Vaga*, pp. 148–9, no. 46, and pp. 118–19, no. 22; and Schoch, Mende and Scherbaum, *Das druckgraphische Werk*, vol. I, pp. 206–8, no. 83 (entry by Rainer Schoch), and vol. II, pp. 246–8, no. 174 (entry by Anna Scherbaum), for the prints.

102 David Ekserdjian, 'Garofalo e le sue fonti', *MuseoinVita*, 9–10 (2019), fig. 8, available at www.museoinvita.it, accessed 1 September 2022; and Schoch, Mende and Scherbaum, *Das druckgraphische Werk*, vol. II, pp. 229–31, no. 168 (entry by Anna Scherbaum), and vol. I, pp. 70–72, no. 20 (entry by Rainer Schoch), for the prints.

103 Chris Fischer, *Fra Bartolommeo et son atelier: Dessins et peintures des collections françaises*, exh. cat., Musée du Louvre, Paris (1994–5), pp. 52–3, no. 27 recto, for the drawing; and Schoch, Mende and Scherbaum, *Das druckgraphische Werk*, vol. I, pp. 73–5, no. 21 (entry by Rainer Schoch); and Annamaria Petrioli Tofani, ed., *L'officina della maniera*, exh. cat., Galleria degli Uffizi, Florence (1996–7), pp. 272–3, nos 92–92a–92b (entry by Maria Sframeli); and Schoch, Mende and Scherbaum, *Das druckgraphische Werk*, vol. I, pp. 155–6, no. 63 (entry by Matthias Mende), and vol. I, pp. 32–3, no. 3 (entry by Rainer Schoch).

3 Paintings

1 Fedja Anzelewsky, *Dürer: Das malerische Werk*, 2 vols (Berlin, 1991).

2 Ibid., vol. I, pp. 131–2, no. 19, and vol. II, plate 21, fig. 26, for the portrait.

3 Ibid., vol. I, pp. 132–3, for Faber's account.

4 Ibid., vol. I, pp. 25, 57–61, and pp. 132–40, nos 20–38, figs 16–26, and vol. II, plates 23–31, figs 28–37.

5 Friedrich Winkler, *Die Zeichnungen Albrecht Dürers*, 4 vols (Berlin, 1936–9), vol. I, pp. 98–9, no. 150; and Walter L. Strauss, *The Complete*

Drawings of Albrecht Dürer, 6 vols and 2 supplements (New York, 1974), vol. 11, pp. 650–51, 1502/32.

6 Winkler, *Zeichnungen*, vol. 1, pp. 113–14, no. 167, where it is rightly observed that this study was reused in the artist's *Martyrdom of the 10,000* woodcut (Rainer Schoch, Matthias Mende and Anna Scherbaum, *Albrecht Dürer: Das druckgraphische Werk*, 3 vols (Munich, London and New York, 2001–4), vol. 11, pp. 41–4, no. 104 (entry by Dagmar Eichberger)); and Strauss, *Drawings*, vol. 1, pp. 422–3, 1496/15.

7 Anzelewsky, *Das malerische Werk*, vol. 1, pp. 29–30, and pp. 140–41, nos 39–40, and vol. 11, plates 47–52, figs 57–63.

8 Ibid., vol. 1, p. 28, fig. 2, p. 57, and pp. 156–62, nos 50–54, figs 44–8, and vol. 11, plate 32, figs 38–9.

9 Schoch, Mende and Scherbaum, *Das druckgraphische Werk*, vol. 1, pp. 114–15, no. 40; Hans Rupprich, ed., *Dürer: Schriftlicher Nachlass*, 3 vols (Berlin, 1956–69), vol. 1, p. 154; and Jeffrey Ashcroft, *Albrecht Dürer: Documentary Biography*, 2 vols (New Haven, CT, and London, 2017), vol. 1, p. 558, for Dürer's reference to it as 'die Weihnachten'.

10 Anzelewsky, *Das malerische Werk*, vol. 1, pp. 60–61, and pp. 160–62, no. 50, fig. 49, and vol. 11, plate 53, fig. 64.

11 Ibid., vol. 1, pp. 60–61, and pp. 176–7, no. 70, and vol. 11, plates 65–9, figs 77–81.

12 Ibid., vol. 1, pp. 36, 60–61, 73–5, and pp. 178–83, nos 72–5, figs 63–8, and vol. 11, plates 71–80, figs 83–92.

13 Ibid., vol. 1, pp. 43, 75–7, and pp. 176–7, no. 70, and vol. 11, plates 111–14, figs 125–8.

14 Anzelewsky, *Das malerische Werk*, vol. 1, p. 220.

15 Schoch, Mende and Scherbaum, *Das druckgraphische Werk*, vol. 11, pp. 41–4, no. 104 (entry by Dagmar Eichberger), for the woodcut of the same subject.

16 Ibid., pp. 43–4, 61–2, and pp. 221–8, nos 107–15, figs 97–104, and vol. 11, plates 115–20, figs 129–35.

17 Schoch, Mende and Scherbaum, *Das druckgraphische Werk*, vol. 11, pp. 274–6, no. 184 (entry by Anna Scherbaum); Winkler, *Zeichnungen*, vol. 11, pp. 153–4, no. 507; and Strauss, *Drawings*, vol. 111, pp. 1216–17, 1510/7, for a drawing of the actual crown.

18 Anzelewsky, *Das malerische Werk*, vol. 1, pp. 44, 62–4, and pp. 230–33, nos 107–15, figs 97–104, and vol. 11, plates 123–30, figs 138–45.

19 Winkler, *Zeichnungen*, vol. 11, pp. 118–19, no. 445; and Strauss, *Drawings*, vol. 11, pp. 1060–61, 1508/23.

20 Schoch, Mende and Scherbaum, *Das druckgraphische Werk*, vol. II,
     pp. 343–4, no. 222 (entry by Erich Schneider).
21 Winkler, *Zeichnungen*, vol. II, p. 156, no. 511; and Strauss, *Drawings*,
     vol. III, pp. 1286–7, 1511/17.
22 Anzelewsky, *Das malerische Werk*, vol. I, pp. 54–5, 79–80, and
     pp. 280–86, nos 183–4, figs 153–4, and vol. II, plates 169–73,
     figs 185–90.
23 Ronald Lightbown, *Mantegna: With a Complete Catalogue of the Paintings,
     Drawings and Prints* (Oxford, 1986), pp. 452–4, no. 52, plates 153–64,
     and fig. 17, for Mantegna's family chapel; and Filippo Pedrocco,
     Titian: The Complete Paintings (London, 2001), pp. 308–9, no. 270, for
     Titian's *Entombment* in the Accademia in Venice, which was intended
     for the altar of the Cappella del Cristo in the Frari, where he wanted
     to be buried.
24 Winkler, *Zeichnungen*, vol. IV, p. 64, no. 873; and Strauss, *Drawings*,
     vol. IV, pp. 2290–91, 1525/9; Winkler, *Zeichnungen*, vol. IV, p. 66,
     no. 878; and Strauss, *Drawings*, vol. IV, p. 2226, 1525/11, for an Apostle
     study of 1523 that was adapted for the figure of St Paul.
25 Winkler, *Zeichnungen*, vol. IV, pp. 62–4, nos 870–72; and Strauss,
     Drawings, vol. IV, pp. 2310–15, 1526/3–5.
26 Anzelewsky, *Das malerische Werk*, vol. I, pp. 129–30, nos 16–17 and
     vol. II, plates 16–20, figs 20–25.
27 Peggy Grosse, 'Dürer's Madonnas?', in *The Early Dürer*, ed. Daniel
     Hess and Thomas Eser, exh. cat., Germanisches Nationalmuseum,
     Nuremberg (2012), pp. 236–44.
28 Anzelewsky, *Das malerische Werk*, vol. I, pp. 142–4, nos 43–4, fig. 27,
     and vol. II, plates 33–8, figs 40–47; and Jane Campbell Hutchison,
     Albrecht Dürer: A Biography (Princeton, NJ, 1990), p. 41, for the fact
     that Agnes's mother's maiden name was Kunigunde Haller.
29 Christopher S. Wood, *Albrecht Altdorfer and the Origins of Landscape*
     (London, 1993), p. 268, fig. 193, for a large-scale painting of the
     latter subject dated 1537 by Albrecht Altdorfer.
30 Anzelewsky, *Das malerische Werk*, vol. I, pp. 177–8, no. 71, and
     vol. II, plate 70, fig. 82. Regardless of its status, it is evidently a
     close-up variation on the theme of the *Madonna with the Iris* from
     Dürer's workshop in the National Gallery, for which see Christof
     Metzger, ed., *Albrecht Dürer*, exh. cat., Albertina, Vienna (2019–20),
     pp. 158–9 and 450, no. 54, where it is attributed to Hans Baldung
     Grien.
31 Hess and Eser, *Early Dürer*, pp. 332–3, nos 51–2, for both pictures.

32 Anzelewsky, *Das malerische Werk*, vol. I, pp. 233–4, no. 120, and vol. II,
   plates 131–2, figs 146–7.
33 Ibid., vol. I, p. 246, no. 130, and vol. II, plate 141, fig. 156.
34 Ibid., vol. I, pp. 244–5, no. 127, and vol. II, plate 138, fig. 153.
35 Ibid., vol. I, pp. 259–61, no. 147, figs 135–9, and vol. II, plate 158,
   fig. 174.
36 Winkler, *Zeichnungen*, vol. III, pp. 38–40, nos 574–7; and Strauss,
   Drawings, vol. III, pp. 1764–7, 1519/5–6, pp. 1772–3, 1519/9,
   pp. 1912–33, 1520/5.
37 Anzelewsky, *Das malerische Werk*, vol. I, pp. 277–8, no. 181, and vol. II,
   plate 167, fig. 183.
38 Ibid., vol. I, pp. 120–21, nos 5–6, and figs 10–11, and vol. II, plates
   5–7, figs 5–10, for the first two, and vol. I, pp. 70–71, and pp. 122–4,
   no. 9, fig. 12, and vol. II, plate 8, fig. 11, for the *Christ*.
39 Ibid., vol. I, pp. 126–8, nos 13–14, fig. 15, and vol. II, plates 13–14,
   figs 17–18. See also David Carritt, 'Dürer's "St Jerome in the
   Wilderness"', *Burlington Magazine*, XCIX/656 (1957), pp. 363–6; and
   Susan Foister and Peter van den Brink, *Dürer's Journeys: Travels of a
   Renaissance Artist*, exh. cat., National Gallery, London (2021–2),
   pp. 196–7, nos 82 and 84.
40 Foister and Van den Brink, *Journeys*, p. 294, no. 84, where the
   'Selected Literature' omits its original publication.
41 Winkler, *Zeichnungen*, vol. I, p. 48, no. 65; and Strauss, *Drawings*, vol. I,
   pp. 232–3, 1494/17.
42 Carritt, *Jerome*.
43 Anzelewsky, *Das malerische Werk*, vol. I, pp. 189–90, nos 83–5, figs
   86–9, and vol. II, plates 87–9, figs 97–8.
44 Ibid., vol. I, pp. 188–9, no. 82, and vol. II, plates 85–6, figs 99–102.
45 Ibid., vol. I, pp. 206–10, no. 98, figs 86–9, and vol. II, plate 101,
   fig. 114.
46 Ibid., vol. I, pp. 245–6, nos 128–9, and vol. II, plates 139–40,
   figs 154–5.
47 Ibid., vol. I, pp. 252–3, no. 138, and vol. II, plate 151, fig. 166.
48 Ibid., vol. I, pp. 263–5, no. 162, fig. 140, and vol. II, plate 160,
   fig. 176.
49 Winkler, *Zeichnungen*, vol. IV, pp. 24–7, nos 788–92; and Strauss,
   Drawings, vol. IV, pp. 2000–2005, 1521/2–4, and pp. 2008–11,
   1521/2–4.
50 Anzelewsky, *Das malerische Werk*, vol. I, pp. 81–2, and pp. 216–21,
   no. 105, figs 93–6, and vol. II, plates 63–4, figs 75–6, and especially

vol. I, p. 172, fig. 57, for the copy. See also Winkler, *Zeichnungen*, vol. I, pp. 173–4, no. 250; and Strauss, *Drawings*, vol. II, pp. 518–19, 1500/8, for a drawing that must be a reliable copy of a now lost first idea for the composition.

51 Alison Wright, *The Pollaiuolo Brothers: The Arts of Florence and Rome* (New Haven, CT, and London, 2005), pp. 98–102, figs 72–3.

52 Erwin Panofsky, *The Life and Art of Albrecht Dürer*, 2 vols (Princeton, NJ, 1943), vol. I, p. 91, and vol. II, p. 20, no. 105.

53 G. Bauch, 'Zur Cranachforschung', *Repertorium für Kunstwissenschaft*, XVII (1894), pp. 421–35, esp. p. 432; Anzelewsky, *Das malerische Werk*, vol. I, pp. 171–3, no. 67; and Pausanias, *Description of Greece*, ed. J. G. Frazer, 6 vols (London, 1898), vol. I, pp. 399–400 (VIII.xxii.3–6).

54 Anzelewsky, *Das malerische Werk*, vol. I, p. 82, and pp. 251–2, no. 137, and vol. II, plate 150, fig. 165.

55 Winkler, *Zeichnungen*, vol. II, pp. 113–14, nos 435–6; Strauss, *Drawings*, vol. II, pp. 1054–7, 1508/20–21; and Klaus Albrecht Schröder and Maria Luise Sternath, *Albrecht Dürer*, exh. cat., Albertina, Vienna (2003), pp. 373–6, nos 122–3.

56 Winkler, *Zeichnungen*, vol. II, pp. 112–13, no. 434; and Strauss, *Drawings*, vol. II, pp. 996–7, 1507/1, for the drawing; and Anzelewsky, *Das malerische Werk*, vol. I, pp. 212–16, no. 104, and vol. II, plates 108 and 110, figs 122 and 124, for the painting.

57 Livy, *History of Rome*, ed. B. O. Foster, 4 vols (London, 1919–26), vol. I, pp. 198–205.

58 Anzelewsky, *Das malerische Werk*, vol. I, p. 82, for its possible connection with a statue reproduced in a woodcut in Jakob von Strassburg's *Triumph of Caesar*. Since it was published in Venice in 1504, Dürer could easily have seen the print – or the presumptive original of the statue reproduced in it – during his months there in 1506.

59 Innis H. Shoemaker and Elizabeth Broun, *The Engravings of Marcantonio Raimondi*, exh. cat., Spencer Museum of Art, Lawrence, KS, Ackland Art Museum, Chapel Hill, NC, and Wellesley College Art Museum, Wellesley, MA (1981–2), pp. 94–5, no. 20; and Gustav Pauli, *Hans Sebald Beham: Ein kritisches Verzeichniss seiner Kupferstiche, Radirungen und Holzschnitte* (Strasbourg, 1901), p. 93, no. 82-11.

60 See Sabine Haag, Christiane Lange, Christof Lange, Christof Metzger and Karl Schütz, *Dürer – Cranach – Holbein. Die Entdeckung des Menschen: Das deutsche Porträt um 1500*, exh. cat., Kunsthistorisches

Museum, Vienna, and Kunsthalle, Munich (2011), p. 89, no. 41
(entry by Christof Metzger), for the identification.

61 Anzelewsky, *Das malerische Werk*, vol. I, pp. 82–3, and pp. 210–11,
    nos 99–100, and vol. II, plates 105–6, figs 118–19.

62 Ibid., vol. I, pp. 131–2, no. 19, and vol. II, plate 21, fig. 26.

63 Winkler, *Zeichnungen*, vol. IV, p. 76, no. 897; and Strauss, *Drawings*,
    vol. IV, pp. 2252–3, 1524/1, for the drawing; and Schoch, Mende and
    Scherbaum, *Das druckgraphische Werk*, vol. II, pp. 236–7, no. 98 (entry
    by Matthias Mende), for the engraving.

64 Anzelewsky, *Das malerische Werk*, vol. I, pp. 256–9, nos 145–6, and
    vol. II, plates 153–7, figs 168–73, for the paintings; and Schoch,
    Mende and Scherbaum, *Das druckgraphische Werk*, vol. II, pp. 456–9,
    no. 252 (entry by Dagmar Eichberger), for the woodcut.

65 Winkler, *Zeichnungen*, vol. III, pp. 33–4, no. 567, and pp. 68–9, no. 635;
    and Strauss, *Drawings*, vol. III, pp. 1736–7, 1518/19 and pp. 1756–7,
    1519/11.

66 Schoch, Mende and Scherbaum, *Das druckgraphische Werk*, vol. I,
    pp. 221–3, no. 89, and pp. 233–5, no. 97 (entries by Matthias
    Mende), for the prints; and Winkler, *Zeichnungen*, vol. III, p. 34,
    no. 568, and vol. IV, pp. 75–6, no. 896; and Strauss, *Drawings*,
    vol. III, pp. 1744–5, 1518/23 and vol. IV, pp. 2216–17 1523/6, for
    the drawings.

67 Schoch, Mende and Scherbaum, *Das druckgraphische Werk*, vol. I,
    pp. 241–2, no. 101 (entry by Matthias Mende), for the engraving;
    and Winkler, *Zeichnungen*, vol. IV, p. 78, no. 901, for the drawing.

68 Schoch, Mende and Scherbaum, *Das druckgraphische Werk*, vol. I,
    pp. 243–6, no. 102 (entry by Matthias Mende), for the print;
    Winkler, *Zeichnungen*, vol. IV, pp. 33–4, no. 805; and Strauss, *Drawings*,
    vol. IV, pp. 1934–5, 1520/16, for the drawing; and Foister and
    Van den Brink, *Journeys*, pp. 216–17, nos 94–5 and fig. 120, for
    the whole episode. See also Rupprich, *Nachlass*, vol. I, p. 156; and
    Ashcroft, *Documentary Biography*, vol. I, p. 561, where the phrase
    'noch einmahl conterfet' ('portrayed once again') implies a
    previous sitting.

69 Anzelewsky, *Das malerische Werk*, vol. I, pp. 144–9, nos 45–6, and figs
    28–36, and vol. II, plates 39–40 and 42, figs 48–9 and 51–2.

70 Ibid., vol. I, pp. 164–6, nos 60–65, and fig. 51, and vol. II,
    plates 57–60, figs 68–71.

71 Ibid., vol. I, pp. 190–91, no. 92, and fig. 73, vol. II, plate 90, fig. 103.

72 Ibid., vol. I, pp. 203–4, no. 95, and vol. II, plate 102, fig. 115.

73 Winkler, *Zeichnungen*, vol. IV, p. 7, no. 746, pp. 18–19, nos 770–71, 77 and 775, and pp. 20–21, no. 780; and Strauss, *Drawings*, vol. IV, pp. 1928–9, 1520/13, pp. 1964–7, 1520/31–2, pp. 2096–7, 1521/57.

74 Anzelewsky, *Das malerische Werk*, vol. I, pp. 205–6, no. 97, and vol. II, plate 104, fig. 117, vol. I, pp. 248–9, no. 133, and vol. II, plates 147–8, figs 162–3, vol. I, pp. 254–5, no. 143, and vol. II, plate 152, fig. 167, vol. I, pp. 265–7, nos 163–5, and vol. II, plates 161–3, figs 177–9, vol. I, pp. 275–6, no. 178, and fig. 151, and vol. II, plates 164, fig. 180, and vol. I, pp. 278–80, no. 182, and vol. II, plate 168, fig. 184.

75 Ibid., vol. I, pp. 162–3, nos 56–8, and vol. II, plates 55–6, figs 66–7, vol. I, pp. 204–5, no. 96, and vol. II, plate 103, fig. 116, vol. I, pp. 276–7, no. 179, and fig. 152, and vol. II, plates 165–6, figs 181–2.

76 Machtelt Brüggen Israëls, *Piero della Francesca and the Invention of the Artist* (London, 2020), pp. 220–21, for Leon Battista Alberti's observation in his treatise *On Painting* that painting 'represents the dead to the living many centuries later'.

4 Drawings

1 Christof Metzger, ed., *Albrecht Dürer*, exh. cat., Graphische Sammlung Albertina, Vienna (2019–20), pp. 37–49, for a step in the right direction.

2 Klaus Albrecht Schröder and Maria Luise Sternath, *Albrecht Dürer*, exh. cat., Albertina, Vienna (2003), pp. 116–17, no. 1.

3 Friedrich Winkler, *Die Zeichnungen Albrecht Dürers*, 4 vols (Berlin, 1936–9); and Walter L. Strauss, *The Complete Drawings of Albrecht Dürer*, 6 vols and 2 supplements (New York, 1974), are the standard catalogues of Dürer's drawings.

4 Fritz Koreny, *Albrecht Dürer und die Tier- und Pflanzenstudien der Renaissance*, exh. cat., Albertina, Vienna (1985), pp. 119–21, no. 36.

5 Koreny, *Tier- und Pflanzenstudien*, pp. 114–18, no. 35; and Fedja Anzelewsky, *Dürer: His Art and Life* (London, 1980), pp. 114–15, figs 107–8.

6 See Giulia Bartrum, *Albrecht Dürer and His Legacy*, exh. cat., British Museum, London (2002), pp. 242–3, nos 193–4, for both the *Virgin and Child with a Monkey* and the *Fisherman's House on a Lake*, from which it borrows the eponymous house.

7 See also Arnold Nesselrath, 'Albrecht Dürer's Silverpoint Sketchbook', in Susan Foister and Peter van den Brink, *Dürer's*

Journeys: Travels of a Renaissance Artist, exh. cat., National Gallery, London (2021–2), pp. 165–83.

8   Winkler, *Zeichnungen*, vol. 11, pp. 90–100, nos 380–400 and 402–9; and Strauss, *Drawings*, vol. 11, p. 914, 1506/9–29 and vol. 11, pp. 944–5, 1506/30, pp. 948–9, 1506/32, pp. 952–9, 1506/34–7, pp. 978–9, 1506/49 for early examples of such techniques dating from 1506.

9   Winkler, *Zeichnungen*, vol. 1, p. 24, no. 24; and Strauss, *Drawings*, vol. 1, pp. 52–3, 1491/6, for a very early example.

10 Winkler, *Zeichnungen*, vol. 1, p. 63, no. 85; and Strauss, *Drawings*, vol. 1, pp. 280–81, 1495/10, for a dated example from 1495 already discussed from an entirely different perspective in Chapter Two.

11 E. H. Gombrich, 'Leonardo's Method for Working Out Compositions', in *Norm and Form: Studies in the Art of the Renaissance 1* (Oxford, 1971), pp. 58–63.

12 Winkler, *Zeichnungen*, vol. 1, p. 27, no. 32; and Strauss, *Drawings*, vol. 1, pp. 148–9, 1493/7, for the former; and Winkler, *Zeichnungen*, vol. 1V, pp. 29–30, no. 800; Strauss, *Drawings*, vol. 1V, pp. 2024–5, 1521/14; and Foister and Van den Brink, *Journeys*, pp. 42, 56–7 and 293, no. 17, for the latter. See also Dirk de Vos for three eminently comparable cushions in Rogier van der Weyden's *Annunciation* in the Louvre, which may suggest Dürer was inspired by Netherlandish precedents.

13 Rolf Quednau, 'Raphael und "alcune stampe di maniera tedesca"', *Zeitschrift für Kunstgeschichte*, XLVI (1983), pp. 129–73, especially p. 131, fig. 1; Hans Rupprich, ed., *Dürer: Schriftlicher Nachlass*, 3 vols (Berlin, 1956–69), vol. 1, p. 158; and Jeffrey Ashcroft, *Albrecht Dürer: Documentary Biography*, 2 vols (New Haven, CT, and London, 2017), vol. 1, p. 563, for his purchase of 'ein Rötelstein' (a piece of red chalk) for a Stüber on his journey to the Netherlands.

14 Otto Pächt, *Van Eyck: Die Begründer der altniederländischen Malerei* (Munich, 1993), pp. 109–10, 112–13, figs 63–4, and plate 9.

15 Ibid., pp. 86–7, 205–6, fig. 52, and plate 13.

16 Lorne Campbell, *The Fifteenth Century Netherlandish Schools*, National Gallery Catalogues (New Haven, CT, and London, 1998), pp. 174–211, and esp. figs 12–13.

17 David Ekserdjian, 'Copying Drawings in the Renaissance: Animal Studies, an Altarpiece by Orazio Gentileschi and a Drawing by Raphael', *Colnaghi Studies Journal*, IX (2021), pp. 31–40, esp. p. 31.

18 David Ekserdjian, 'The Tip of the Iceberg: Barocci's Postmortem
   Inventory and the Survival of Renaissance Drawings', in *Federico
   Barocci: Inspiration and Innovation in Early Modern Italy*, ed. Judith W. Mann
   (Abingdon, 2018), pp. 154–73.

19 Anzelewsky, *Dürer*, p. 129, fig. 119.

20 Winkler, *Zeichnungen*, vol. II, pp. 99–100, nos 404–7; and Schröder
   and Sternath, *Dürer*, pp. 335–6, no. 105, pp. 350–54, nos 107–8
   (entry by Heinz Widauer).

21 Winkler, *Zeichnungen*, vol. I, pp. 36–7, no. 49, pp. 55–6, no. 73, pp. 65–6,
   no. 88, p. 173, no. 249, pp. 22–3, and vol. II, no. 295, p. 53, no. 328;
   and Strauss, *Drawings*, vol. I, pp. 166–7, 1493/16, pp. 276–7, 1495/8,
   pp. 306–7, 1495/23, and vol. II, pp. 572–3, 1501/3, pp. 694–5,
   1503/21, pp. 636–7, 1502/23, for examples of both types.

22 Winkler, *Zeichnungen*, vol. I, p. 82, nos 108–9, and p. 87, no. 115; and
   Strauss, *Drawings*, vol. I, pp. 362–5, 1495/51–2 and pp. 404–5, 1496/6.

23 Winkler, *Zeichnungen*, vol. I, pp. 86–7, no. 114; and Strauss, *Drawings*,
   vol. I, pp. 400–401, 1496/4.

24 Winkler, *Zeichnungen*, vol. I, pp. 23–4, no. 23, Strauss, *Drawings*,
   vol. I, pp. 50–51, 1491/5; and Bartrum, *Legacy*, p. 98, no. 27, for
   the drawing; and Bartrum, *Legacy*, p. 99, no. 28, for the print.

25 Winkler, *Zeichnungen*, vol. I, p. 26, no. 29; Strauss, *Drawings*, vol. I,
   pp. 144–5, 1493/5; and Bartrum, *Legacy*, p. 101, no. 31.

26 Bartrum, *Legacy*, pp. 156–7, no. 96, for the original; and Heinrich
   Theodor Musper, 'Das Original der "Windischen Bäuerin" von
   Albrecht Dürer', *Pantheon*, XXIX (1971), pp. 474–82, for the copy.

27 Koreny, *Tier- und Pflanzenstudien*, pp. 96–7, no. 28.

28 Winkler, *Zeichnungen*, vol. I, pp. 54–5, no. 69; and Strauss, *Drawings*,
   vol. I, pp. 268–9, 1495/4. Winkler, *Zeichnungen*, vol. I, pp. 43–6,
   nos 58–60; and Strauss, *Drawings*, vol. I, pp. 220–25, 1494/11–13,
   are all dated 1494, but are not first ideas.

29 Bartrum, *Legacy*, p. 156, no. 95.

30 Rainer Schoch, Matthias Mende and Anna Scherbaum, *Albrecht
   Dürer: Das druckgraphische Werk*, 3 vols (Munich, London and New
   York, 2001–4), vol. I, pp. 103–4, no. 36 (entry by Rainer Schoch),
   and vol. II, pp. 232–4, no. 169 (entry by Anna Scherbaum).

31 Peter van den Brink, *Dürer war hier: Eine Reise wird Legende*, exh. cat.,
   Suermondt-Ludwig-Museum, Aachen (2021), pp. 402–3,
   figs 259–60.

32 Winkler, *Zeichnungen*, vol. IV, pp. 46–54, nos 837–51, and pp. 55–6,
   nos 855–6; Strauss, *Drawings*, vol. IV, pp. 2144–5, 1521/81,

pp. 2148–9, 1521/83–9, pp. 2164–77, 1521/91–7, pp. 2186–7,
1522/4, and pp. 2180–83, 1521; and Stijn Alsteens, 'Dürer's Virgin
and Child with Saints of 1521–22: An Archducal Commission?',
in Foister and van den Brink, *Journeys*, pp. 129–45.

33   Alsteens, 'Virgin and Child'.
34   Mauro Lucco and Giovanni Carlo Federico Villa, *Antonello da Messina:
     l'opera completa*, exh. cat., Scuderie del Quirinale, Rome (2006),
     pp. 226–31, no. 34 (entry by Mauro Lucco).
35   Alsteens, 'Virgin and Child', p. 136, fig. 63.
36   Ibid., p. 138, no. 64.
37   Ibid., pp. 138 and 296, no. 63.
38   Ibid., p. 137, fig. 64.
39   Ibid., figs 65–6.
40   Ibid., pp. 132–3, nos 57 and 60–61, and fig. 59.
41   Winkler, *Zeichnungen*, vol. 11, p. 94, no. 388; Strauss, *Drawings*, vol. 11,
     pp. 918–19, 1506/11; and Fedja Anzelewsky, *Dürer: Das malerische Werk*,
     2 vols (Berlin, 1991), vol. 1, pp. 233–4, no. 120, and vol. 11, plates
     131–2, figs 146–7.
42   Andrea Emiliani, *Federico Barocci (Urbino, 1535–1612)*, 2 vols (Ancona,
     2008), vol. 1, p. 312, for a letter of 19 November 1574, in which
     Federico Barocci in Urbino reassures the patrons of his *Madonna del
     Popolo* for Arezzo that all he needs to know is whether the light
     comes from the left or the right.
43   Winkler, *Zeichnungen*, vol. 11, pp. 99–100, no. 403; Strauss, *Drawings*,
     vol. 11, pp. 948–9, 1506/32; and Schröder and Sternath, *Dürer*,
     pp. 354–6, no. 109, for a female head study that has sometimes been
     associated with the *Madonna of the Siskin*.
44   Winkler, *Zeichnungen*, vol. 11, p. 100, no. 408; Strauss, *Drawings*,
     vol. 11, pp. 946–7, 1506/31; and *West European Drawing of XVI–XX
     Centuries Kunsthalle Collection in Bremen: Catalogue* (Moscow, 1992),
     pp. 98–9, no. 22.
45   Winkler, *Zeichnungen*, vol. 11, p. 100, no. 409; and Strauss, *Drawings*,
     vol. 11, pp. 950–51, 1506/33.
46   Winkler, *Zeichnungen*, vol. 11, pp. 91–2, no. 382; and Strauss, *Drawings*,
     vol. 11, pp. 914–15, 1506/9.
47   Schröder and Sternath, *Dürer*, pp. 332–4, nos 100–103.
48   Ibid., pp. 326–30, no. 97.
49   Winkler, *Zeichnungen*, vol. 11, p. 131, no. 464; and Strauss, *Drawings*,
     vol. 11, pp. 1038–9, 1508/12.
50   Schröder and Sternath, *Dürer*, pp. 360–62, nos 111–12.

51 Winkler, *Zeichnungen*, vol. IV, pp. 62–4, nos 870–72; and Strauss, *Drawings*, vol. IV, pp. 2310–15, 1526/3–5.

52 Anzelewsky, *Das malerische Werk*, vol. I, pp. 79–80, and pp. 280–86, nos 183–4, and vol. II, plates 169–73, figs 185–90.

53 Winkler, *Zeichnungen*, vol. II, pp. 64–5, no. 345; Strauss, *Drawings*, vol. II, pp. 874–5, 1505/17; and Schoch, Mende and Scherbaum, *Das druckgraphische Werk*, vol. I, pp. 206–8, no. 83 (entry by Rainer Schoch).

54 Winkler, *Zeichnungen*, vol. III, pp. 82–3, no. 669; Strauss, *Drawings*, vol. III, pp. 1632–3, 1516/5; and Schoch, Mende and Scherbaum, *Das druckgraphische Werk*, vol. I, pp. 174–8, no. 70 (entry by Matthias Mende).

55 Winkler, *Zeichnungen*, vol. III, pp. 82–3, no. 669 and plate XIX; and Strauss, *Drawings*, vol. III, pp. 1632–3, 1516/5.

56 Winkler, *Zeichnungen*, vol. III, pp. 48–9, no. 589–90; and Strauss, *Drawings*, vol. IV, pp. 2006–7, 1521/5, and vol. III, pp. 1282–3, 1511/15, for the drawings; and Schoch, Mende and Scherbaum, *Das druckgraphische Werk*, vol. I, pp. 174–8, no. 70 (entry by Matthias Mende), for the print.

57 Winkler, *Zeichnungen*, vol. II, pp. 20–22, nos 291–4; and Strauss, *Drawings*, vol. II, pp. 690–93, 1503/19–20, pp. 696–7, 1503/22, and pp. 734–5, 1504/1

58 Compare Winkler, *Zeichnungen*, vol. II, pp. 20–21, no. 291; Strauss, *Drawings*, vol. II, pp. 692–3, 1503/20; and Schoch, Mende and Scherbaum, *Das druckgraphische Werk*, vol. II, pp. 254–6, no. 177 (entry by Anna Scherbaum).

59 Compare Winkler, *Zeichnungen*, vol. II, p. 22, no. 294, Strauss, *Drawings*, vol. II, pp. 638–9, 1502/24; and Schoch, Mende and Scherbaum, *Das druckgraphische Werk*, vol. II, pp. 235–7, no. 170 (entry by Anna Scherbaum).

60 Compare Winkler, *Zeichnungen*, vol. II, pp. 21–2, no. 292, Strauss, *Drawings*, vol. II, pp. 634–5, 1502/22; and Schoch, Mende and Scherbaum, *Das druckgraphische Werk*, vol. II, pp. 246–8, no. 174 (entry by Anna Scherbaum).

61 Compare Winkler, *Zeichnungen*, vol. II, p. 22, no. 293, Strauss, *Drawings*, vol. II, pp. 734–5, 1504/1; and Schoch, Mende and Scherbaum, *Das druckgraphische Werk*, vol. II, pp. 246–8, no. 174, and pp. 254–6, no. 177 (entries by Anna Scherbaum).

62 Winkler, *Zeichnungen*, vol. II, pp. 22–3, nos 295–6; Strauss, *Drawings*, vol. II, pp. 694–7, 1503/21–22; and Schröder and Sternath, *Dürer*, pp. 380–81, no. 75.

63 Giulia Bartrum, ed., *Dürer Unseen* (London, 2022), for this drawing.

5 Prints

1 David Landau and Peter Parshall, *The Renaissance Print, 1470–1550*
   (New Haven, CT, and London, 1994), pp. 84–5, figs 74–5, for two
   early examples.
2 Rainer Schoch, Matthias Mende and Anna Scherbaum, *Albrecht
   Dürer: Das druckgraphische Werk*, 3 vols (Munich, London and New
   York, 2001–4), vol. II, pp. 232–4, no. 169, and pp. 226–8, no. 167
   (entries by Anna Scherbaum).
3 David Ekserdjian, 'The Northern Renaissance Response to the
   Antique before the Sack of Rome', *Colnaghi Studies Journal*, VIII
   (2021), pp. 14–29.
4 Hans Rupprich, ed., *Dürer: Schriftlicher Nachlass*, 3 vols (Berlin,
   1956–69), vol. I, and Jeffrey Ashcroft, *Albrecht Dürer: Documentary
   Biography*, 2 vols (New Haven, CT, and London, 2017), vol. I, for the
   complete journal; and Rupprich, *Nachlass*, vol. I, p. 164, and Ashcroft,
   Documentary Biography, vol. I,
   p. 272, for Jacopo de' Barbari and the *St Jerome* engraving.
5 Luca Baroni, *Incisori tedeschi del Cinquecento* (Milan, 2020), p. 76,
   fig. 1.41.
6 Giorgio Vasari, *Le opere di Giorgio Vasari con nuove annotazioni e commenti
   di Gaetano Milanesi*, 8 vols and index (Florence, 1878–85), vol. V,
   pp. 396–403.
7 Schoch, Mende and Scherbaum, *Das druckgraphische Werk*, vol. II,
   pp. 467–70, no. 266 (entry by Dagmar Eichberger), for a woodcut
   portrait of 1522, and vol. I, pp. 241–6, nos 101–2 (entries by
   Matthias Mende), for two portrait engravings dated 1526, and
   thus only slightly later.
8 Christof Metzger, ed., *Albrecht Dürer*, exh. cat., Albertina,
   Vienna (2019–20), pp. 86, fig. 2, pp. 90–91 and 446–7,
   nos 9–12.
9 Giulia Bartrum, *Albrecht Dürer and His Legacy*, exh. cat., British
   Museum, London (2002), p. 171, no. 115, for the *Entombment*,
   and p. 119, no. 50, for the woodblock for *Hercules*.
10 Jan Johnson, 'Woodcut', in *The Dictionary of Art*, ed. Jane Turner,
   34 vols (London, 1996), vol. XXXIII, pp. 345–67, esp. pp. 347–8
   and 351–3; and Landau and Parshall, *Print*, pp. 21–3.
11 See respectively William M. Ivins Jr, 'Notes on Three Dürer
   Woodblocks', *Metropolitan Museum Studies*, II/1 (1929), pp. 102–11;
   and Bartrum, *Legacy*, p. 119, no. 50.

12 Amy Namowitz Worthen, 'Engraving', in *Dictionary of Art*, vol. X, ed. Turner, pp. 379–9, esp. pp. 379–81 and 384–5; and Landau and Parshall, *Print*, pp. 23–7.

13 David P. Becker, 'Drypoint', in *Dictionary of Art*, vol. IX, ed. Turner, pp. 307–10, esp. pp. 307–8; and Schoch, Mende and Scherbaum, *Das druckgraphische Werk*, vol. I, pp. 157–8, no. 64 (entry by Rainer Schoch), pp. 158–60, no. 65 (entry by Anna Scherbaum), and pp. 161–2, no. 66 (entry by Rainer Schoch).

14 Ad Stijnman, 'Etching', in *Dictionary of Art*, vol. X, ed. Turner, pp. 547–60, esp. pp. 547–9; Landau and Parshall, *Print*, pp. 27–8; and Schoch, Mende and Scherbaum, *Das druckgraphische Werk*, vol. I, pp. 206–8, no. 83, and pp. 210–12, no. 85 (entries by Rainer Schoch).

15 Fedja Anzelewsky, *Dürer: His Art and Life* (London, 1980), p. 83, fig. 70, and p. 127, fig. 117.

16 Schoch, Mende and Scherbaum, *Das druckgraphische Werk*, vol. II, pp. 418–20, no. 240 (entry by Matthias Mende).

17 Ibid., vol. I, pp. 100–101, no. 34 (entry by Rainer Schoch), pp. 116–17, no. 41 (entry by Anna Scherbaum), pp. 135–7, no. 138 (entry by Bernd Mayer), vol. II, pp. 418–20, no. 240 (entry by Matthias Mende), vol. I, pp. 82–3, no. 25, and pp. 89–90, no. 30 (entries by Rainer Schoch), vol. II, pp. 112–15, no. 129 (entry by Rainer Schoch) and pp. 453–6, no. 251 (entry by Matthias Mende), pp. 140–44, nos 140–41 (entries by Bernd Mayer), and pp. 383–8, no. 237 (entry by Thomas Schauerte).

18 Ibid., vol. I, pp. 103–4, no. 36, pp. 206–8, no. 83, pp. 210–12, no. 85 (entry by Rainer Schoch), and p. 213, no. 86 (entry by Anna Scherbaum), and vol. II, pp. 133–4, no. 137 (entry by Bernd Mayer) for prints where the Christ Child is suckling.

19 Ibid., vol. I, pp. 226–7, no. 91 (entry by Anna Scherbaum), and vol. II, pp. 378–9, no. 235 (entry by Rainer Schoch), for prints where the Christ Child is swaddled.

20 Ibid., vol. I, pp. 209–10, no. 84 (entry by Anna Scherbaum).

21 Ibid., vol. I, pp. 92–5, no. 32 (entry by Rainer Schoch). See also Susan Foister and Peter van den Brink, *Dürer's Journeys: Travels of a Renaissance Artist*, exh. cat., National Gallery, London (2021), p. 106, no. 50, and especially the catalogue's cover, for a spectacular enlarged detail of the landscape.

22 Schoch, Mende and Scherbaum, *Das druckgraphische Werk*, vol. I, pp. 74–6, no. 114, pp. 84–6, no. 118, pp. 90–91, no. 122, pp. 94–5,

no. 122 (entries by Peter Krüger), pp. 73–8, nos 21–2, pp. 95–9,
no. 33 (entries by Rainer Schoch).

23 Jacques de Voragine, *La légende dorée*, 2 vols (Paris, 1967), vol. II,
p. 306.

24 Schoch, Mende and Scherbaum, *Das druckgraphische Werk*, vol. I,
pp. 110–13, no. 39 (entry by Rainer Schoch). See also Alan Shestack,
Master LCz and Master WB (New York, 1971), p. 28, fig. 19, and p. 32,
fig. 23, for two earlier background chamois in an engraving of the
Temptation of Christ by the Master LCz and a woodcut in the *Swabian
Chronicle* of 1486, both of which Dürer may very possibly have known.

25 Maryan W. Ainsworth, *Gerard David: Purity of Vision in an Age of
Transition* (New York, 1998), p. 222, fig. 210, for Gerard David's
St Jerome in the Wilderness; and Elisabeth Dhanens, *Hubert and Jan van
Eyck* (Antwerp, 1980), pp. 366, 370–71, fig. 232, for Van Eyck's
St Jerome in His Study.

26 Schoch, Mende and Scherbaum, *Das druckgraphische Werk*, vol. I,
pp. 174–8, no. 70 (entry by Matthias Mende); and Foister and
Van den Brink, *Journeys*, p. 116, for an enlarged detail.

27 Lorne Campbell, *The Fifteenth Century Netherlandish Schools*, National
Gallery Catalogues (New Haven, CT, and London, 1998),
pp. 174–211, for the most obvious case in point, Jan van Eyck's
Arnolfini Wedding.

28 Angelo Walter, ed., *Gemäldegalerie Alte Meister Dresden: Katalog der
ausgestellten Werke* (Dresden, 1982), pp. 246–7, no. 1397; and Arthur
Wheelock Jr, ed., *Johannes Vermeer*, exh. cat., National Gallery of Art,
Washington, DC, and Mauritshuis, The Hague (1996), p. 35, fig. 6,
p. 52, fig. 6, pp. 108–13, no. 5, pp. 128–33, no. 8, pp. 170–75, no. 16,
pp. 186–9, no. 19.

29 Schoch, Mende and Scherbaum, *Das druckgraphische Werk*, vol. I,
pp. 68–70, no. 19 (entry by Rainer Schoch).

30 Friedrich Winkler, *Die Zeichnungen Albrecht Dürers*, 4 vols (Berlin,
1936–9), vol. I, pp. 147–8, no. 213, vol. III, pp. 66–7, nos 628–9;
and Walter L. Strauss, *The Complete Drawings of Albrecht Dürer*, 6 vols
and 2 supplements (New York, 1974), vol. III, pp. 1248–9, 1510/28,
vol. VI, pp. 2974–5, no. XW.213, and pp. 3062–3, no. XW.628, for
examples.

31 Winkler, *Zeichnungen*, pp. 151–2, no. 217; and Strauss, *Drawings*, vol. VI,
no. XW.217.

32 Schoch, Mende and Scherbaum, *Das druckgraphische Werk*, vol. I,
pp. 169–73, no. 69 (entry by Matthias Mende), for the print; and

Bartrum, *Legacy*, p. 156, no. 95, for the drawing in charcoal of *Death Riding a Horse*, which is monogrammed and dated 1505, and inscribed with the words 'ME/ [M]ENTO/ MEI' ('Remember me'), which are presumably to be imagined as being spoken by the crowned skeleton, who is Death.

33 Julius Held, *Dürers Wirkung auf die niederländische Kunst seiner Zeit* (The Hague, 1931), pp. 137–8, for a complete list of all the prints referred to in the diary, and the number of copies given or sold.

34 Schoch, Mende and Scherbaum, *Das druckgraphische Werk*, vol. II, pp. 208–10, no. 164 (entry by Anke Fröhlich).

35 Joseph Heller, *Das Leben und die Werke Albrecht Dürer's*, 2 of 3 planned vols (Bamberg, 1827), vol. II.2, pp. 503–4.

36 Erwin Panofsky, *The Life and Art of Albrecht Dürer*, 2 vols (Princeton, NJ, 1943), vol. I, pp. 151–4, and vol. II, p. 29, no. 205, and fig. 207.

37 Joachim Sandrart, *Teutsche Akademie der Bau-, Bild- und Mahlerey-Künste* (Nuremberg, 1675), p. 223.

38 Klaus Albrecht Schröder and Maria Luise Sternath, *Albrecht Dürer*, exh. cat., Albertina, Vienna (2003), pp. 412–13, no. 137 (entry by Matthias Mende). See also Metzger, ed., *Albrecht Dürer*, pp. 360, 375, and 461, no. 170, for the observation that the knight in question belonged to a cavalry unit that had been established by Maximilian in that very year.

39 Winkler, *Zeichnungen*, vol. I, p. 177, no. 255; and Strauss, *Drawings*, vol. II, pp. 620–21, 1502/15.

40 Winkler, *Zeichnungen*, vol. II, pp. 77–8, nos 360–61; and Strauss, *Drawings*, vol. II, pp. 706–9, 1503/27–8.

41 Schröder and Sternath, *Dürer*, pp. 414–15, no. 138 (entry by Matthias Mende).

42 Both left feet of the horse, as well as the left forefoot and both back feet of Death's mount, are 'grounded' by the shadows they cast, but these details take a bit of finding, and their corresponding absence when it comes to the dog is even less obvious.

43 Bartrum, *Legacy*, pp. 186–7, no. 127. For a quotation of the dog from the print in a painting of *Diana the Huntress* in the Louvre by an anonymous artist of the School of Fontainebleau, see André Chastel, *French Art: The Renaissance 1430–1620* (Paris and New York, 1995), p. 174.

44 Winkler, *Zeichnungen*, vol. I, pp. 79–84, nos 106–11, and esp. p. 84, no. 111; and Strauss, *Drawings*, vol. I, pp. 236–7, 1494/19, pp. 340–41, 1495/40, and pp. 360–67, 1495/50–53, and esp. pp. 236–7, 1494/19.

45 Schröder and Sternath, *Dürer*, pp. 414–15, no. 138 (entry by Matthias
    Mende).
46 Schoch, Mende and Scherbaum, *Das druckgraphische Werk*, vol. I,
    pp. 117–19, no. 42 (entry by Anna Scherbaum).
47 Francis Haskell and Nicholas Penny, *Taste and the Antique: The Lure of
    Classical Sculpture, 1500–1900* (New Haven, CT, and London, 1982),
    pp. 252–5, no. 55, fig. 129.
48 Schoch, Mende and Scherbaum, *Das druckgraphische Werk*, vol. I,
    pp. 65–7, no. 18 (entry by Anna Scherbaum), pp. 73–5, no. 21
    (entry by Rainer Schoch), and pp. 179–85, no. 71 (entry by
    Matthias Mende).
49 Ibid., vol. I, pp. 206–8, no. 83 (entry by Rainer Schoch).
50 Ibid., vol. I, pp. 27–8, no. I (entry by Rainer Schoch).
51 Stanley Wells and Gary Taylor, eds, *The Complete Oxford Shakespeare*,
    3 vols (Oxford, 1987), vol. II, p. 587 (*A Midsummer Night's Dream*,
    Act III, Scene 2, line 9).
52 Charles Ilsley Minott, *Martin Schongauer* (New York, 1971),
    pp. 120–21, nos 88 and 90.
53 Winkler, *Zeichnungen*, vol. I, pp. III–12, no. 164; and Strauss,
    Drawings, vol. I, pp. 424–5, 1496/16, where it is still accepted as
    autograph; and Schoch, Mende and Scherbaum, *Das druckgraphische
    Werk*, vol. I, pp. 56–9, nos 14–15 (entries by Rainer Schoch).
54 Schoch, Mende and Scherbaum, *Das druckgraphische Werk*, vol. I,
    pp. 54–5, no. 13 (entry by Rainer Schoch).
55 Ibid., pp. 53–4, no. 12 (entry by Rainer Schoch).
56 Ibid., pp. 194–6, nos 76–7, and pp. 261–7, no. 88 (entries by Anna
    Scherbaum), and pp. 169–73, no. 69 (entry by Matthias Mende).
57 Giuseppe Basile, *Giotto: The Arena Chapel Frescoes* (London, 1993).
58 Ibid., pp. 31–72.
59 Ibid., and Schoch, Mende and Scherbaum, *Das druckgraphische
    Werk*, vol. II, pp. 226–42, nos 167–72.
60 Wolfgang Kemp, *The Narratives of Gothic Stained Glass* (Cambridge, 1997).
61 Michael A. Michael, *Stained Glass of Canterbury Cathedral* (London, 2004).
62 Otto Demus, *The Mosaic Decoration of San Marco, Venice* (Chicago, IL,
    and London, 1988).
63 Floridus Röhrig, *Der Verduner Altar* (Klosterneuburg, 2004); and
    Helmut Buschhausen, 'The Klosterneuburg Altar of Nicholas of
    Verdun: Art, Theology and Politics', *Journal of the Warburg and Courtauld
    Institutes*, XXXVII (1974), pp. 1–32.
64 Panofsky, *Life and Art*, vol. I, pp. 99–103.

65 Ibid., pp. 97–8.

66 Ibid., p. 96, for the chronology.

67 Michelangelo's frescoes on the ceiling of the Sistine Chapel of much
the same date are an exception, but not least because he realized he
had miscalculated the scale of the first half to be completed when he
saw it after the removal of the scaffolding.

68 Metzger, *Dürer*, pp. 202 and 453, no. 78, for the identical motif in an
illumination Dürer added to a printed edition of Theocritus
published in 1496, which must be of much the same date, and André
Chastel, 'L'ardita capra', *Arte Veneta*, 29 (1975), pp. 146–9, for the
latter iconography.

69 Schoch, Mende and Scherbaum, *Das druckgraphische Werk*, vol. II,
pp. 256–9, no. 178, and pp. 265–7, no. 181 (entries by Anna
Scherbaum).

70 Ibid., pp. 268–70, no. 182 (entry by Anna Scherbaum).

71 Ibid., pp. 235–7, no. 170 (entry by Anna Scherbaum).

72 Baroni, *Incisori*, pp. 91, 98–101, where the small-scale reproductions
mean it is possible to scan the complete sets at a glance.

73 Ibid., pp. 100, 91 and 98.

74 *Légende dorée*, vol. 1, pp. 70–71.

75 Schoch, Mende and Scherbaum, *Das druckgraphische Werk*, vol. II,
pp. 259–62, no. 179 (entry by Anna Scherbaum).

76 Ilsley Minott, *Schongauer*, p. 64, no. 7; and Panofsky, *Life and Art*,
vol. 1, pp. 100–101. The dragon tree (*Dracaena draco*) is not
native to Europe, but grows in Morocco and Macaronesia.

77 Schoch, Mende and Scherbaum, *Das druckgraphische Werk*, vol. II,
pp. 262–5, no. 180 (entry by Anna Scherbaum).

78 Wolfgang Waetzoldt, *Albrecht Dürer und seine Zeit* (Vienna, 1935),
pp. 135–7, for an absorbing but very different account of Dürer's
engagement with the subject.

79 Schoch, Mende and Scherbaum, *Das druckgraphische Werk*, vol. II,
pp. 185–8, no. 156 (entry by Anke Fröhlich).

80 Ibid., vol. 1, pp. 131–2, no. 46 (entry by Anna Scherbaum).

81 Winkler, *Zeichnungen*, vol. II, p. 31, no. 298, Strauss, *Drawings*, vol. II,
pp. 772–3, 1504/21; and Metzger, *Dürer*, pp. 332–6, and especially
p. 332, fig. 21, as a copy after Dürer.

82 Schoch, Mende and Scherbaum, *Das druckgraphische Werk*, vol. II,
pp. 302–3, no. 196 (entry by Erich Schneider).

83 Ibid., vol. II, p. 345, no. 223 (entry by Erich Schneider); and
Waetzoldt, *Dürer*, p. 137, for its purpose.

84 Schoch, Mende and Scherbaum, *Das druckgraphische Werk*, vol. I,
    pp. 200–202, no. 80 (entry by Rainer Schoch).
85 Winkler, *Zeichnungen*, vol. III, p. 51, no. 598; and Strauss, *Drawings*,
    vol. IV, pp. 2256–7, 1524/3.
86 Winkler, *Zeichnungen*, vol. III, p. 46, no. 584; and Strauss, *Drawings*,
    vol. III, pp. 1610–11, 1515/74.
87 Winkler, *Zeichnungen*, vol. III, pp. 46–7, no. 585; Strauss, *Drawings*,
    vol. III, pp. 1732–3, 1518/17; and Schröder and Sternath, *Dürer*,
    pp. 402–3, no. 134 (entry by H. Widauer).
88 Winkler, *Zeichnungen*, vol. III, p. 47, no. 586; and Strauss, *Drawings*,
    vol. IV, pp. 2258–9, 1524/4.
89 Winkler, *Zeichnungen*, vol. IV, pp. 28–9, nos 797–8; Strauss, *Drawings*,
    vol. IV, pp. 1980–81, 1520/39, and pp. 2036–7, 1521/20; and Dana
    E. Cowen, 'Albrecht Dürer's Late Passion Drawings: The Oblong
    Passion in Context', in Foister and Van den Brink, *Journeys*,
    pp. 241–51, and esp. pp. 243–4, fig. 130 and no. 106.
90 Winkler, *Zeichnungen*, vol. IV, p. 72, no. 891; and Strauss, *Drawings*,
    vol. IV, pp. 2258–9, 1524/4.
91 Schoch, Mende and Scherbaum, *Das druckgraphische Werk*, vol. II,
    pp. 393–412, no. 238 (entry by Thomas Schauerte); and Metzger,
    Dürer, pp. 386–99 and 462, no. 176.
92 Schoch, Mende and Scherbaum, *Das druckgraphische Werk*, vol. I,
    pp. 101–3, no. 35, pp. 105–7, no. 37, and vol. II, pp. 448–53,
    nos 249–50, pp. 460–67, nos 253–5, pp. 484–5, no. 258 (entries by
    Rainer Schoch), pp. 514–16, no. A15 (entry by Thomas Schauerte),
    pp. 531–4, nos A25–6 (entries by Rainer Schoch). For the knots, see
    ibid., vol. II, pp. 145–57, nos 142–7 (entries by Matthias Mende),
    and for the projections see ibid., vol. II, pp. 430–35, nos 243–4
    (entries by Rainer Schoch).
93 Ibid., vol. II, pp. 319–474, no. 277 (entry by Berthold Hinz).
94 Ibid., vol. III, pp. 275–6, no. 274 (entry by Peter Schreiber).
95 Lynne Lawner, *I Modi – The Sixteen Pleasures: An Erotic Album of
    the Italian Renaissance* (London, 1988).

Conclusion

1 Joseph Leo Koerner, *The Moment of Self-Portraiture in German Renaissance
    Art* (Chicago, IL, and London, 1993).
2 Claudia Lichte, ed., *Tilman Riemenschneider: Werke seiner Blütezeit*, exh. cat.,
    Mainfränkisches Museum, Würzburg (2004), pp. 37 and 359.

3 Giulia Bartrum, *Albrecht Dürer and His Legacy*, exh. cat., British
  Museum, London (2002), pp. 266–82.
4 Fritz Koreny, *Albrecht Dürer und die Tier- und Pflanzenstudien der
  Renaissance*, exh. cat., Albertina, Vienna (1985), for Hoffmann;
  and Peter van den Brink, *Dürer war hier: Eine Reise wird Legende*,
  exh. cat., Suermondt-Ludwig-Museum, Aachen (2021), p. 480,
  fig. 322, for Brueghel.
5 Bartrum, *Legacy*, p. 266.
6 Alessandro Zuccari, *I Caravaggeschi: Percorsi e protagonisti*, 2 vols
  (Milan, 2010), vol. II, p. 545; and Rainer Schoch, Matthias Mende
  and Anna Scherbaum, *Albrecht Dürer: Das druckgraphische Werk*, 3 vols
  (Munich, London and New York, 2001–4), vol. II, pp. 286–7,
  no. 186 (entry by Erich Schneider).
7 Gregory Martin, *The Flemish School*, National Gallery Catalogues
  (London, 1970), pp. 68–73, especially p. 69; and Christopher Baker
  and Tom Henry, *The National Gallery: Complete Illustrated Catalogue*
  (London, 1995), p. 224, for an illustration.
8 Letizia Treves, *Beyond Caravaggio*, exh. cat., National Gallery, London
  (2016–17), pp. 66–9, no. 8 (entry by Aidan Weston-Lewis);
  Schoch, Mende and Scherbaum, *Das druckgraphische Werk*, vol. II,
  pp. 171–3, no. 152.
9 Schoch, Mende and Scherbaum, *Das druckgraphische Werk*, vol. I,
  pp. 110–13, no. 39 (entry by Anna Scherbaum).
10 José López-Rey, *Velázquez*, 2 vols (Cologne, 1996), vol. II,
  pp. 264–7, no. 107; and Schoch, Mende and Scherbaum,
  Das druckgraphische Werk, vol. I, pp. 110–13, no. 39 (entry by
  Rainer Schoch).
11 Jane Campbell Hutchison, *Albrecht Dürer: A Biography* (Princeton,
  NJ, 1990), pp. 188–9.
12 Kenneth Clark, *Rembrandt and the Italian Renaissance* (New York, 1966),
  p. 205.
13 Ibid., p. 51, fig. 41.
14 Koerner, *Moment of Self-Portraiture*, p. 250, fig. 125.
15 Luis-Martin Lozano, *The Complete Paintings of Frida Kahlo*
  (Cologne, 2021), p. 46.
16 Lawrence Gowing, *Lucian Freud* (London, 1982), p. 201, fig. 162.
17 Fedja Anzelewsky, *Dürer: Das malerische Werk*, 2 vols (Berlin, 1991),
  vol. II, plates 169–70, and figs 185a and 186.
18 Maureen Hart Hennessey and Anne Knutson, *Norman Rockwell:
  Pictures for the American People*, exh. cat., Norman Rockwell Museum,

Stockbridge, MA, and elsewhere (1999–2002), pp. 77 and 185, where the various precursors are identified and discussed by Robert Rosenblum.

19 Pierre Mac Orlan, *Le quai des brumes* (Paris, 1964), pp. 43 and 135.

20 Günter Grass, *Aus dem Tagebuch einer Schnecke* (Reinbek bei Hamburg, 1974), pp. 197–213.

BIBLIOGRAPHY

Acidini Luchinat, Cristina, ed., *The Chapel of the Magi: Benozzo Gozzoli's Frescoes in the Palazzo Medici-Riccardi Florence* (London, 1994)

Aikema, Bernard, 'La pala di Cingoli', in *Lorenzo Lotto: Atti del Convegno Internazionale di Studi per il v Centenario della Nascita* (Asolo, 1980), ed. Pietro Zampetti and Vittorio Sgarbi (Venice, 1981), pp. 443–56

—, and Andrew John Martin, *Dürer e il rinascimento tra Germania e Italia*, exh. cat., Palazzo Reale, Milan (2018)

Ainsworth, Maryan W., *Gerard David: Purity of Vision in an Age of Transition* (New York, 1998)

Anzelewsky, Fedja, *Dürer: Das malerische Werk*, 2 vols (Berlin, 1991)

—, *Dürer: His Art and Life* (London, 1980)

—, 'Eine Gruppe von Malern und Zeichnern aus Dürers Jugendjahren', *Jahrbuch der Berliner Museen*, XXVII (1985), pp. 35–59

Aretino, Pietro, *Dialogues*, trans. Raymond Rosenthal (New York, 1994)

Ashcroft, Jeffrey, *Albrecht Dürer: Documentary Biography*, 2 vols (New Haven, CT, and London, 2017)

Bailey, Martin, *Dürer* (London, 1998)

Baker, Christopher, and Tom Henry, *The National Gallery: Complete Illustrated Catalogue* (London, 1995)

Bambach, Carmen, *Michelangelo: Divine Draftsman and Designer*, exh. cat., Metropolitan Museum of Art, New York (2017–18)

Baroni, Luca, *Incisori tedeschi del Cinquecento* (Milan, 2020)

Bartrum, Giulia, *Albrecht Dürer and His Legacy*, exh. cat., British Museum, London (2002)

—, ed., *Dürer Unseen* (London, 2022), pp. 95–111

Basile, Giuseppe, *Giotto: The Arena Chapel Frescoes* (London, 1993)

Bauch, G., 'Zur Cranachforschung', *Repertorium für Kunstwissenschaft*, XVII (1894), pp. 421–35

Bauer, Herbert, and Georg Stolz, *Engelsgruss und Sakramentshaus in St Lorenz zu Nürnberg* (Königstein im Taunus, 1974)

Bindman, David, and Henry Louis Gates Jr, eds, *The Image of the Black in Western Art*, vol. II: *The Early Christian Era to the Age of Discovery*, 2 parts (Cambridge, MA, and London, 2010)

Bober, Phyllis Pray, and Ruth Rubinstein, *Renaissance Artists and Antique Sculpture: A Handbook of Sources* (London, 1986)

Brüggen Israëls, Machtelt, *Piero della Francesca and the Invention of the Artist* (London, 2020)

Buck, Stephanie, and Stephanie Porras, eds, *The Young Dürer: Drawing the Figure*, exh. cat., Courtauld Gallery, London (2013–14)

Buschhausen, Helmut, 'The Klosterneuburg Altar of Nicholas of Verdun: Art, Theology and Politics', *Journal of the Warburg and Courtauld Institutes*, XXXVII (1974), pp. 1–32

Butterfield, Andrew, ed., *Verrocchio: Sculptor and Painter of Renaissance Florence*, exh. cat., National Gallery of Art, Washington, DC (2019–20)

Campbell, Caroline, et al., *Mantegna and Bellini*, exh. cat., National Gallery, London, and Gemäldegalerie, Staatliche Museen zu Berlin (2018–19)

Campbell, Lorne, *The Fifteenth Century Netherlandish Schools*, National Gallery Catalogues (New Haven, CT, and London, 1998)

Campbell Hutchison, Jane, *Albrecht Dürer: A Biography* (Princeton, NJ, 1990)

Carritt, David, 'Dürer's "St Jerome in the Wilderness"', *Burlington Magazine*, XCIX/656 (1957), pp. 363–6

Chastel, André, 'L'ardita capra', *Arte Veneta*, XXIX (1975), pp. 146–9

—, *French Art: The Renaissance 1430–1620* (Paris and New York, 1995)

Clark, Kenneth, *The Nude: A Study of Ideal Art* (Harmondsworth, 1960)

—, *Rembrandt and the Italian Renaissance* (New York, 1966)

Cordellier, Dominique, and Paola Marini, *Pisanello: Le peintre aux sept vertus*, exh. cat., Musée du Louvre, Paris (1996)

—, and Bernadette Py, *Musée du Louvre, inventaire général des dessins italiens: Raphaël, son Atelier, ses copistes* (Paris, 1992)

Crawford Luber, Katherine, *Albrecht Dürer and the Venetian Renaissance* (Cambridge, 2005)

Dal Pozzolo, Enrico Maria, *Giorgione* (Milan, 2009)

Dalli Regoli, Gigetta, *Lorenzo di Credi* (Cremona, 1966)

—, *Verrocchio, Lorenzo di Credi, Francesco di Simone Ferrucci* (Paris, 2003)

Demus, Otto, *The Mosaic Decoration of San Marco, Venice* (Chicago, IL, and London, 1988)

De Voragine, Jacques, *La légende dorée*, 2 vols (Paris, 1967)

Dhanens, Elisabeth, *Hubert and Jan van Eyck* (Antwerp, 1980)
Edelstein, Bruce, and Davide Gasparotto, *Miraculous Encounters: Pontormo
     from Drawing to Painting*, exh. cat., Morgan Library and Museum,
     New York, and J. Paul Getty Museum, Los Angeles (2018–19)
Eisler, Colin, *Dürer's Animals* (Washington, DC, and London, 1991)
Ekserdjian, David, 'Copying Drawings in the Renaissance: Animal
     Studies, an Altarpiece by Orazio Gentileschi and a Drawing by
     Raphael', *Colnaghi Studies Journal*, IX (2021), pp. 31–41
—, 'A Dürer Drawing and a Classical Torso', *Master Drawings*, XXXII/3
     (1994), pp. 273–4
—, 'Establishing a Norm for the High Renaissance: Raphael and the
     Dissemination of a Style', in *Modello, regola, ordine: Parcours normatifs
     dans l'Italie du Cinquecento*, ed. Hélène Miesse and Gianluca Valenti
     (Rennes, 2018), pp. 217–35
—, *The Italian Renaissance Altarpiece: Between Icon and Narrative* (New Haven,
     CT, and London, 2021)
—, 'La nascita dell'entomologia e gli inizi della natura morta',
     in *Natura morta: rappresentazione dell'oggetto – oggetto come rappresentazione*,
     ed. Costanza Barbieri and Damiana Frascarelli, Convegno
     internazionale di studi, Napoli, Accademia di Belle Arti, 11–12
     December 2008 (Naples, 2010), pp. 23–8
—, 'Mantegna's Lost *Death of Orpheus*', in *Gedenkschrift für Richard Harprath*,
     ed. Wolfgang Liebenwein and Anchise Tempestini (Munich and
     Berlin, 1998), pp. 144–9
—, 'The Northern Renaissance Response to the Antique before
     the Sack of Rome', *Colnaghi Studies Journal*, VIII (2021), pp. 14–29
—, *Parmigianino* (New Haven, CT, and London, 2006)
—, 'The Portrait in Renaissance Italy and Lorenzo Lotto: Past, Present,
     and Future', in *Los retratos de Lorenzo Lotto*, ed. Enrico Maria Dal
     Pozzolo (Madrid, 2022), pp. 8–17
—, 'A Print Source for Botticelli: A Devil by the Master E.S.', *Apollo*,
     CXLVIII/441 (1998), pp. 15–16
—, 'Raphael's Small Madonnas and Holy Families: A Question
     of Influence', in *Studi raffaelleschi*, I, ed. Barbara Agosti, Anna
     Maria Ambrosini Massari and Silvia Ginzburg (Urbino, 2022),
     pp. 10–31
—, 'Regional Riches', *Apollo* (July–August 2017), pp. 94–5
—, 'Spigolature intorno al "Catalogo generale dei dipinti e delle
     miniature delle collezioni civiche veronesi" (2010)', *Verona illustrata*,
     28 (2015), pp. 35–9

—, 'The Tip of the Iceberg: Barocci's Postmortem Inventory and the
    Survival of Renaissance Drawings', in *Federico Barocci: Inspiration and
    Innovation in Early Modern Italy*, ed. Judith W. Mann (Abingdon, 2018),
    pp. 154–73
—, and Tom Henry, *Raphael*, exh. cat., National Gallery, London (2022)
Emiliani, Andrea, *Federico Barocci (Urbino, 1535–1612)*, 2 vols (Ancona, 2008)
Ferri, Ferruccio, ed., *Le poesie liriche di Basinio* (Turin, 1925)
Foister, Susan, and Peter van den Brink, *Dürer's Journeys: Travels of a
    Renaissance Artist*, exh. cat., National Gallery, London (2021–2)
Frabetti, Giuliano, *L'autunno dei manieristi a Ferrara* (Ferrara, 1978)
Friedländer, Max J., *Landscape – Portrait – Still Life: Their Origin and
    Development* (Oxford, 1949)
Fuchs, Franz, 'Eine neue Notiz zu Dürers Krankheit und Tod', *Mitteilungen
    des Vereins für Geschichte der Stadt Nürnberg*, CVII (2020), pp. 279–88
Gasparotto, Davide, ed., *Giovanni Bellini: Landscapes of Faith in Renaissance
    Venice*, exh. cat., J. Paul Getty Museum, Los Angeles (2017–18)
Grass, Günther, *Aus dem Tagebuch einer Schnecke* (Reinbek bei Hamburg, 1974)
Grosshans, Rainald, *Maerten van Heemskerck: Die Gemälde* (Berlin, 1980)
Haag, Sabine, Christiane Lange, Christof Lange, Christof Metzger and
    Karl Schütz, *Dürer – Cranach – Holbein. Die Entdeckung des Menschen:
    Das deutsche Porträt um 1500*, exh. cat., Kunsthistorisches Museum,
    Vienna, and Kunsthalle, Munich (2011)
Hart Hennessey, Maureen, and Anne Knutson, *Norman Rockwell:
    Pictures for the American People*, exh. cat., Norman Rockwell Museum,
    Stockbridge, MA, and elsewhere (1999–2002)
Haskell Francis, and Nicholas Penny, *Taste and the Antique: The Lure of
    Classical Sculpture, 1500–1900* (New Haven, CT, and London, 1982)
Held, Julius, *Dürers Wirkung auf die niederländische Kunst seiner Zeit*
    (The Hague, 1931)
Heller, Joseph, *Das Leben und die Werke Albrecht Dürer's*, 2 of 3 planned vols
    (Bamberg, 1827)
Herrmann Fiore, Kristina, ed., *Dürer e l'Italia*, exh. cat, Scuderie del
    Quirinale, Rome (2007)
Hess, Daniel, and Thomas Eser, eds, *The Early Dürer*, exh. cat.,
    Germanisches Nationalmuseum, Nuremberg (2012)
Hoare, Philip, *Albert and the Whale* (London, 2021)
Humfrey, Peter, *Lorenzo Lotto* (New Haven, CT, and London, 1997)
—, *The Altarpiece in Renaissance Venice* (New Haven, CT, and London, 1993)
Ilsley Minott, Charles, *Martin Schongauer* (New York, 1971)
Isherwood, Christopher, *Goodbye to Berlin* [1939] (London, 2003)

Ivins, William M. Jr, 'Notes on Three Dürer Woodblocks', *Metropolitan
     Museum Studies*, II/I (1929), pp. 102–11
Jameson, Anna, *Legends of the Madonna as Represented in the Fine Arts*
     (London, 1903)
Kahsnitz, Rainer, ed., *Veit Stoss in Nürnberg: Werke des Meisters und seiner Schule
     in Nürnberg und Umgebung* (Munich and Berlin, 1983)
Kemp, Wolfgang, *The Narratives of Gothic Stained Glass* (Cambridge, 1997)
Knab, Erwin Mitsch, and Konrad Oberhuber, *Raphael: Die
     Zeichnungen* (Stuttgart, 1983)
Koerner, Joseph Leo, *Bosch and Bruegel: From Enemy Painting to Everyday Life*
     (Princeton, NJ, 2017)
—, *The Moment of Self-Portraiture in German Renaissance Art* (Chicago, IL, and
     London, 1993)
Koreny, Fritz, 'Albrecht Dürer und die Niederlände', in *El siglo de Durero:
     Problemas historiográficos*, ed. Mar Borobia (Madrid, 2008), pp. 333–44
—, *Albrecht Dürer und die Tier- und Pflanzenstudien der Renaissance*, exh. cat.,
     Albertina, Vienna (1985)
—, 'A Coloured Study by Martin Schongauer and the Development of
     the Depiction of Nature from Van der Weyden to Dürer', *Burlington
     Magazine*, CXXXIII/1062 (1991), pp. 588–97
Kotková, Olga, '"The Feast of the Rose Garlands": What Remains of
     Dürer?', *Burlington Magazine*, CXLIV/1186 (2002), pp. 4–13
Kurz, Otto, 'Huius Nympha Loci: A Pseudo-Classical Inscription and
     a Drawing by Dürer', *Journal of the Warburg and Courtauld Institutes*, XVI
     (1953), pp. 171–7
Landau, David, and Peter Parshall, *The Renaissance Print, 1470–1550*
     (New Haven, CT, and London, 1994)
Lavin, Irving, 'Divine Grace and the Remedy of the Imperfect:
     Michelangelo's Signature on the St Peter's Pietà', *Artibus et Historiae*,
     XXXIV/68 (2013), pp. 277–327
Lawner, Lynne, *I Modi – The Sixteen Pleasures: An Erotic Album of the Italian
     Renaissance* (London, 1988)
Levenson, Jay A., Konrad Oberhuber and Jacquelyn L. Sheehan, *Early
     Italian Engravings from the National Gallery of Art*, exh. cat., National
     Gallery of Art, Washington, DC (1973)
Levey, Michael, *Albrecht Dürer* (London, 1964)
Lichte, Claudia, ed., *Tilman Riemenschneider: Werke seiner Blütezeit*, exh. cat.,
     Mainfränkisches Museum, Würzburg (2004)
Lightbown, Ronald, *Mantegna: With a Complete Catalogue of the Paintings,
     Drawings and Prints* (Oxford, 1986)

Livy, *History of Rome*, ed. B. O. Foster, 4 vols (London, 1919–26)

Lognon, Jean, Raymond Cazelles and Millard Meiss, *The 'Très Riches Heures' of Jean, Duke of Berry* (New York, 1969)

López-Rey, José, *Velázquez*, 2 vols (Cologne, 1996)

Lozano, Luis-Martin, *The Complete Paintings of Frida Kahlo* (Cologne, 2021)

Lübbeke, Isolde, *The Thyssen-Bornemisza Collection: Early German Painting, 1350–1550* (London, 1991)

Lucco, Mauro, and Giovanni Carlo Federico Villa, *Antonello da Messina: l'opera completa*, exh. cat., Scuderie del Quirinale, Rome (2006)

Mac Orlan, Pierre, *Le quai des brumes* (Paris, 1964)

Marciari, John, and Suzanne Boorsch, *Francesco Vanni: Art in Late Renaissance Siena*, exh. cat., Yale University Art Gallery, New Haven, CT (2013–14)

Martin, Gregory, *The Flemish School*, National Gallery Catalogues (London, 1970)

Metzger, Christof, ed., *Albrecht Dürer*, exh. cat., Albertina, Vienna (2019–20)

Meyer zur Capellen, Jürg, *Raphael: The Paintings*, 3 vols (Landshut, 2001–9)

Michael, Michael A., *Stained Glass of Canterbury Cathedral* (London, 2004)

Musper, Heinrich Theodor, 'Das Original der "Windischen Båuerin" von Albrecht Dürer', *Pantheon*, XXIX (1971), pp. 474–82

Nesselrath, Arnold, 'Raphael's Gift to Dürer', *Master Drawings*, XXXI/3 (1993), pp. 376–89

Pace, Claire, *Lives of Adam Elsheimer* (London, 2006)

Padoa Rizzo, Anna, 'Firenze e Europa nel Quattrocento: la "Vergine del Rosario" di Cosimo Rosselli', in *Studi di Storia dell'Arte in onore di Mina Gregori*, ed. M. Boskovits (Florence, 1994), pp. 64–9

Panofsky, Erwin, *The Life and Art of Albrecht Dürer*, 2 vols (Princeton, NJ, 1943)

Parker, K. T., *Catalogue of the Collection of Drawings in the Ashmolean Museum*, vol. II: *Italian Schools*, 2 vols (Oxford, 1972)

Parma, Elena, *Perino del Vaga: tra Raffaello e Michelangelo*, exh. cat., Palazzo Te, Mantua (2001)

Parshall, Peter, Stacey Sell and Judith Brodie, *The Unfinished Print*, exh. cat., National Gallery of Art, Washington, DC (2001)

Pauli, Gustav, *Hans Sebald Beham: Ein kritisches Verzeichniss seiner Kupferstiche, Radirungen und Holzschnitte* (Strasbourg, 1901)

Pausanias, *Description of Greece*, ed. J. G. Frazer, 6 vols (London, 1898)

Pedrocco, Filippo, *Titian: The Complete Paintings* (London, 2001)

Petrioli Tofani, Annamaria, ed., *L'officina della maniera*, exh. cat., Galleria degli Uffizi, Florence (1996–7)

Pignatti, Terisio, *Giorgione: Complete Edition* (London, 1971)
Piper, David, *Treasures of the Ashmolean Museum: An Illustrated Souvenir of the Collections* (Oxford, 1995)
Popham, A. E., *The Drawings of Leonardo da Vinci* (London, 1946)
Quattrini, Cristina, *Bernardino Luini: Catalogo generale delle opere* (Turin, 2019)
Quednau, Rolf, 'Raphael und "alcune stampe di maniera tedesca"', *Zeitschrift für Kunstgeschichte*, XLVI (1983), pp. 129–73
Ringbom, Sixten, *Icon to Narrative: The Rise of the Dramatic Close-Up in Fifteenth-Century Devotional Painting*, 2nd edn (Doornspijk, 1983)
Röhrig, Floridus, *Der Verduner Altar* (Klosterneuburg, 2004)
Rossi, Marco, *Giovannino de Grassi: La corte e la cattedrale* (Cinisello Balsamo, 1995)
Röver-Kann, Anne, *Albrecht Dürer: Das Frauenbad von 1496*, exh. cat., Kunsthalle Bremen (2001)
Rupprich, Hans, ed., *Dürer: Schriftlicher Nachlass*, 3 vols (Berlin, 1956–69)
Sandrart, Joachim, *Teutsche Akademie der Bau-, Bild- und Mahlerey-Künste* (Nuremberg, 1675)
Scarpellini, Pietro, *Perugino* (Milan, 1984)
Schmid, F. Carlo, 'Prints after the Antique up to 1869', *Print Quarterly*, XXXVIII/2 (2021), pp. 184–7
Schoch, Rainer, Matthias Mende and Anna Scherbaum, *Albrecht Dürer: Das druckgraphische Werk*, 3 vols (Munich, London and New York, 2001–4)
Schoen, Christian, *Albrecht Dürer. Adam und Eva: Die Gemälde, ihre Geschichte und Rezeption bei Lucas Cranach d. Ä. und Hans Baldung Grien* (Berlin, 2001)
Schröder, Klaus Albrecht, and Maria Luise Sternath, *Albrecht Dürer*, exh. cat., Albertina, Vienna (2003)
Sgarbi, Vittorio, *Carpaccio* (New York, London and Paris, 1995)
Shearman, John, *Raphael in Early Modern Sources, 1483–1602*, 2 vols (New Haven, CT, and London, 2003)
Shestack, Alan, *Master LCz and Master WB* (New York, 1971)
Shoemaker, Innis H., and Elizabeth Broun, *The Engravings of Marcantonio Raimondi*, exh. cat., Spencer Museum of Art, Lawrence, KS, Ackland Art Museum, Chapel Hill, NC, and Wellesley College Art Museum, Wellesley, MA (1981–2)
Simon, Erika, 'Dürer und Mantegna 1494', *Anzeiger des Germanischen Nationalmuseums* (1971–2), pp. 21–40
Sohm, Philip, 'Giving Vasari the Giorgio Treatment', *I Tatti Studies in the Italian Renaissance*, XVIII/1 (2015), pp. 61–111
Steer, John, *Alvise Vivarini: His Art and Influence* (Cambridge, 1982)

Strauss, Walter L., *The Complete Drawings of Albrecht Dürer*, 6 vols and
    2 supplements (New York, 1974)
—, ed., *The Complete Engravings, Etchings and Drypoints of Albrecht Dürer*
    (New York, 1972)
Strieder, Peter, ed., *1471 Albrecht Dürer 1971*, exh. cat., Germanisches
    Nationalmuseum, Nuremberg (1971)
Stumpel, Jeroen, and Jolein van Kregten, 'In the Name of the Thistle:
    Albrecht Dürer's Self-Portrait of 1493', *Burlington Magazine*,
    CXLIV/1186 (2002), pp. 14–18
Tempestini, Anchise, *Giovanni Bellini: Catalogo completo dei dipinti*
    (Florence, 1992)
Treves, Letizia, *Beyond Caravaggio*, exh. cat., National Gallery, London
    (2016–17)
Turner, Jane, ed., *The Dictionary of Art*, 34 vols (London, 1996)
Ullmann, Ernst, and Elvira Pradel, *Albrecht Dürer: Schriften und
    Briefe* (Berlin, 1984)
Unterkircher, Franz, *Le Livre du cueur d'amours espris* (London, 1975)
Van den Brink, Peter, *Dürer war hier: Eine Reise wird Legende*, exh. cat.,
    Suermondt-Ludwig-Museum, Aachen (2021)
—, 'A Tale of Two Drawings: Albrecht Dürer and Gossart's Lost
    Middelburg Altarpiece', in *Ingenium at Labor: Studia ofiarowane Profesorowi
    Antoniemu Ziembie z okazji 60. Urodzin* (Warsaw, 2020), pp. 109–17
Vasari, Giorgio, *Le opere di Giorgio Vasari con nuove annotazioni e commenti
    di Gaetano Milanesi*, 8 vols and index (Florence, 1878–85)
—, *Lives of the Artists*, intro. and notes by David Ekserdjian, 2 vols
    (London, 1996)
Waetzoldt, Wolfgang, *Albrecht Dürer und seine Zeit* (Vienna, 1935)
Walter, Angelo, ed., *Gemäldegalerie Alte Meister Dresden: Katalog der ausgestellten
    Werke* (Dresden, 1982)
Wells, Stanley, and Gary Taylor, eds, *The Complete Oxford Shakespeare*,
    3 vols (Oxford, 1987)
*West European Drawing of XVI–XX Centuries: Kunsthalle Collection in Bremen:
    Catalogue* (Moscow, 1992)
Wheelock, Arthur Jr, ed., *Johannes Vermeer*, exh. cat., National Gallery
    of Art, Washington, DC, and Mauritshuis, The Hague (1996)
Winkler, Friedrich, *Die Zeichnungen Albrecht Dürers*, 4 vols (Berlin,
    1936–9)
Wolf, Norbert, *Dürer* (Munich, Berlin, London and New York, 2010)
Wood, Christopher S., *Albrecht Altdorfer and the Origins of Landscape*
    (London, 1993)

Woods, Kim W., *Making Renaissance Art* (New Haven, CT, and
    London, 2007)
Woods Marsden, Joanna, *Renaissance Self-Portraiture: The Visual
    Construction of Identity and the Social Status of the Artist* (New Haven, CT,
    and London, 1998)
Wright, Alison, *The Pollaiuolo Brothers: The Arts of Florence and Rome*
    (New Haven, CT, and London, 2005)
Zeri, Federico, and Elizabeth Gardner, *A Catalogue of the Collection
    of the Metropolitan Museum of Art. Italian Paintings: Florentine School*
    (New York, 1971)
Zitzlsperger, Philipp, *Dürers Pelz und das Recht im Bild: Kleiderkunde
    als Methode der Kunstgeschichte* (Berlin, 2008)
Zuccari, Alessandro, *I Caravaggeschi: Percorsi e protagonisti*, 2 vols
    (Milan, 2010)

ACKNOWLEDGEMENTS

Discussions of the patronage of visual art during the Renaissance often seek to distinguish between work that is commissioned and work that is not, between what might be described as 'made to measure' and 'off the peg'. Seen in those terms, my main debt of gratitude goes to François Quiviger and Michael Leaman, for the simple reason that this book would never have come to be written if they had not approached me, however much I may have dreamt of working on such a project over the years.

Next come three Dürer specialists – Giulia Bartrum, Peter van den Brink and Christof Metzger – who reassured me that I was on more or less the right track, while at the same generously removing numerous banana skins from my path.

Third in order are the people who tried to teach me German at Westminster School and Trinity College, Cambridge, and succeeded to the extent that I can – admittedly with a dictionary at my side – reasonably comfortably read the requisite Dürer literature: Hugo Garten, Christopher Martin, Roger Paulin, Ernst Sanger and Christopher Wightwick.

More general help and support of a variety of kinds I owe to Jean-Luc Baroni, Hugo Chapman, Anthony Crichton-Stuart, Achim Gnann, George Goldner, Katrin Henkel, Joseph Koerner, Fritz Koreny, Meg Koster, Michael Levey, Alessandro Nova, Cliff Schorer and Nicolas Schwed, never forgetting my eternally long-suffering family.

Finally, I give thanks for a book that is not in the Bibliography to this one, the two volumes and 1968 pages of Wolgang Hütt's *Albrecht Dürer 1471 bis 1528: Das gesamte graphische Werk*, which I was able to buy for a song as a young graduate student, and whose contents I have done my best to learn off by heart since I acquired it over four decades ago.

PHOTO ACKNOWLEDGEMENTS

The author and publishers wish to express their thanks to the below sources of illustrative material and/or permission to reproduce it. Some locations of artworks are also given below, in the interest of brevity:

Agnews Gallery, London: 50; © The Albertina Museum, Vienna: 1, 4, 8, 11, 17, 18, 19, 20, 21, 23, 24, 25, 26, 41, 45, 46, 47, 49, 51, 53, 54, 55, 57, 58; Alte Pinakothek, Munich (CC BY-SA 4.0): 10, 33, 34, 37, 60; The British Museum, London: 43; Duomo di Pistoia (photo Francesco Bini/Sailko, CC BY 3.0): 27; Galleria degli Uffizi, Florence: 15, 36; Gemäldegalerie, Staatliche Museen zu Berlin: 29, 39, 40; © Gemäldegalerie Alte Meister, Staatliche Kunstsammlungen Dresden (photo Elke Estel/Hans-Peter Klut): 32; Graphische Sammlungen, Klassik Stiftung Weimar: 2; The J. Paul Getty Museum, Los Angeles: 16; Kunsthalle Bremen: 5, 12, 44; Kunsthistorisches Museum, Vienna: 6, 31, 38; Kupferstichkabinett, Staatliche Museen zu Berlin: 3, 22, 48; © The Lucian Freud Archive, all rights reserved 2023/Bridgeman Images: 59; The Metropolitan Museum of Art, New York: 13, 42; Musée du Louvre, Paris: 7; Museo Nacional del Prado, Madrid: 9, 14; Museo Nacional Thyssen-Bornemisza, Madrid: 30; Národní galerie, Prague: 28; The National Gallery, London: 35; National Gallery of Art, Washington, DC: 52; Victoria and Albert Museum, London: 56.

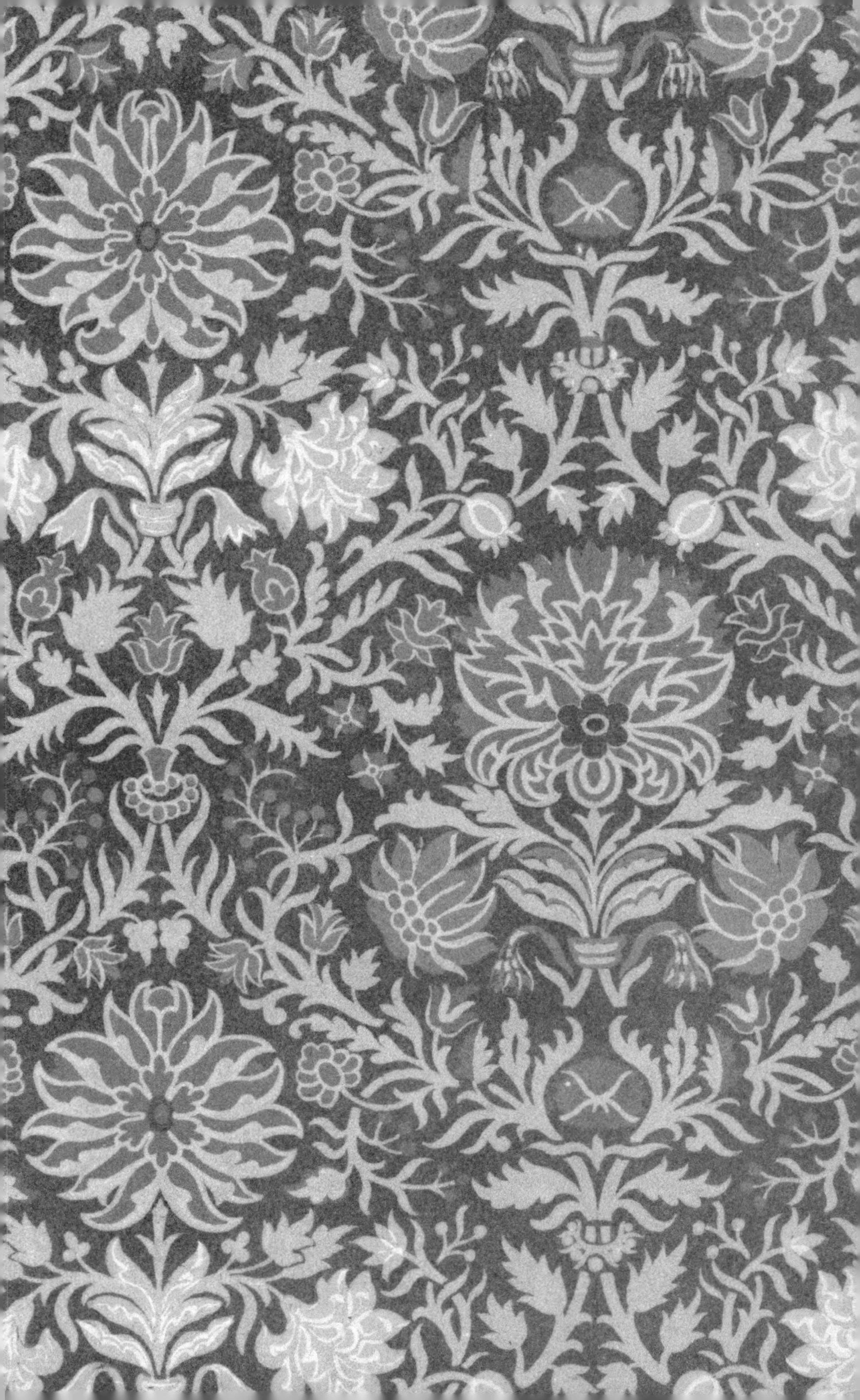